Praise for *Wherever You Go, There They Are*

"A smart, edgy writer . . . As a memoirist, Gurwitch succeeds by evoking emotions that cut to the core of our humanity, and giving us laughs along the way."

—Mort Zachter, *Los Angeles Review of Books*

"A vivacious confessional . . . The memoir's madcap joy is the entire Gurwitch clan of scenery chewers. . . . With her moonshine-smuggling forebears and her brothel matron great-grandmother, Gurwitch joins the shell-shocked ranks of dysfunctional-family chroniclers Augusten Burroughs and Sean Wilsey."

—Natalie Beach, *O, The Oprah Magazine*

"Reading Annabelle Gurwitch feels like staying up all night in a free-wheeling conversation with my funniest, wisest, most magnetic friend. *Wherever You Go, There They Are* is a required remedy for everyone desperate for a good, hard laugh at the vexing, heart-swelling madness we call family."

—Maria Semple, author of *Today Will Be Different*
and *Where'd You Go, Bernadette*

"Annabelle Gurwitch tackles every life passage, epic or trivial, with a courageous wit that makes even the darkest moments more bearable. *Wherever You Go, There They Are* hilariously explores the frustrations, catastrophes, and unforgettable thrills of navigating life with that gaggle of lunatics known as family."

—Heather Havrilesky, author of *How to Be a Person
in the World* and *Disaster Preparedness*

"Annabelle Gurwitch claims to be related to her nutty family, but I suspect she's really the secret love child of Nora Ephron and Groucho Marx. She's an old-fashioned wit for the postmodern age, a curmudgeon with a deep well of empathy and a genuinely good soul. I'm so glad she's back with another book."

—Meghan Daum, author of *The Unspeakable*

"Once I started *Wherever You Go, There They Are*, I couldn't put it down. This book is hysterically, laugh-out-loud funny—take it on an airplane and be prepared to enjoy your flight."

—Judy Greer, actress and author of
I Don't Know What You Know Me From

"Anyone can tell jokes. Annabelle Gurwitch does something much cleverer: every sentence [in *Wherever You Go, There They Are*] has a delicious and charming turn of wit."

—Richard Dawkins, author of *The God Delusion*

"I love spending time under the spell of Annabelle Gurwitch, who lived all these crackpot adventures so we don't have to. Her unforgettable stories about family and other disasters remind us how insane this world can be, and how necessary our laughter."

—Sarah Hepola, author of *Blackout: Remembering the Things
I Drank to Forget*

"I had to invent a word to describe this book. It's 'luffaw': a guffaw with a poignant 'awww' as well. You'll relate to Annabelle Gurwitch's stories about finding your people and working with the ones you were given."

—Jen Kirkman, author of *I Can Barely Take Care of Myself*

"Annabelle Gurwitch takes a sharp-eyed, un-fool-able, and hilarious look at her family's loopy pursuit of the American Dream in *Wherever You Go, There They Are*. Wherever she goes, you'll want to follow her!"

—Barbara Ehrenreich, author of *Nickel and Dimed*

"Annabelle Gurwitch's book is *really* funny. That is, when you aren't choking up, you'll be laughing. Her parents are lovably infuriating and her travels among atheists, secular humanists, and new-agey summer campers are not only hysterical, but important, and a reminder that family is where you find it."

—Julia Sweeney, author of *If It's Not One Thing, It's Your Mother* and *God Said Ha!*

"Annabelle Gurwitch picks up the mantles of Nora Ephron and David Sedaris with unapologetic irreverence and lovably brutal self-deprecation. As she ponders why families are so impossible to escape, you'll want to hold your own crazy loved ones closer and perhaps—like Annabelle—even consider breastfeeding your cat."

—Faith Salie, author of *Approval Junkie*

"In *Wherever You Go, There They Are* Annabelle Gurwitch takes inspiration from her own life to examine that most horrible of all human conditions: family. She makes a compelling case for community, while arguing for a definition that eschews tribalism. This hilarious and insightful book reminds me why I'm so, so happy that I didn't have children!"

—Bill Maher

"Sagacious wit and soulful insights with a dash of Nora Ephron."

—Cynthia Romanowski, *Coast* magazine

wherever you go, there they are

STORIES ABOUT MY FAMILY
YOU MIGHT RELATE TO

Annabelle Gurwitch

BLUE RIDER PRESS | *New York*

blue
rider
press

An imprint of Penguin Random House LLC
375 Hudson Street
New York, New York 10014

Blue Rider Press is a registered trademark and its colophon
is a trademark of Penguin Random House LLC

The Library of Congress has cataloged the hardcover edition
of this book as follows:

Names: Gurwitch, Annabelle author.
Title: Wherever you go, there they are : stories about my
family you might relate to / Annabelle Gurwitch.
Description: New York : Blue Rider Press, 2017.
Identifiers: LCCN 2016052134 (print) | LCCN 2017014631
(ebook) | ISBN 9780399574900 (Ebook) |
ISBN 9780399574887 (hardcover)
Subjects: LCSH: Gurwitch, Annabelle—Family. |
Actors—United States—Biography. | Television
personalities—United States—Biography. | Gurwitch,
Annabelle—Humor. | Families—Humor.
Classification: LCC PN2287.G797 (ebook) |
LCC PN2287.G797 A3 2017 (print) | DDC 818/.602—dc23

Printed in the United States of America
1   3   5   7   9   10   8   6   4   2

BOOK DESIGN BY NICOLE LAROCHE

Blue Rider Press hardcover: April 2017
Blue Rider Press paperback: April 2018
Blue Rider Press paperback ISBN: 9780399574894

For Shirley and Harry

CONTENTS

what we talk about when we talk about family: an introduction

Long before I'd ever heard the phrase "what we talk when about when we talk about," I was talking about what we talk about when we talk about family. I remember looking around the Thanksgiving table, my grandmother noisily sucking the bone marrow of a turkey leg, my mom silently stewing over some perceived slight, while a cousin made fun of my theatrical aspirations. *There's been a mistake*, I said to myself, *I can't possibly be related to these people!* Much of my life has been spent in search of a family with whom I share more than a genetic predisposition toward moles and the overshare. This begs the question: Is family our blood relations, our friends, our neighbors, our pets, the people we work with, pray with, and, dare I add, party with?

The desire to join a different family isn't unique to me. We're living in a time when your family of origin determines your economic future almost as certainly as it did in medieval times. No wonder so many of us suffer from a moderate to severe case of family envy.

There are folks for whom family evokes the warm embrace of unconditional love—or, at least, that's what I hear. To me, it's nothing short of astounding that the phrase "we'll treat you like family" has positive associations when time spent with family so often feels like a hostage situation.

Of course that's using the narrowest definition of family, the type that implies blood relation. One of the hallmarks of modern life across the globe is the advent of what sociologists refer to as "supplemental families." These chosen families are loosely defined as close-knit tribes you spend a fixed part of your life with; whose members develop their own set of customs, hierarchies, and unique family dynamics. Confederacies, sisterhoods, and even cults have not only sustained me in difficult times, they remain an essential part of my life; even though there have been numerous undertakings I would characterize as looking for tribe in all the wrong places. If I've learned anything, it's that no matter how hard you try to escape your crazy family, you just end up in another crazy family.

To explore the importance and insanity of family, it seemed compulsory to include an overview of my family of origin. It felt necessary to write about my parents, and then, it seemed essential to write about their parents, and then it seemed impossible, for context, not to include the circumstances by which we arrived on American shores in hopes of living the American dream. What emerged was a narrative that is not atypical of many second-generation Americans. We are certainly "colorful," as we say about people of questionable character in the South, but I hope our exploits at the margins of polite society won't distract from the larger truth, which is that my family is not so different from your family and every other immigrant family.

A funny thing happened after completing the book: both the world and my family underwent major upheavals. Since the book was published, I've been stunned to witness, not only in America, but around the world, how the temptation toward tribalism has fueled a rise in anti-Semitism, racism, and other-ization of all kinds. How many outsiders can we absorb into our ranks and still retain our identity? Who is the *us* and who is the *them*? Even the most conventional definition of family is being questioned. Proposed legislation by the Trump administration posits that grandparents, aunts, and uncles are not close enough relations to qualify one for citizenship. Unskilled laborers? Not welcome. Most of my family would have been disqualified on both of these accounts! In reconstructing the making of my American family, I am reminded how fraught each passage, how unfathomable the sacrifices, how insubstantial the differences among all who are displaced. Now, each time I see photographs of migrants crossing the Mediterranean or chancing the desperate trek north from Latin America, I see the faces of my ancestors.

Nor did I anticipate the changes in my immediate family. While writing this book, I was caring for my parents as their health had declined precipitously and their finances were precarious. At that time, I was smack in the middle of what I've since learned has been termed the "Daughter Trap." Two thirds of the approximately forty-three million Americans caring for aging relatives are women. More often than not, in families where there are adult children, it's the female offspring who are corralled into filling the gap between medical professions and home health workers. Okay, in my case we have no male siblings, but I certainly relate to the trap. Between my mother firing me for showing up at her hospital bed with my shirt untucked, the huge hit on my income, and the debilitating powerlessness I experienced while navigating one health-care quagmire after another, I often felt as though I was sinking in quicksand. At one point, I was so frustrated with my inability to get my mother a desperately needed appointment with a psychologist, I pretended to be a doctor so I could reach her GP on his personal number. Still, I prefer to think of that time as the "Daughter Opportunity." After a lifetime of rocky relations, I was able to usher my parents out of this world with some modicum of dignity. Most of us are robbed of that chance through the cornucopia of indignities that the random universe provides: car accidents, bathroom mishaps, disease, wars, natural disasters. Careening off the deck of a cruise ship isn't just a plot point in Jonathan Franzen's *The Corrections*—every year an average of twenty people fall overboard!

I was working on the final pass of edits for this book when my father had a stroke and died a few weeks later. My mother followed him swiftly. The Daughter Opportunity offered me a chance to practice a selflessness I didn't know I was capable of. During her last days, my mother informed the hospice staff that she was immensely proud of the work I was doing in the community. It was only months later that I realized that during that entire week at her bedside, she'd mistaken me for my philanthropic sister. In what could be seen as an expression of love—although I suspect it was her way of ensuring she wasn't overshadowed in death as she'd been in life—she made her exit on the morning of my dad's memorial service. I gave the tribute to the mother who I only came to appreciate in the final chapter of her life.

I'd made a pact with my mom years earlier: I wouldn't publish stories I suspected would upset her until after she'd passed. She was uncomfortable with me sharing the extent of our financial ups and downs, whereas my father was untroubled by any such concerns. I never had the heart to tell her that the details of the many lawsuits and bankruptcies were easily accessible with a simple Google search. When she was diagnosed with stage-four breast cancer in 2011, I began a timeline for writing, but my mother was like the Energizer Bunny: she kept going and going, to the point where we joked that she was determined to outlive me to keep me from revealing family secrets. Ultimately, I didn't invite either of my parents to read drafts of this manuscript, and it seems strange and impossible that neither lived long enough to see this book in which they play a central role. My beloved uncle Jack (also pictured on the cover of this book), as well as several cousins, passed just prior to the book's release. My remaining relatives are now anxiously checking moles that have changed shape.

I believe my mother would be heartened to know that I've embraced the admonition often repeated by my paternal grandmother Rebecca, to "stay close to your family." I was able to visit with Jack just prior to his death and heal the longstanding rift between him and my mother.

"Hi, this is your mother, Shirley Gurwitch," was my mom's preferred phone greeting, and I think she'd delight in how it drives my son just as crazy as it drove me now that I've adopted her salutation.

My dad would have gotten a kick out of hearing that the audience for the book launch in Miami was mainly comprised of attorneys, both those who'd represented him and others who'd sued him. The consensus was that he cut a memorable swath and that "he sure knew how to party." I also received condolences from my father's poker buddies at the Gulfstream Park racetrack and casino. That my dad "sure knew how to party" were also among the last words spoken by both my mother and uncle. In this book, you'll read about many of my dad's exploits in the swinging seventies, but I'm thankful that there are a myriad of tawdry adventures that I will never know about. Other family members have told me they enjoyed this book, at least those that are still speaking to me.

I returned to Alabama after receiving a generous invitation to present this book in an event cosponsored by the two Jewish congregations in Mobile: Springhill Avenue Temple and Ahavas Chesed Synagogue. I was truly looking forward to this, especially because back in my grandparents' time and even my parents' day, despite their isolation deep in the Bible Belt, these two congregations operated entirely independent of each other. As we circled Mobile in a tiny propeller plane, the captain made an announcement: "We don't have a lot of gas." *We don't have a lot of gas?* "We're trying to outrun the lightning storm." *What lightning storm?* "We might head to Jackson." *Oh, my, god. I'm going to die. You can't ever go home again. Everybody knows that! Especially Southerners! I've tempted fate. Why did I come back to Mobile? I'm being sucked back in by my ancestors who are angry that I left, and I'm going to be buried in the family plot.*

We landed safely, but I'd missed the event. I did make it to a reading at Page and Palette—the bookstore on the eastern shore of Mobile Bay—where they made a margarita in my honor, the terribly named but delicious Gurwitcharita. And members of my chosen family in Mobile, a collection of artists, writers, and foodies, treated me to dinner at Sunset Pointe restaurant, where Chef Panini Pete "treats you like family."

Come to think of it, maybe the time has come to retire that phrase. I propose that should we want to express love, affection, and solidarity with our fellow humans, we say, "we'll treat you like cherished friends who we rarely get to see." My fondest wish is that after reading these stories about my family, which you might relate to, you'll be inspired to expand your notion of cherished friends to include even those you have yet to meet.

"You kids promised to walk the dog and give him baths and you never did,"
said my mother and every other parent in the history of the world.

we live down the street from cat town

Moo Goo Gai Pan was a swashbuckling adventurer who sailed the seven seas carousing and plundering and generally yo-ho-ho-ing it up. At least, that was Pan's MO according to my father, Harry Gurwitch. If my dad has one talent, it's the ability to spin a yarn. Pan and his exploits were our bedtime stories during the six or so months in 1967 that our family crashed at my aunt Gloria's home in Wilmington, Delaware.

I was in kindergarten and had just gotten the hang of buttoning myself into my Wright School for Girls pinafore when my parents packed up Mom's wood-paneled Chevy Caprice station wagon and drove north from Mobile to Wilmington. We arrived with only the suitcases that fit in the car.

We pulled up to the house and my mother took to her bed in a nylon peignoir set. It wasn't actually her bed, it was the twin bed with a Snoopy comforter in my cousin Shari's bedroom, and she didn't emerge again for several months. Shirley Gurwitch was "in mourning for her life," to borrow from Chekhov. Aunt Gloria and Uncle Jack folded my sister and me into their brood. My maternal grandmother, Frances, slipped money to Gloria and Jack every week to feed and clothe us. My mother says she still has PTSD from the trauma of having to move back home and in with her sister.

My mother had big little-girl dreams. Her childhood diaries hint at a desire to become an actress, an aspiration that she was too shy to pursue and would not have gone over well with her parents.* Whereas my father's family was colorful and risk taking, my mother's was unassuming and hardworking. Frances wanted to go into nursing, but only the boys in her family got educations and she ended up a clerk in the county welfare department. My mother's father, Johnny Maisel, was a movie projectionist. The work was anything but glamorous. The profession attracted taciturn loners who were strong enough to manipulate the heavy machinery and handy with electrical appliances. Johnny so rarely spoke, in fact, that no one realized he had Alzheimer's until we started getting phone calls from strangers in Baltimore after he'd gone out to get bread and milk in Wilmington.

My mother loved dreaming the day away in the cool darkness of the movie theater, but she only once worked up the courage to audition for a play. "Dinner is served," she unmemorably announced

---

* Even when I found regular work on a soap opera, Frances continued to send letters urging me to keep up my typing skills. (I neglected to tell her I had cheated my way through typing in high school.)

as Tweeny, a junior domestic worker, in her high school production of the equally forgettable British comedy *The Admirable Crichton*. It was her debut and swan song.

I recently had lunch with Muriel, who looked up to my mother, her slightly older cousin, when they were undergraduates at the University of Delaware. "Your mother was pretty and studious and I wanted to be just like her." Muriel became a science and engineering professor at MIT, but by then, my mother had already met my father. She'd represented the Maisels, who could only afford one train ticket, at a family wedding in Mobile. My father was assigned to escort her during her stay. There were lavish parties, teas, and dances, and my mom was seduced by the Southern hospitality.

After graduating with a degree in sociology, she had a brief tenure as a first-grade teacher. My mother has never made it a secret that she doesn't really like children. She lasted exactly two days. Instead of enrolling in graduate school she threw herself at the tall, dark, and handsome Southerner she'd met in Mobile, not realizing that she was marrying into a family of bootleggers, gamblers, and fabulists. That was just the first of a lifetime of miscalculations.

My sister, Lisa, says we snuck out of Mobile in the middle of the night, which may or may not be an accurate account, but to us kids it sure felt like our life had crashed and burned without warning. In reality, the trajectory was years in the making. There was the failure of an insurance company, the demise of a used-car dealership, and the short sale of a local radio station to a Christian broadcasting group, silver mines that didn't pan out, then a shady situation that tanked a real estate development in Toulminville, a suburb of Mobile. All I knew was that one day we were tooling around town in

Dad's Silver Cloud Rolls-Royce with the mahogany pull-down trays and the next we were homeless.

Returning to Wilmington penniless broke my mother's spirit, but my sister and I had Moo Goo to keep us going. Lisa, my three cousins, and I hung on every word that Big Daddy, as our cousins dubbed our six-foot-four father with his booming Southern drawl, told of Moo Goo's derring-do. None of us recall the piratey particulars other than that the stories bordered on Orientalism and that his adventures ended abruptly with the news that Moo Goo had acquired a lady friend and Dad wouldn't be able to tell us any more of the story until we were all much, much older. Apparently, we still aren't old enough, because to this day we don't know what became of the couple. It wasn't until many years later that I discovered that Moo Goo Gai Pan is a Cantonese chicken and vegetable stir-fry and not a dashing thrill seeker.

Is it possible that my dad cooked up the Moo Goo stories to help us cope with the stress of living under one roof? Maybe. Was he casting himself as the Pied Piper, a welcome distraction from his new job, a Willy Loman-esque grind of selling Fuller brushes door-to-door? Maybe. Or he was just fucking with us. What I do know is that Moo Goo entered our lives in the winter of 1967 and held us in his sway until we could afford to move into our own apartment.

Poor Mom. Even before our financial troubles, my sister was easygoing and eager to please, while I was born to make her life difficult.

"Your first word was 'no' and you never stopped saying it," is my mom's characterization of me from the age of eighteen months to this morning.

For too many years to be considered endearingly quirky, I refused to eat anything other than fried chicken, butter, and grape juice. This kind of pickiness is recognized now in the *DSM* as an eating disorder called "selective eating," but back in the day the official diagnosis was "a royal pain in the ass." Exactly how unkempt and unruly I was is something that members of my family never tire of repeating, and heralded the entrance of another outlandish fictional character into our lives.

I think of this as the story called "How It's a Miracle I Didn't End Up in a Straitjacket." Lucky the Leprechaun, the mascot for the General Mills cereal Lucky Charms, stars in one of the most recognizable and memorable ad campaigns of all time. Those magically delicious commercials played over and over on our twenty-four-inch black-and-white TV screen and must have made a deep impression on my big sister. Lisa, seven at the time, calling up skills that would one day make her a successful CEO, decided to come to my mother's rescue by enlisting the services of my imaginary friend, inspired by Lucky, who went by the name The Little Man.

I was five years old, lying on my bed, doing something patently criminal, like licking S & H Green Stamps and sticking them to my forehead or trying to untangle one of the wads of bubble gum that was always getting stuck in my long hair,* when a high-pitched voice introduced himself as The Little Man. That my sibling was hiding under my bed pretending to be a little person who wanted me to eat my vegetables was more implausible than the perfectly reasonable explanation: I was having a conversation with a friendly,

---

* Peanut butter gets gum out of hair. My mother never made us PB&J sandwiches because all of our peanut butter ended up in my hair.

if somewhat fiber-obsessed, neighborhood leprechaun. Thus began my relationship with The Little Man. The Little Man came on sweetly but in no time was issuing orders left and right.

Uh-oh, you might be thinking, *is this* that *kind of story?* It seems to be headed somewhere it is *not going.* Still, isn't it bad enough that my imaginary friend's idea of a good time was getting me to wash behind my ears or lay out my clothes for school? He was not above bestowing small gifts and rewards for completed chores. If I, say, brushed my teeth, I'd find a piece of candy on my pillow, which would seem to be totally contradictory, but I suppose all in all, it paid off, because I only had three cavities growing up. My sister also taught me to read, an act she refuses to characterize as anything mercenary, but not long after I sounded out *Fun with Dick and Jane*, notes began appearing from the little guy: *Make your bed, set dinner table, put dirty clothes in hamper.*

Even though my sister prefers to maintain the fiction that she only wanted to help me, other cousins remember it differently. "Didn't The Little Man order Annabelle to bring us milk and cookies?" my cousin Robin said at a family gathering last year. Little or not, I was working for the man.

TLM was kind enough to relocate to Delaware with us, and with my mother on "bed rest," he turned into a real taskmaster. Lisa recruited my three cousins into the act and in any room where I might wander, he'd be lying in wait. *Take the trash out! Do your homework! Brush your hair—all the way to the back!* a note would read or I'd hear barked in my direction. I can't for the life of me remember how it all blew up, but I must have been traumatized because I was sent to see *someone.*

The child psychologist was heavily bearded and stood all of five foot one. He looked so much like how I'd pictured The Little Man that I refused to speak to him. I still wonder if the constant reminders of my slovenly ways turned me into the kind of person who, to this day, if I'm not vigilant, makes a good candidate for *Hoarders*.* Both TLM's unmasking and Moo Goo's hooking up with a gal pal coincided with our move to an apartment of our own, but it was the distraction of our new dog that kept me from reporting my family to social services.

"You kids promised to walk the dog and give him baths and you never did," said my mother and every other parent in the history of the world. Sure, my sister and I didn't want to actively participate in caring for a new pet, but with an apartment and a pet, it seemed like we were a normal family again.

Petey was a Peekapoo, sort of an also-ran hybrid of a Pekingese and poodle.† One of the most prominent features of the Peekapoo is what has been termed its "hilarious attachment" to its owners. Our Peekapoo liked to be with us so much that he preferred to urinate on our feet rather than be separated from us by even a few inches.

Our Petey was a barking hairball who collected everything in his path. Leaves, twigs, crumbs, even bits of poop were regularly found clinging to his scrawny body. His smashed-in Pekingese nose was often runny. He was a hot hairy mess, but that didn't dampen our enthusiasm for him, or so I thought.

---

* My son likens riding in my car to driving around inside that junk drawer that's next to the fridge, but I haven't gotten gum stuck in my hair in at least fifteen years.

† Pekingese are extremely popular with actresses. It's so common to see those furry faces peeking out of celebrities' handbags that you might think these puppies are standard accessories, like a change purse.

In 1972, my father landed a business opportunity in Florida. It was the beginning of a story he hoped would be titled "How We Got Rich." He rented a house for us in a gated island community in Biscayne Bay where the archbishop of Miami, deposed Nicaraguan dictator Somoza, and reclusive billionaire Howard Hughes owned compounds, and estates had names like Casa Tranquila and Palacio del Eden. One of the island families kept the guardhouse stocked with ice-cream sandwiches —*as many as you wanted, for free*—for kids walking home from school. My father was one of those dads who was always producing quarters from behind your ears, but this was his best trick yet. The only thing was, the lease didn't allow for pets. I imagine that this was something of a relief to my mother, who along with not liking children was never really a pet person, and it must have seemed like a good way to soften the blow to tell my sister and me that Petey would join us later. His flight kept getting delayed. Then his flight was canceled. A few times. Flights from Wilmington to Miami were surprisingly unpredictable. A month after the move, the letter arrived.

> *Dear Annabanana and Leelee,*
>
> *I am fine, I miss you, but I will not be joining you in Florida. I am living with your dad's secretary, Caroline. I have had such a good time staying here that I don't want to leave. I have become Italian and I love spaghetti. We have it a lot!*
>
> *Love,*

I've always assumed that my parents really did give the dog to Caroline, Dad's secretary, even if the provenance of that paw print was rather sketchy, but as I type this page, it's clear: that canard was as much of a fantasy as my elfin overlord or the swashbuckling stir-fry.

Over the years, I worked Petey into countless comedy sketches and television appearances, much to my parents' mortification. I swore to myself that if I ever had children, I would never, ever, ever "Petey" them, which is why I was surprised that when my son asked why he didn't have a sibling, I assured him that he did.

"I don't know how to break it to you, but our cat, Stinky, is actually your sister, Amelia," I told Ezra when he was about the same age as I was when The Little Man befriended me.

Wide eyes.

"We put her in a cat costume for Halloween and the fur grew over the zipper."

Wider eyes.

I wasn't consciously coming up with this fabrication. It could be that I am a pathological liar, a diagnosis marked by chronic fictionalizing, something I freely admit I am guilty of. During my actressing years, I regularly testified to fluency in several languages with which I have only a passing familiarity and to being able to carry a tune, which makes me just plain ridiculous, as both are so easily disproven.

Is it possible I was engaging in the kind of teasing that you don't get when you're a singleton, or feeling guilty for failing to give him a sibling? Maybe. Ezra had endured years of surgeries to correct anomalies associated with a congenital birth defect and I thought it would be beneficial for him to be a big brother, but I couldn't muster the energy for another child.* Or maybe I was just fucking with him, relishing that ineffable jolt of pleasure you get when you test just how far you can stretch the truth with your children.

I can't say that my son believed that he had a sister named Amelia any more than he believed in the Easter Bunny or the Tooth Fairy, but I delighted in watching Ezra's eyes light up with the spark of imagination, or terror, as he'd feel for the zipper. I'd like to say that was as far as I took that story, but it's not. When Stinky the cat died, I couldn't let Amelia go as well—that would have been tragic—so Amelia had to be sent Elsewhere. Sometimes I'd say she was recovering from an unspecified illness, but I eventually settled on her being at boarding school, which had the added benefit of a veiled threat along the lines of *We could send you away too if you don't [fill in the blank]* and was just plausible enough to keep Ezra guessing.† It worked. Over the years, Amelia's notoriety has only grown.

One afternoon, when Ezra was in ninth grade, he and a group of his friends marched in tandem into my home office.

"Where is my sister, Mom? My friends don't believe me," Ezra demanded.

"She's at a boarding school in Canada."

"Prove it."

I picked up the phone and dialed a number at random. As luck

---

* VACTERL is an acronym for the constellation of birth defects. All were repaired except that he has a single kidney. "Well, you forgot to give me a second kidney, Mom," is his go-to when I'll ask why he forgot to clean his room/tell me he'll be home late/complete a school assignment, and it's hard to argue with that.

† I also said she had "issues," which is why she didn't come and visit us from this boarding school/institution. Just shoot me.

would have it, I'd phoned a social services center in Quebec. It was after hours and we reached a recording in both English and French that sounded enough like what I'd just described that the teenagers screamed with a kind of mad glee. Even I entertained the idea that I might actually have a daughter.

I sighed. "See, she's in Canada and has gone native. If you want to speak to her, you'll need to learn French." I threw up my hands in feigned exasperation and exited for dramatic effect.

When I told my sister about the latest chapter in the saga of Ezra's sister, Amelia, she said, "You're a weirdo," and, "It's like magical realism," and I racked my brain trying to remember if *One Hundred Years of Solitude* has a happy ending.*

"You know, I never connected it to our family," she went on to say, "but when I couldn't fall asleep at night, I used to ask my husband to tell me the story of our sons' births, and if I was really anxious, I'd ask him to tell me about the deals we closed when we worked at the same law firm."

"You asked him to recount the details of corporate real estate closings?"

"These were really complicated contracts."

Now who's the weirdo?

I THOUGHT ABOUT what she said for weeks, bristling at the notion of promoting anything bordering on magical thinking. I like to believe that I've provided my son with a modicum of security and a realistic understanding of the workings of the world.

---

* It doesn't.

"You want to be an indie rock star? That's great, but I hope you like Subway!"

Losing our home didn't just leave a mark on our mother. A day doesn't go by when I don't picture myself pushing all of my belongings in a shopping cart. I am stunned and awed by people's ability to function in the world. How does everyone do it? How do they manage to make their lives work? How secure are their family's finances? What kind of secrets are they keeping? I'll look at a home and wonder what *their* story is and whether they'll ever have to get out of Dodge in the middle of the night.

I'VE LIVED IN the same home since my son was born, in the hills of Los Feliz, a neighborhood bordering on the eastern end of the Santa Monica Mountains. With its steep inclines, once I deduced that I could avoid that scorching Southern California sun by exercising at night, I quit the gym and started going on evening runs. A bonus is that the neighborhood is an architect's worst nightmare. Each home was built with seemingly little thought to the style of neighboring properties. A Spanish colonial abuts a New England colonial. Some are ranch style with xeriscaping and seem appropriate to a desert clime, while others, with their merlons and hoardings, look like they've been airlifted from the Scottish Highlands. Others have so many competing designs, it's a reminder of what they say about makeup: you have to choose between eyes and lips. I lose myself in elaborate fantasies about the people who live in these homes as I run.

When Ezra was in middle school he started joining me a few

nights a week.* We delighted in rating the hominess quotient of the houses on our route, creating lurid backstories and weaving family mythologies into a tapestry we call "There's No Place Like Homey Home."

Neighboring houses that are twins: The lives of the people who live in these houses mirror the lives of those who live next door; they find themselves thinking the thoughts of their neighbors. They must be careful not to meet because when two parallel universes collide, it causes a disruption in the matrix and entropy occurs.†

Houses with naked porch light bulbs and tinfoil over a window: These people don't put sheets on their mattresses and eat meals off paper plates, and there's at least one closet with a cache of empty vodka bottles. The inhabitants are embroiled in a contentious custody battle, so who can blame them for hitting the sauce? There's a cousin "with issues" living in the back bedroom who only emerges once a day to eat bowls of dry cereal.

Houses with a prefab bump-out bay window in the kitchen: These people have squirreled away money in their IRAs instead of renovating the entire kitchen. Don't take no for an answer—you should be able to sell them at least two boxes of candy bars for school fund-raisers.

Sometimes our notions have proven to be right. There's a boxy McMansion on our block that so closely resembles a bank branch, I've been tempted to stick my ATM card into the mail slot. A family

---

* I have no doubt he was just trying to get out of doing homework, but I enjoyed the pretense that he wanted to spend time with me.

† This is also the premise of the J. J. Abrams series *Fringe*.

of bronze deer are posed on the front lawn, although a closer look reveals that their hooves are chained to the ground. We noticed the owners installing more and more elaborate security systems. First they put a metal fence, then they added a locked gate on the driveway, cameras, and bars on the windows. Even the second-story ones. Not long after the bars went up, we read in the paper the house was owned by an Armenian Mafia don. He put in solid-gold toilet seats just prior to getting arrested and sent to prison. The deer were really the clue; those padlocks on their hooves looked a lot like house-arrest monitoring bracelets.

It was while conducting our epistemological investigation of homey homes that we discovered Cat Town. At least, that's what we call it.

There's a set of eight historic bungalows known as the Snow White Cottages just down the street from our home. Built in 1932, they're adjacent to property where the original Walt Disney studios were located, now a food store. The stucco and brick storybook cottages have lopsided, sloping shingled roofs, miniature paned windows, and exposed wooden beams that outline their edges. A shaded, vaguely foreboding, winding path connects the tiny houses. Locals claim that indie rocker Elliott Smith wrote his heartbreaking lamentations in a claw-foot attic bathtub in one of the bungalows. They were featured in David Lynch's *Mulholland Drive*. One of the animators who worked on *Snow White* is rumored to have lived there and used them as the models for the dwarfs' cottage in the film.

We dubbed it Cat Town because we've never seen anyone there. Not a single person walking in or out in seventeen years. Only cats padding down the pathways or peering out of one of the narrow windows. How they've managed on their own has become an elaborately detailed, slightly macabre story we've made up, and when I say "we," I mean me.

I told Ezra to be careful when passing by because when the cats get lonely they breathe their magical cat breath into the mouths of neighborhood children. The breath casts a spell over them and the kids play with the cats for hours on end. "If you ever notice you've lost a few hours, Ezra, it's probably because you were hypnotized in Cat Town."

"But how do they pay rent, Mom?"

"Well, when the last human who lived there died, the cats tore into a sofa, took out the filling, and taxidermied her. They control her like a puppet with strings. You know how cats love string? They use the strings like levers, wrapping them around their claws, so she can write out rent checks by hand."

I'd noticed him rolling his eyes at my more recent demented twists to Cat Town, but then, things took a turn for the transitional. I was running errands in the neighborhood when I noticed that a padlocked metal fence had gone up around the perimeter. I was heartsick.

"I guess we were wrong; there's no way cats put that fence up. You need an opposable thumb to work that lock," I said to Ezra when I returned home.

His eyes lit up with that familiar spark of terror or imagination, and he sat me down and calmly explained that the felines of Cat Town suspected that humans were onto them but since the advent of computer touch screens they'd become self-reliant. "See, now they don't have to worry about writing checks or typing into computers. One of the cats dragged an iPad back to the bungalows with his teeth; a city council cat tapped the screen with his paw and ordered a locksmith. That was a *combination lock* you saw, wasn't it, Mom?"

"Well, yes it was, as a matter of fact."

"The kitties work that combination lock by grasping the dial in their mouths and turning it," he added, and then bounded out of the house. I was grateful for his crackerjack improvisation and struck with a "What on earth was I was thinking, concocting these lunatic fairy tales?" pang of guilt. This was not the plan—or was it?

I've been toying with the idea of creating a family mission statement. I read an article about how Stephen Covey, who authored *The 7 Habits of Highly Effective People*, posited that families should borrow from corporations to create "a clear, compelling vision of what [their] family is all about."* Covey's family came up with this:

"The mission of our family is to create a nurturing place of faith, order, truth, love, happiness, and relaxation, and to provide opportunity for each individual to become responsibly independent, and effectively interdependent, in order to serve worthy purposes in society."

That is the mission statement of people who would seem to belong to a different species than my family. I have friends who've crafted statements that are less ambitious: "We love nature. Our

---

* A family mission statement is the same kind of mythologizing that motivated the Crusades and inspired international air guitar competitions. How important is it? Historian Yuval Harari writes in *Sapiens* that creating shared fictions allowed Homo sapiens to achieve dominance over Neanderthals, who didn't have the brain capacity to conceive of strategies to unite large groups.

family's mission is to spend time in the great outdoors and leave no trace." I was hoping to borrow from the Nike slogan—"The mission of our family is to just do it"—or to use the tagline from *Alien* as a jumping-off point: "In our family no one can hear you scream."

My husband and son made merciless fun of me. "You can't find your keys every morning, and you want to make a mission statement?"

"Yes! It will be good for us. A mission statement works like the unifying theory that Einstein was searching for. He was convinced there was an all-encompassing, coherent theoretical framework of physics. A 'theory of everything' that fully explains and links together all physical aspects of the universe. Once we have that, we'll know where we came from, who we are, and where we're going. As I understand it, it hasn't panned out, but we're talking about the whole universe, and there are just three of us. Our mission statement will bring the world into sharper focus and surely that will help me locate my keys every day." They weren't buying it, but I am my father's daughter in more ways than I'd like to admit.

I watched from the front door as Ezra's lanky frame disappeared down the street to meet up with Harmony Tiger Lily or someone else he hangs out with whom I don't know because he's seventeen and so independent. Ezra will be leaving us to go to college next year and I'll still be living down the street from Cat Town. A family mission statement formed in my head: "We're a family that tells tall tales to add a little magic to our realism."

The torch has been passed down, as we say about the teachings of the Torah, *l'dor v'dor*, from generation to generation. Or he was just fucking with me.

I'm not sure why I thought Dorothy needed to
wear so much makeup, but it was the 1980s.

there's no people

like show people

In the 1982 blockbuster *Tootsie*, Dustin Hoffman plays an actor, Michael Dorsey, who, despite his visible five o'clock shadow and Mr. Potato Head features, minces his way into America's heart while masquerading as a female actress, Dorothy Michaels, on a trashy daytime television soap opera.

In the film, Hoffman accompanies his costar and BFF, Julie, played by Jessica Lange, to her childhood home. It's an immaculately maintained white-shingled colonial, surrounded by wheat fields, with a sturdy swing on the front porch and glowing embers crackling in the library's fireplace. Julie's childhood bedroom has been lovingly preserved by her doting, big-hearted, but lonely widower father, played by Charles Durning, who, wouldn't you know it, falls head over heels for Hoffman. Hilarity ensues. Spoiler alert: there's a happy ending!

People loved that movie. I loved that movie. It was a huge hit, but the plot was preposterous. Hoffman makes a plausible if hirsute woman, but once we got a glimpse of Lange's background, I laughed so hard, I peed a little in my pants. People who come from stable, loving homes do not go into showbiz.

Gérard Depardieu has been famously quoted as asking, "Who abandoned you?" upon learning that someone is an actor. No one abandoned me, but I learned at a young age that the theatrical community is the mother ship for those of us who don't fit in anywhere else.

Not to say that my first theatrical forays were in any way triumphant. By all accounts, I was a painfully shy child, but by virtue of having a dress shirt and a pulse, I managed to get cast in a production of *How to Succeed in Business Without Really Trying* at my summer camp. There was little in the way of sets or costumes; it was more of an "I've got a barn, let's put on a show" production that attracted campers who preferred hanging out in a barn to swimming laps in the cold lake. I was Secretary Number . . . something. Maybe 35? There were a lot of us in that secretarial pool, which was composed entirely of girls.*

Our big number was an ode to coffee. I will pack my own grounds and espresso maker if I suspect I might have limited access to strong coffee for even an overnight trip, but at twelve I had no idea why anyone would write an entire song about the importance of unfettered access to caffeine.

At one point, the word "coffee" is repeated a number of times. One of our ranks was to shout, "There's no more coffee!" to cue the

---

* Even though it was 1974 and copies of Gloria Steinem's *Ms.* magazine were on newsstands and many of our mothers' nightstands, there were no male secretaries in our pool.

end of the number. I was that office worker. I was supposed to count the number of times we repeated the word "coffee." It might have been two or fifteen or twenty-two thousand—even then I had no aptitude for math, but somehow, I'd been chosen for a role where the ability to sequence numbers was a prerequisite.

On the night of the big show, we were sandwiched in a conga line, making churning motions with our arms, like the wheels of a steam engine, and chanting, "Coffee, coffee, coffee, coffee." I got lost in the sound. The word "coffee" disappeared and we were no longer a group of pimply prepubescents, we were one undulating pimply prepubescent. Suddenly, a voice cried out, "There's no more coffee." Wait . . . that voice was supposed to be mine. Secretary Number 17 or 21 or 33 stepped in and saved the day. I have no idea what profession Secretary someone-other-than-me works in today, but I hope she became a highly sought-after accountant, because it really was impressive how she managed to keep track of all those "coffees." Despite the humiliation of missing my one and only line, I was hooked on a feeling.* It was the kind of kinship enjoyed by that subspecies of Homo sapiens the Homo thespian. It was clear I was headed for membership in the melting pot of teenage malaise: the high school drama club.

Thespian Troupe 391 was the cheerleading squad for stoners, closeted gay people, class clowns, kids looking for an outlet for outsized melancholy or exuberance, kids with secrets, kids who were too fat/too thin/too tall/too small, kids with low self-esteem/ undeservedly high opinions of themselves, kids with terrible acne

---

* I was also high on believing in Blue Swede's "Hooked on a Feeling," which hit the airwaves in 1974.

they hoped could be concealed with stage makeup, and that undiagnosed ADHD kid who had animated opinions on subjects of little to no importance. Except for the gay part, which I consider a failure of my imagination, you could have put me in any of those categories at one time or another.

Now that it's acceptable, at least in many urban communities, to identify as LGBTQIA* in high school, theater seems to attract a distinctly different breed of young person than in the past. The cast of *Glee* has much better skin and is more well-adjusted than the angst-ridden misfits depicted in *Fame*, the *Glee* of my generation.

Those years of moving around the country and financial ups and downs left their mark on me. I had accumulated an unarticulated repository of grief. Actors typically list special talents on their résumés. These range from the genuinely intriguing (speaks seven languages, Olympic javelin medalist, or hula hooper) to the mystifying (sings exceptionally off-key, ability to manufacture on-screen chemistry with Tom Cruise, or "fast talker"). One of my special talents was taking plays that contained a kernel of sadness and making that the central feature of the drama. Onstage at Miami Beach Senior High School, I was the most put-upon Cinderella ever. My performance wrung tears out of dry eyes, mostly mine, since I'd taught myself to cry on cue during the hundreds of hours spent honing this skill in my bathroom mirror. I turned *The Wizard of Oz* into a Greek tragedy. When I noted, as Dorothy, "We're not in Kansas anymore," it wasn't an observation, it was a primal

---

* "QIA"—"questioning, intersex, asexual"—is the latest addition to the "LGBT" acronym. I would like to suggest new nomenclature: "I'm all the things."

scream. The majority of the cast was stoned, which also slowed the pace down considerably; our version clocked in at about three hours. But we killed. Literally. Our audience was bused in from the neighboring retirement homes and ambulances were regularly stationed outside the auditorium. On several occasions, we were asked to pause while an elderly person was carried out on a stretcher. Honestly, it wasn't the biggest deal; Miami Beach was lousy with *alter cockers* (that's Yiddish for "farty old people," but not in a mean way, just in the endearingly gaseous way that you get when you're old), so this kind of scene was not unfamiliar to us. We never learned the fate of those senior citizens, but it's possible that we bored them into a merciful passing, which, come to think of it, isn't the worst way to go.

Those long hours of rehearsing, and even longer hours of pretending to rehearse but screwing off together, fostered a kind of intimacy—though I wouldn't have used that word at that time— that appealed to me. I had been indoctrinated into keeping family secrets. It wasn't hard to follow my mother's directive "If someone asks what your father does, don't answer them," because I genuinely didn't know, but it was unsettling to be warned that if the phone rang I should tell creditors that my parents weren't at home. My parents weren't home from 1971–80.

A play has well-defined rules, dialogue and blocking that are repeated each time the play is staged. Relationships, no matter how volatile, resolve with reliability. The emotional timbre might vary from performance to performance, but Brutus is always the betrayer in *The Tragedy of Julius Caesar*. If an actor blurts out, "Et tu, *Mark Anthony?*" that's a production that's gone off the rails.

This temporary abolition of ordinary existence provided a tonic to the unpredictability of my family life.* Every time I'd do a play, it was like being rescued from a sinking ship and put into a lifeboat. I'm sure people on sports teams feel buoyed in much the same way, except that in a play you also get to pretend to be someone else whose last name doesn't set them up for constant ribbing on the order of "Are you a good witch or a Gurwitch?"

If a young person who's been bitten by the drama bug manages to avoid being incarcerated or institutionalized, they might head off to college to study theater. Once there, they will quickly discover that there are distinct tribes in the nation of show people.

You've got your musical theater types. These hambones live to sing show tunes and are never happier than when in the company of their brethren. These folk are not unlike American tourists traversing distant lands. When they happen upon someone who looks like they might be from their hometown, their faces light up in recognition. Broadway babies will throw out a line from *Gypsy*, "If ya want to bump it . . . ," and if "Bump it with a trumpet!" comes back to them, abandon all hope; they'll "stay all night and sing 'em all."†

Then there are the straight (not necessarily literally) theater geeks. We often have cats or children or both cats and children named Stella or Maggie.‡ Tragically, we not only name our off-

---

* An irony is that when working in TV, script revisions, varied locations, and rotating directors are the norm. It's the opposite of the comfort of stepping into the same world over and over that plays can provide.

† If you're a show person, you know I'm paraphrasing Judy Garland. This footnote was not intended for you.

‡ If you're a show person, you know I am referring to Maggie from *Cat on a Hot Tin Roof* and Stella from *A Streetcar Named Desire*. You don't need this footnote either.

spring after characters, our roles often bleed into our lives. I once dated someone who instructed me to hand-wash his underpants because "Hamlet doesn't do laundry!"

Show people, all kidding aside, are often humanists who want to tell uplifting and impactful stories. However, there are other, saner careers in which to pursue these lofty ideals that don't involve wearing pancake makeup and delivering dialogue like, "I've been building hot tubs in Kuwait. They're very popular 'cause it's a nice way to relax with your wives." That memorable line was spoken, without a trace of irony, by the enormously talented and genuinely philanthropic George Clooney when he was on *The Facts of Life.* But it's like what David Mamet says about people who pursue a life in the theater: "Those with something to fall back on invariably fall back on it. Those of you with nothing to fall back on, you will find, are home."

At New York University, I discovered a rarefied variety of show person: the experimental theater artist. The avant-garde movement questioned the relevance of the kind of "legit" theater I'd been exposed to growing up, promoted social and political change, and was possibly unhygienic. Our studies included spending a great deal of time rolling around on top of each other naked. If you've ever been to a corporate retreat where you work on "building trust" by closing your eyes, falling backward, and having the group catch you, this is much like that, except for us, building trust was an extreme sport. One particularly memorable assignment involved a noted performance artist convincing us to run barefoot and blindfolded through the streets of downtown New York—he really missed his calling on Wall Street.

This theater aesthetic was pioneered by French surrealist play-

wright Antonin Artaud in the 1920s. Artaud theorized in his semi-
nal writing on the Theater of Cruelty that Western theater had
fallen into a lassitude and needed a lacerating wake-up call. Not
everyone goes to the theater for a lashing "assault on the senses,"*
but that it was an unpopular art form was a bonus. I felt special being a part of something that most people couldn't possibly understand. I can only assume that supporters of a return to the gold
standard are attracted by a similar outsider status.

There might be some sort of genetic predisposition toward ideo-
logically driven fraternities. I was warned against just this kind of
thing by my grandmother Frances. One of her aunts had to be
begged to leave when the family was emigrating from Russia, because she was a Bolshevik sympathizer. She wound up as a union
organizer in a garment factory, never married, and might have
even "liked girls." There was also a cousin who was rumored to
have fallen under the spell of this very same degenerate theater
crowd and ended up driving a cab, but I was undeterred. I had no
plan B.

I'm going to include here a few sentences from the mission statement of Mabou Mines, one of the theater companies whose aesthetic
and esprit de corps spoke to me: *"The most incendiary of experimental
ensembles. Originally associated with the conceptual art movement, performance art and minimalist music, Mines is an artist-driven ensemble
confederation, generating original works and re-imagined adaptations of
classic works through collaboration among its members."*

---

* Would it surprise you to also learn that Artaud ended up in a straitjacket?
Still, he remains one of the most influential figures in modern theater.

If you are not moved to your core by those words, congratulations, you are no doubt living a life of moral virtue and are probably gainfully employed. When I read this kind of manifesto, I am tempted to sell my wedding ring, hitchhike across the country, and build sets for their next production.

Even more intoxicating to me was that this world was organized much like the FLDS faction of Mormonism, minus the unflattering rayon dresses, starched hair, and prohibition against drinking coffee. In the absence of the promise of fame and fortune, these theater companies were led by visionaries running the gamut from benevolent dictators to maternal or paternal gurus who attracted grateful acolytes. Bingo. I had found my people.

A month into college, the avuncular Richard Schechner, founder of the Performance Group, whose bacchanalian production of *Dionysus* in '69 was legendary in the experimental world, gave a lecture on the connection of rituals and rites of passage of the ancient world to modern theater to my Introduction to Theater 101 seminar. "I want to follow you around," I announced to him afterward. His ex-wife was already my acting teacher and our class took turns babysitting his son; I promptly enrolled in the Performance Studies department, and would have offered to shine his shoes given the opportunity. As it happened, Schechner was directing a Jacobean tragedy and he needed a young actress to play a lady-in-waiting trying to wheedle her way to a higher status in the royal court. It was a perfect match, given my desire to suffer stylishly onstage. The next thing I knew, I was starring in a production Off-Broadway at iconic producer Joseph Papp's Public Theater, home to the New York Shakespeare Festival. I had no idea Schechner had a reputation for encouraging women to follow him home. He was a father figure, a mentor, a guru, you name it, and, for the record, he never made a pass at me.*

The Public Theater houses numerous stages within its walls. Mabou Mines was performing in one space and a concert adaptation of *Alice's Adventures in Wonderland*, *Alice in Concert*, starring Meryl Streep, was closing out their run. Streep can channel sadness like nobody's business. She wept while hitting the high notes! I must have seen that show a dozen times, hoping to one day be known as the Meryl Streep of my generation. At my costume fitting, I was issued a pair of knee pads to wear under my Jacobean-style gown. Sliding them on, I saw that Meryl Streep's name was crossed out and mine was written in its place. That's the closest I've ever gotten to becoming the Meryl Streep of my generation, but it seemed like an auspicious beginning.

The play closed before it opened. I resumed my classwork, headed to London for a semester abroad, and had just returned to New York when my dad phoned with the news that his latest business had gone belly-up. There was no money for me to continue my education. My parents declined to share their tax returns with me, effectively nixing my chances of getting financial aid.

Just like Mobile, this belly flop was years in the making. What did them in was Abscam. In what became an infamous sting operation in the late 1970s, an FBI agent posed as an Arab sheik and offered congressmen (or entrapped them into taking, depending on

---

* My cousin David worked briefly with Schechner. David drove a cab while he was in the theater company but ended up leaving the theater and opening a chiropractic practice. He had a plan B.

which side of the transaction you were on) bribes for casino licenses and building permits. The FBI rented a yacht and invited local businesspeople to give the sheik some social cred. Is it any wonder my dad was invited into the fold? Casinos? Kickbacks? A mysterious investor with millions to spare? My mother says she knew that the whole thing was fishy because they were served Cheez Whiz on Ritz crackers at a cocktail party. Despite being raised in a working-class family, she has always had an innate elegance and an eye for quality. They never went to another party, but when the sting came to light, my parents were investigated, as often happens in these sorts of situations, and the IRS opened an audit. That's how it came out that they hadn't filed their taxes in years, although that information wasn't shared with me until much later. All I knew at the time was that once again, it seemed like the floor had dropped out from beneath us.

Armed with the confidence you can only muster when you're nineteen and have been cast in exactly one professional production, I was certain I could find a place in the theater scene, but downtown New York was gentrifying; theater companies weren't expanding and couldn't absorb us next-gen avant-wannabes. I needed to start a theater family of my own, and I needed to make money to do that.

I worked odd jobs and pounded the pavement, as the saying goes, sliding my picture and résumé under the doors of casting offices all over town until one day I got lucky. In the early 1980s, at any hour of the day or night, the saddest clothing sale in North America was taking place in Greenwich Village, on the corner of Astor Place that was home to the 1,800-pound sculpture known as the Cube. The bedraggled denizens of the Lower East Side sold the clothing right off their backs, and that's how a grubby black leather motorcycle jacket saved my life. I put that jacket on and didn't take it off for the next four years. Wearing that jacket, I was able to get cast as "punky but non-threatening chick" in commercials and landed the role of a gang girl on the soap opera *Guiding Light*. My Brechtian-alienation style of acting didn't play well in this arena, but the head writer, Pamela Long Hammer, a former Miss Alabama, took pity on a fellow Southerner. A part that was scheduled for a handful of appearances turned into three years of intermittent employment.

A group of us formed a collective to try to catch the proverbial last wave of the avant-garde scene. One of our fellow students, Peter, emerged as our director. That he was Austrian carried a lot of weight with us because the favored writers of the alienated include those barrel-of-laughs crowd-pleasers Kafka, Wedekind, and Büchner. Peter wore vintage suits with pants held up by rope in lieu of a belt. He smoked Gitanes, was squatting in the back of an art gallery, and carried his belongings in a cardboard suitcase. He appeared to have emerged straight out of a Beckett play. We didn't work on traditional acting skills like diction, projection, and script interpretation. We were more interested in dating each other and dreaming up ways to make an audience work as hard as possible to understand what we were doing.

Our first outing was a meditation on the loss of innocence and the death of glamour, or maybe it was the other way around. We got ourselves booked at the Pyramid Club, a downtown venue.*

We premiered with our exploration of innocence, the highlight

---

* My parents came to the Pyramid. They'd heard the East Village was a jungle and thought it would be hilarious if they wore the matching Abercrombie & Fitch safari outfits they'd gotten for a trip to the Amazon.

of which was when a talented sprite of an actress got her period for the first time. This effect was to be achieved by breaking a sandwich baggie filled with ketchup in her panties. We never rehearsed this pivotal moment, but the concept seemed plausible. After her several failed tries at clapping her legs together hard enough to break the bag, I reached over and squashed it myself, which was greeted with hilarity from the audience. The condimented actress and I vowed we would always remember this as our worst moment onstage. We were wrong.

For the next week's installment we were set to depict the decline and fall of glamour by evoking the silent-film era. Footage of us frolicking in an abandoned lot wearing vintage gowns was to accompany our performance. On the evening of the show, three of us posed in a series of choreographed gestures, but the projector broke down, as did the tiny portable cassette player with our soundtrack. Ever resourceful, our director jumped onto the stage and beat out a rhythm on a mop and pail. As we slowly sank to the floor, a metaphor for our demise, people yelled, "Come on, die already!" during the entire half hour it took us to descend to the stage. We couldn't have been more pleased with the response.

In what we hoped would be our splashy international debut, Peter secured funding for us to stage *Mörder, Hoffnung der Frauen*— *Murderer, Hope of Women*—a play so controversial that the author, Secessionist painter Oskar Kokoschka, was run out of town following its premiere.* We were to perform this colossal downer at the Vienna International Theater Fest, a prestigious gathering of pretentious artists. When I told the producers of *Guiding Light*

---

* It might take an entire other book to explain the plot of that play.

about the gig, my character was written off the show under the pretense of a very long European vacation. How Gina Daniels, who was trying to wheedle her way to a higher status in Springfield, afforded this vacay was as mysterious as the comas people were always falling into on those shows. These flights of fancy have never troubled the audience for the soaps. When I landed at the Munich airport, I was swarmed by a group of American soap fans.

"Oh my God, it's Gina Daniels," they cried in unison. "Soap operas are real!"

Once in Vienna, we worked and lived communally, even sharing underwear.* How were we received? From the moment we stepped onstage, the crowd booed. When I swung a real dead chicken over my head as I paced the stage, the audience seemed just as confused as I was. The play was about something important. Love, loss . . . poultry? It really didn't matter. We were engaged in heated late-night discussions of art in broken English. I took up with a local, drank *kaffee mit schlag*, and went to work each day in a palace. I was in heaven.

When we returned to New York we were invited to stage the show at the Guggenheim Museum. It was the dead of winter. We had small, polite audiences, mostly docents of the museum. After the show, the audience cleared out quickly and quietly. I trudged home alone through the snow each night. The notoriously cruel John Simon summed up the production in *New York* magazine with one word: "WHY?"

---

* This was instituted by our member from Iceland, where almost everyone is related. People raise children communally, so why not share panties?

That was the last show we did together. The movie *Wall Street* came out, with its catchy tagline "Greed is good," and with those words, materialism officially supplanted nihilism in New York. My fellow experimental theater classmate Wendy Hammers remembers the exact moment she knew the climate had changed: "The day a Gap opened up on St. Marks Place in the East Village. I stood on the corner and cried." It was only 1987, but the eighties were officially over.

We drifted apart. Peter headed back to Austria, others to academia, and I concentrated on getting work in television and films. I threw in my lot with another kind of show people, show-*business* people, people who were interested in building careers, not tearing down commercial theater. Actors working in television and films often forge fellowships of sorts, especially on long-running shows, but on big-budget productions, money, power, and celebrity can divide casts into castes.*

Once in Los Angeles, I scored a gig as one of Candice Bergen's ill-fated secretaries on *Murphy Brown*. Secretary Number 10 was an actress who came to work in character as, you guessed it, Maggie from *Cat on a Hot Tin Roof* and Eliza Doolittle from *My Fair Lady*. It launched my comedic television career. I didn't even own a television at that time.

I am fortunate to have enjoyed the perks of working on big-budget productions. Among them are unlimited access to fresh

---

* Theater is far more egalitarian. Whether your role is large or small, you need to be present at the theater for the entirety of the production, while actors can be starring in the same film but never meet. Also, actors typically share dressing rooms in plays, while a movie star might have a caravan of trailers.

coffee and having someone knock on the door of your private dressing room to inquire, "Do you have time to try on a cute skirt?" As a writer, I spend a lot of time on coffee runs to and from a shared office with writers whose company I truly enjoy. It's a privileged existence. Still, I can't tell you how much I wish someone would ask me if I have time to try on a cute skirt. Yes. "Yes, I would love to" will always be the answer.

Given my early exposure, the drama bug is like a virus lying dormant in my system and it doesn't take much to trigger a full-blown case. In 2013, I was offered a juicy role in a play by a well-regarded playwright, but what really sweetened the deal was that the production ran through the holiday season. A night at the theater provides audiences a welcome respite from those carbohydrate-laden meals from Thanksgiving through New Year's, and working in the theater provides the perfect excuse for begging off your family's festivities.*

It had been several years since I'd done a theatrical production and I assumed that at this point in my life I was immune to the kind of bonding that had taken place in the casts of my youth. We were scheduled for three weeks of rehearsal at a theater located deep in the San Fernando Valley. The Valley has an undeservedly bad reputation. There are neighborhoods with quaint restaurants and friendly enclaves where kids shoot hoops in the street. Then there's this part of the Valley: chop shops, warehouses, and parking lot barbecue pits smoking the kind of mystery meats that make me

---

* Napping during a play is more prevalent during the carb-laden-meal holidays, but actors prefer nappers to unwrappers. No matter how slowly you open that fucking candy, we can hear it onstage!

question if we should really be letting our cats roam freely on the streets.

The theater was located in the shadow of the clown. That's the thirty-two-foot, luridly bright, neon, macabre mascot of the landmark Circus Liquor in North Hollywood. Alicia Silverstone gets mugged in *Clueless* right under the clown. Snoop Dogg features the clown in one of his videos. It says something about the clientele that Circus has its own line of baby apparel. Try not to imagine who would put their baby in a Circus Liquor onesie. Just don't do it.

The transition from writing desk to rehearsals was disorienting. Despite working with the actors and support staff for eight hours a day, sharing meals and coffee breaks, during the first week of rehearsal, I couldn't remember anyone's name. I managed to learn that one of the actors in the cast voiced a small mammal on my son's favorite animated cartoon series, and I came home every night and announced, "I'm working with the squirrel from *Rick and Morty*." And every night Ezra would correct me: "Bill plays a raccoon on *Regular Show*." I had such mixed feelings that I kept getting lost on the way to work and arrived so tardily every day I was sure I'd be fired within the week.

I was playing a tough but benign Jewish mama, circa 1940. The majority of the cast was in their early twenties and playing, to hilarious effect, the grade school classmates of my eleven-year-old daughter. By this time, I'd already portrayed a mother on-screen, but this was the first go-round as the matriarch of a theater family.* The show featured several holiday pageants, so dozens of wigs and

---

* If I play your mother on-screen, you're likely to do well: Shia LaBeouf and Vincent Kartheiser have played my progeny.

elaborate costumes, and an outrageous number of props, were foisted upon us. "Where the fuck is my frankincense?" you'd hear whispered above the din as actors furiously swapped out their Pilgrim hats for Magi headpieces. It was a colorful chaos that reminded me of the themed birthday parties I hosted when my son was little, and something cracked open in my heart.

Resistance is futile. I was the first person in the cast to say, "I love you," as we left the theater each night.

Casts typically make the holidays festive. Our dressing room resembled a department store window: we had a tree and a menorah, candy canes were hung from the makeup lights, we secret Santaed, and I was more than happy to let my onstage role translate to production mother hen.

I stepped in to broker truces in dressing-room squabbles recognizable to anyone from a large family. "Meghan gets to have her wig put on first every night, it's not fair! I've got to get onstage too" sounds a lot like "Heather's been in the shower so long, it's not fair! I need to get in the bathroom too." One afternoon during the run of the show, I spent hours rummaging through my bedroom closet. "Girls, I've brought clothes, some of my favorite things, and I'm sure there's enough for all of you!" I said as I entered our dressing room, brimming with maternal affection. They tore into the loot. A few choice pieces were meted out, but most of it was deemed uncool. They'd treated me with exactly the same deference as my actual child. Roasted!*

The performers, directors, writers, designers, stagehands, and

---

* According to my son, "roasted" is the new "scorched," which was the old "dissed," replacing the now positively archaic "burned."

stage managers that make up theatrical tribes aren't the only artistic communities that form filial bonds. Musicians regularly hold fund-raisers for collaborators who fall ill; visual artists share lives and work spaces; even Larry Page, cofounder of Google, that techie confederation of digital artists, proudly declared, "Google isn't just a company, it's a family." You'd have to Google that to see if his employees agree.

I can't speak for the other arts, but our fraternities have great staying power, much like childhood friendships forged on the play-ground.* I count several members of Thespian Troupe 391 among my nearest and dearest. On the other hand, a theater feud can be lasting and downright Hatfield and McCoy. If you're a mainstay in one director's set, you can expect to never work on a rival's pro-ductions; it's that intense.

A few years back, I found myself being interviewed by an engaging young journalist named Sam for a TV series I was head-lining. At the end of our conversation, he mentioned his last name: Schechner. As in my mentor Richard Schechner's son, whom I'd last seen when he was three years old. I'm sure there are people who have gone to greater lengths than reminding a journalist that they changed their diapers to get a good write-up in the *WSJ*, but I don't know of an example offhand.

I can't even count how many times in my life I've wished I weren't a show person. Foiled by math, again! If it weren't for pe-rennially confusing milliliters and milligrams, I could have gone into medicine and been useful in the way that Doctors Without

---

* Chimps and gorillas that bond through playing together as youngsters form alliances that continue throughout their lives.

Borders gets to swoop in and do something like fix fistulas instead of having honed the ability to cry on cue.* But lately, I have been struck by how one of the concepts, that of the restorative power of entering "time without time," or liminality, which I learned about from Schechner, is more essential than ever. In the ancient world, early humans developed ritualized forms of play that created a poetic world alongside the world of nature, and in this way created a liminal state. Participating in this sacred suspension of time contributed to the cohesiveness of their community.†

Schechner has developed a slew of improvisational techniques to reinforce the singularity of the theatrical event and unify the performers and audience. He'll direct his actors to wait until the audience is completely silent before speaking or moving. So if someone coughs or rustles, the performers freeze until you can hear a pin drop in the theater. Often the audience catches on and begins to play along with the performers. They'll calibrate the speed of scenes by either making sounds or shushing their neighbors so the action can continue. It's electrifying. Directors regularly incorporate these kind of elements into shows now. What was once avant-garde is now de rigueur as producers seek to provide compelling

---

* Some parents teach their kids how to cook or play ball. I challenged my son to cry-offs and relished beating him to the tears.

† Anthropologists have long posited that synchronous activities like dancing, singing, praying, and even deep breathing in groups lead to "collective effervescence"—positive emotions that break down the boundaries between self and group. People speak of the experience of joining in the hajj, the pilgrimage to Mecca, in these terms.

reasons for people to tear themselves away from binge-watching *Transparent.**

In the recent past, there were many more opportunities for communal transcendence. You might have glimpsed it in a religious service or on a hike or airplane, but there are few places now beyond the reach, temptation, and distraction of our devices. There is nothing more depressing to me than walking into a restaurant and seeing diners sitting together but transfixed by their individual screens. Except when I'm that jerk. Theater remains one of the precious few spaces where the outside world ceases to exist. Kind of like sex, except that your playbill provides more information about the people you're engaging with than you might glean during a Tinder hookup.

At theaters around the world, at seven thirty p.m., the stage manager announces, "The house is open," to let us know you have arrived at our home. When you step through those doors, we welcome you, however briefly, into our tribe. And, if you're going to the theater? Let's face it, you're probably show people too.

---

* I am that person who finds it hard to tear myself away from binge-watching *Transparent.*

Dauphin Island Bridge

Dauphin Island, Alabama

There would be white sand, grand parties, casinos, the full resort life.

massacre island

Growing up, I pined for the day when I'd receive a letter or call informing me that I'd inherited something of value, maybe a castle or, even better, a musty but elegant classic six in a prewar building just off of Central Park West, left to me by a forgotten spinster aunt or long-lost cousin.

My paternal grandmother, Rebecca, was fond of sending care packages. These boxes started arriving when I went off to college in New York. You just couldn't convince her that stuffed cabbage, even when wrapped in layers of waxed paper and tinfoil, sealed in plastic, and then covered in tinfoil again, didn't travel well. Home-made banana bread was always included, along with old-world reminders to "stay close to the family" and the dangers of "catching a cold *down there*."* As the years went by, she sent increasingly

---

* Becca layered long silk drawers under her girdle, topped that with panties and nylons under both dresses and pantsuits. Her brassieres resembled iron

disparate and eccentric items. The last package arrived on my door-step in 1991, a year before she died. It contained: two teaspoons, a steak knife, an opened box of aspirin, the emerald green brocade tunic she'd worn to my Bat Mitzvah, a signed copy of Isaac Bashevis Singer's *The Spinoza of Market Street*, and an extension cord coiled around a tattered eggshell-blue Tiffany box lid, upon which she'd made the notation *in case I ever get a little house of my own again*. Wouldn't you know it? My grandmother received a gift from Tiffany and all I got was the lid to the box! Still, I treasure these totems and accepted that they represented the totality of my inheritance, when the news I'd longed for finally arrived.

"Your land is taking a beating," my dad says on the phone.

"Whaaaat?"

It's August 25, 2005. My husband and I have wrangled a short vacation in Vermont, driving through historic towns, stopping at rustic inns with good wine lists, while CNN broadcasts coverage of Hurricane Katrina barreling across the Gulf Coast. I can't remember which family members are still scattered across the South, but Dad calls with an update: our friends in NOLA and the few cousins left in Mobile have made it to higher ground, but my Dauphin Island property is in trouble. I have no idea what he's talking about.

He tells me that a quarter-acre lot, located on a barrier island thirty-five miles south of Mobile in the Gulf of Mexico, that once belonged to my grandmother is now mine. Well, mine and several other family members'. Rebecca intended to leave the land to her three children—my father; his brother, Bert; and their sister,

---

lungs. She never wore a dress without a long slip. Watching her dress was both mesmerizing and terrifying.

Phyllis—but neither my dad nor his brother wanted assets in his name, as they'd both filed for bankruptcy (not the first time for either) when the will was written. I consider offering up some kind of clever axiom like "The family that prays together stays together," but no words come to mind that rhyme with "bankruptcy." That is why my sister; I; Uncle Bert's kids, Michael and Mindy; and Aunt Phyllis inherited her land. Dad has been paying our share of the taxes for Lisa and me since Rebecca's death in 1992. Why am I only hearing about this now?

"Her will has never been probated. Things move slowly in the South."

"So, is that 'Dolphin,' like the mammal?"

"It's French. It was named for Louis XIV's great-grandson and heir, *le dauphin*."*

"Sounds fancy to me."

I GIDDILY REPORT the news to my husband: "We've inherited an *island*! Let's build a summer home! We're rich! We've got land!" I'm over the moon. Our house carries a mortgage, our cars are leased, our son belongs to the future, but this plot of land is owned outright. I Google the island and it's not just some unlucky sandbar being battered by the storm, it's my land. I feel the kind of pride of ownership that comes with actual ownership.

"What's the place like?" my husband says, getting caught up in my excitement.

"I have no idea. I've never been there."

---

* "Dauphin" also is the French word for "dolphin."

Thus begins a ten-year fascination with my island and deep dive into our family's Southern roots.

Four hundred and ninety years before the call from my dad, a Spanish explorer followed the gulf coastline up from Florida and mapped the island, but it wasn't until January 31, 1699, that the French explorer Pierre Le Moyne d'Iberville claimed the territory for France and the island entered recorded history with a catchy and evocative name: Massacre Island.

When d'Iberville landed he encountered massive piles of skeletons, but it wasn't until years later that it would be understood that what he'd come upon wasn't the site of a massacre. The island was dotted with burial mounds left there by the earliest known inhabitants of North America and excavated by a recent storm. Not much is known of these indigenous people, the Mound Builders, a collection of nomadic tribes whose territory included the tributaries of the Mississippi from AD 900 to 1500, except for the expansive earthen formations, something like flat-topped pyramids, that they left behind.

Speculation is that the island was their winter stomping ground. Most likely the Mound Builders succumbed to smallpox or influenza after their first contact with these Eurasian infectious diseases. We do know a lot about their palates: they left millions of clam and oyster shells. Still visible, these enormous piles are evidence of thousands of delicious meals.*

In 1700, the island, which was now the capital of the Louisiana

---

* Just to note, my Northern ancestors kept kosher, but not the Southerners, really: it would be a *shonda*—that's Yiddish for "crime"—to live on the Gulf Coast and not eat shellfish.

French territories, became an important trading post for goods from South America and given the much more welcoming name Îsle Dauphine. Then, during the Civil War, in the Battle of Mobile Bay, on August 8, 1864, as the monitor USS *Tecumseh* hit a mine and began to sink, Admiral David Farragut gave the famous rallying cry "Damn the torpedoes, full speed ahead" and, in what was a decisive victory for the North, took the southernmost outpost of the Confederate army, Fort Gaines. The fort has been lovingly preserved and houses artifacts from early life on the island. Creepy! Historic! Shellfish! My island has it all.

In the aftermath of Katrina, every major news outlet writes about the island as the canary in the coal mine for how climate change is affecting the coastal areas of North America, and I follow this reporting obsessively. "The western end of this Gulf Coast island has proved to be one of the most hazardous places in the country for waterfront property. Since 1979, nearly a dozen hurricanes and large storms have rolled in and knocked down houses, chewed up sewers and water pipes and hurled sand onto the roads," I read, in *The New York Times*, no less. Citing the cost of shoring up the coastline in the face of rising sea levels, scientists are wondering if it isn't time to give up the ghost. "If ever there were a poster child for a barrier island that shouldn't have been developed, it's Dauphin Island, and now we all keep paying for it," says Orrin H. Pilkey, a Duke University coastal geologist. Katrina not only washed away entire homes, forty or fifty beach lots have been swallowed by the sea. I read that FEMA is offering buyouts to landowners.

"Some people are already taking the FEMA buyout, Annabelle. Though those are folks whose land is already underwater," the mayor of the island, Jeff Collier, writes to me in August 2006, in our first correspondence. I call members of my family, imploring them to begin the process of probating the will and issuing a call to completely contradictory actions.

"We should donate our land to the local estuarium."

"We should build a family vacation house!"

"We should sell before the island is completely underwater."

But we're all busy with our lives in Texas; Atlanta; Washington, D.C.; San Francisco; and Los Angeles. We're five owners who live in five different states. Things move slowly in the South, but things move even slower in our family.

Everyone I tell about my inheritance, including my own son, says the same thing: "You're from the South? I didn't know there were Jewish people in Alabama."

More than two million Eastern European Jews came to America between 1887 and the start of World War II. Most arrived at Ellis Island, looking like the bus and truck touring company of *Fiddler on the Roof*, with nothing more than a letter vouching for them from a family member who'd already immigrated, the clothes on their back, and a case of cholera or TB. While the majority settled in big northern cities like New York and Philadelphia, others entered the country through Boston or southern ports like Charleston and Mobile. The Jewish population of Mobile has never been greater than it was in 1918, with more than 2,200 Jews.*

By all accounts, Herschel Ripps, my grandmother Rebecca's father, who went by the anglicized Harry Ripps, came to this country

---

* The Jewish population in Alabama is so low that in 2007, one synagogue offered a fifty-thousand-dollar bonus to Jewish families who would agree to move to Alabama. It worked. As of 2013, the Dothan congregation had grown from thirty-eight to seventy-one families.

after his brother, a furrier by trade, found work tanning leather along the Mississippi and sent word back that money could be made in America. Great-Grandpa Harry arrived on our shores with his mother, Goldie, and his four sons, settling first in Prichard and eventually in Mobile. He'd left his wife, Pesha, and daughters Rebecca and her older sister Freda in Russia, intending to send for them when he'd made his fortune. When word got to them that Pesha died, Harry married another recent Jewish immigrant in Mobile, and when that wife died as well, he married again. Was it because he'd started a new life or that the daughters were less valuable as workers to him, who knows, but they were either farmed out to other family members or placed in orphanages—we really don't know that either, because the two refused to ever discuss it. Ever wonder what kind of people send their children alone on perilous journeys across the globe? My people. The Ripps brothers begged Harry to send for their sisters, so young Rebecca and Freda crossed the ocean on a steamship, in steerage. Rebecca showed up in Mobile with her head shaved. She'd entered the country with a terrible case of lice—a good indication that whatever happened during those lost years, it probably wasn't very good.*

Meanwhile, my grandfather Ike's father, Bert Gurwitch, and his clan left from the same part of Eastern Europe to seek their fortune, stopping first in London, where they opened a tobacco store. Family lore says they had tickets on the *Lusitania* but were engaged in one of those famously endless Jewish good-byes and missed the boat.

---

* We never knew Rebecca's real age, because she lopped off at least a few years to be good marriage material, but nearing sixty, she claimed to be older so she could collect Social Security sooner.

By trade, Bert was a welder in the shipyards, so they followed the work in the busiest coastal cities, starting in Quincy, Massachusetts, then moving south to Charleston, South Carolina; Chickasaw, Alabama; Prichard; and later Mobile.

My grandmother Rebecca always stressed the importance of knowing who someone's "people" were. She never took into account that people might not like us if they considered who our people were.

Malcolm Gladwell wrote in *The New Yorker* in 2014 about "climbing the crooked ladder of success," immigrant families working on the margins to become respectable pillars of society.* These climbers' aim wasn't the establishment of a criminal empire, it was simply advancement of the clan, and that's what motivated the Gurwitch and Ripps families to team up.

Great-Grandpa Bert's welding skills proved invaluable to maintaining the local bootleggers' stills, while Harry had ties with ship captains because his dry goods shop stocked the "slop chests" (slop chests were essentially a ship's general store) for the vessels docking in Mobile. Sugar was one of the biggest imports in those days, and as it's also a key ingredient in making moonshine, the bootleggers were always looking for new ways to score it. If bags of sugar got wet during their journey from the Caribbean, they were legally unsalable, but damp sugar wasn't a problem for the bootleggers. Bert enlisted Harry because of his relationship with the captains, and he became a broker of the sticky stuff, earning him the nickname "Sugar." Funny thing: once Bert and Sugar were in league with the bootleggers, an awful lot of wet sugar started showing up on the docks of Mobile. One of Bert's sons, Isaac, was introduced to

---

* The "crooked ladder" is a term that was coined by sociologist James O'Kane.

Sugar's daughter Rebecca, and my future grandparents got married. I owe my existence to white-lightning moonshine.

Bert's wife, Rose, my great-grandmother, was one enterprising broad. She sold the moonshine from a pickle barrel in her store. You'd tap a sterling silver cup that was attached to the barrel with twine, and she'd pour you a swig for ten cents. Same cup for everyone.* When some "circus people," the Kurfetses, moved in next door, Rose saw a chance to "make a fast dollar," as they say in my family. She sold shots of white lightning to the women waiting to get their fortunes told by Mrs. Kurfets. The more they drank, the more time they'd spend with Mrs. Kurfets, who charged by the minute. If the reading had some particularly bracing content, Rose would sell them another shot on the way out. My cousins have made me take a blood oath not to write that Rose ran a brothel, but she did rent out rooms behind the store to a cadre of single ladies who engaged in remarkably short-lived relationships. No one in the family disputes that during the 1950s, all the boys in the family would drop in on Edna's joint, and when Edna, one of Rose's former tenants, answered the door, you'd say, "The Gurwitches sent me," and she'd show you right in. The only door being a member of my family ever opened led to a brothel.

The Depression hit my family hard. Three generations were living together and everyone worked to put food on the table. Even though Prohibition ended in 1933, Alabama was one of seventeen states that continued to tightly control alcohol distribution, so there

---

* It was probably her Kiddush cup. Many Jewish families, even if poor, have one sterling silver cup used for holiday rituals; the sterling was thought to kill germs.

was still money in moonshine. Before setting off for grade school, my father was charged with marking the sidewalk outside their home with an X in chalk. It was a signal, part of what was sometimes referred to as "the hobo code" among the unemployed, that work was available. Hard-up locals would line up to pick blackberries in exchange for white bread and baloney sandwiches and cups of coffee that Dad would make and serve on the porch. Dad says the sound of corks popping as blackberry wine fermented in the bathtub would wake them up all through the night.

As the country geared up for World War II, my father and his first cousin Billy collected scrap metal in Dad's little red wagon to donate for the war effort. Sometimes this "scrap metal" was copper piping that eight-year-old boys were just small enough to harvest from the crawl spaces under neighbors' homes. When Ike got wind of this, he was pissed. Why donate when there was a fast dollar to be made? He directed them to sell to the local scrap metal dealers instead. They also hustled pool at the Wide Awake Pool Hall and Café, standing on apple crates they stole from the A&P as they took their shots. No one saw the boys coming and they made a lot of bank.*

During the 1940s and well into the '50s, the ladder was, if not crooked, tilted at a perilous angle. Our cousins owned a jewelry and pawn store, Gulf Coast Jewelry and Tobacco. One of their surefire ways of making a fast dollar was to announce a going-out-of-business sale and price things at a great discount. Legally,

---

* Billy grew up to become a dentist. Members of our family were his first patients. I'm glad I didn't know about the pool hustle when I was his patient, but he did have awfully steady hands when examining my teeth.

you could only sell merchandise already in the store, so in the middle of the night, my dad and all the cousins were rounded up to load in more stock. Like pennies in a junk drawer, inventory seemed to magically multiply.

Our family was run by a matriarch, the wife of Becca's older brother, Uncle Sam: Annie Mitchell Ripps, the cousin I'm named for. She brought her father Meyer's wealth into the family, so her opinion carried a lot of weight. Every Sunday, all the family would gather at her home. She made business decisions and even dictated when and how many children you were going to have. But even Annie couldn't solve every problem. President Truman's Justice Department got wind of irregularities with the jewelry store. My dad was sent to Washington, D.C., with fifty thousand dollars strapped to his waist to drop off at the office of a federal prosecutor. The bribe was accepted, but Sam and cousin Joe were found guilty of tax evasion and sent to "camp," as the family referred to it.*

The family didn't just go to "camp" together, they traveled in a pack. Dad and his cousins would sneak out on Saturday nights. The Klan met up just before midnight, and the boys watched them spew their hate-filled rhetoric around a bonfire. Knowing that you are the target of such ire can only bind you closer together.

The private clubs in Mobile restricted Jews, so the women started the Ladies Aid Society and the men founded the Jewish Progressive Club. Both were formed to uplift the community, and the Aid Society and the Progressive hosted parties and sponsored charitable

---

* I can't confirm my dad's part, but the prosecutor was fired and Joe and Sam were rumored to owe over a million dollars, in 1949 dollars.

projects. Planning meetings can really drag on, so the Progressive installed hand-cranked slot machines, nicknamed one-armed bandits, in the back room, and card games were a regular feature, until the police shut the casino down. Everyone in the family played cards, and my grandfather Ike was known as a particularly high roller. One night he lost all of their savings, seventy-five thousand dollars, shooting craps. Rebecca threatened to kill him and Sam had to wrestle the gun away from her.

Becca, Rose, and Annie had an ongoing poker game, playing for pennies lifted from the *pushke*—the charity collection jar. Word has it they were viciously competitive, formed secret alliances, and were rampant cursers and unrepentant cheaters. My dad says that Rose taught him to play poker and shoot craps when he was five. I don't doubt that.

"What is going on here?" I said when I discovered Dad and my then-five-year-old son crowding around a corner of my parents' living room in Florida.

"Grandpa's teaching me to shoot craps!" my son gleefully exclaimed. My father presented him a "legacy gift" on that trip: a set of hand-carved ivory dice and a leather cup given to him by Rose.*

I met my great-grandmother near the end of her life. She was a kindly old lady, five feet at most, who wore blousy housedresses, orthopedic shoes, and wire-rimmed glasses. She spoke only Yiddish but always kissed our cheeks and handed out hard candies

---

* Rose's worldview influenced all the cousins. Billy's kids say their dad taught them that they needed three skills to be successful in life: to putt in golf, count cards when playing gin, and shoot craps. They played craps after dinner like other families played Monopoly.

from a cut-glass bowl in the living room of her modest home. I would never have pegged her for a potty-mouthed moonshiner in league with prostitutes.

My cousin Ruth says she was talking to her dad, Bert Larry, and when she told him, "Cousin Harry said—" he interrupted her, "If Cousin Harry said it, don't believe it," because his reputation as a fabulist is well established in the family. Dad claims that he was sent to New York in 1947 with other young men from the South to pack arms to send to Israel. They loaded guns in shipping containers labeled "Farm Equipment" and stayed at the Waldorf. Only, the next time he told me this story, they bunked at a hostel in Brooklyn. This effort, funded by wealthy Northern Jewish bankers, including the Lehman brothers, is well documented, but whether my father participated, there's no way of knowing. One thing is for sure: during the 1950s, money was flowing into Mobile. Resources were pooled; Dad and his cousins were sent to boarding schools and included in male-bonding adventures, like ferrying over to Havana, where they gambled at the Tropicana, took in live sex acts at the Shanghai Club, and attempted to pick up women, claiming their ROTC uniforms were the official garb of the Royal Canadian Tank Corps.*

Around this time, the family got the idea to offer casino cruises that would run back and forth to Dauphin Island in Mobile Bay. There was very little on the island at that time, just a refreshment stand frequented by people fishing in the waters nearby. All the

---

* The Tank Corps is one of my father's fabulous fictions, but the live sex act show featuring a performer known as Superman, because of his (alleged) eighteen-inch penis, has been confirmed by our cousins and written about in numerous accounts of Havana in the 1950s.

males in the family went on these fishing "rodeos," as they were called, weekend fishing trips off the shores of Dauphin Island. It was on one of these rodeos that someone came up with the idea to pool money together to rent a riverboat, outfit it with slot machines and booze, and spread the word. So many people showed up for the maiden voyage that the boat ran aground a few feet offshore. Luckily, they'd paid off the Coast Guard, who were standing by to escort the boat, so no one was injured.

Other folks saw the potential for making money on the island as well.

The island boosters put out brochures in 1954, touting it as "the Riviera of the South." At the time, there were approximately two hundred full-time human residents—fishermen and their families—not counting the wild goats, cattle, and the occasional alligator that roamed freely. The warmth and wetness of the gulf makes for a fantastic breeding ground for mosquitoes, ticks, and water moccasins, all of which call the island home. An article ran in the *Birmingham Register* headlined "Alabama Marshland Now Valuable Beachfront." My grandparents and other family members bought land in the summer of 1954. This early investor money was used to build a bridge to the island. Our lot cost $2,400 and included a lifetime membership to the country club. The family planned to build summer homes close to each other and enjoy "the romance of a home on an island," as it was described in the brochures. There would be grand parties, casinos, golfing—the full resort life.

Mobilians snapped up all the lots available, and once the bridge was completed in 1955, you could go over to the Sand Dunes Casino, the Fort Gaines Club, or the Isle Dauphine Golf Course and Club. My mom and dad as newlyweds often went to the island to serve as chaperones for hayrides sponsored by the synagogue.

Dauphin Island's growth stalled in the late sixties and early seventies. There were disagreements about how much of the beach was private property and how much was public. The Fort Gaines Club burned down and in 1971 the Sand Dunes Casino was bulldozed, after being vandalized and falling into disrepair. Our cousins built homes on adjoining lots, but in 1979, Hurricane Frederic hit. The storm not only washed houses away, it took the bridge and public beach out. With no bridge for several years, people who might have built on Dauphin Island moved on to places like Gulf Shores or Biloxi, and our family moved on as well.

By the time I came into the picture in the early 1960s, the first American generation of my family, including my father, his siblings, and his cousins, had been sent to college and were becoming professionals: doctors, dentists, and lawyers. Their immigrant parents gained status in the community; they had real estate holdings, and Gurwitch's, which under Rose's watch was a dry goods store, was passed down to Ike and Becca and became an upscale clothing shop. My mother says Annie remained the family matriarch right up until her death, a few months before I was born, which is how I came to be named for her, but it seemed like the family had climbed that ladder. Still, Jews weren't welcome in churchy Mobile. Our cousin Bubba was, by this time, a wealthy and powerful personage in Alabama, but when he applied for membership at the country club in Mobile, they sent him a letter. "We're not taking any of your kind."* So the cousins in my father's generation who had grown up together still socialized and vacationed en masse.

In 1967, my immediate family led the first wave of our clan away from "the bosom of our family," as Becca called it. But soon, Ike and Becca and other cousins followed. We hopped over the Mason-Dixon Line and never went back to Mobile. Not for weddings or holidays, not even for funerals, until Ike died in 1977. Still, I had fond memories of the few weeks in the summers when my sister and I were sent to Atlanta to stay with Becca and Ike. Hot days were spent indoors playing Old Maid and Go Fish. There were weeks-long Marco Polo marathons in the pool at the Standard Club, the one Jewish club in Atlanta, with our cousins; all the while we wondered if that dreaded red chemical line would really trail you if you peed in the pool.† We'd visit Ike's store, now a furniture outlet. All of us kids tore through the living room setups, trying out sofas and chairs, pretending we lived in each of the model rooms. There was also the memorable evening that Ike and Becca took my sister and me, aged eleven and fourteen, to see *Portnoy's Complaint* through the fingers of their hands, which shielded our eyes. I never did get an answer as to why that boy was sniffing his sister's underwear or why we never went to Mobile.

---

* Bubba was a president of AIPAC, the powerful Jewish lobbying group, and donated thirty-six million dollars to the University of Alabama, among other generous donations. When our cousin Robin wanted to join the Betas, a popular citywide sorority, in the late 1970s, she was turned down. It wasn't until 2015 that a Jewish girl was allowed to be presented at Mobile's debutante ball.

† This was an urban myth, and though we believed it, it never stopped anyone from peeing in the pool.

The cousins of my generation are scattered far and wide across the country. We're down to weddings, funerals, and Bar Mitzvahs, and I never made attendance a priority. I even missed Becca's funeral.

After that phone call with my dad, I started paying my share of the property taxes and was determined to see my grandmother's land. Even though I had gigs nearby in New Orleans and northern Florida, I just couldn't get to Dauphin Island. Every year there was another reason that made a trip impossible: too much work, too little money, and then the 2010 Deepwater Horizon BP oil spill, which devastated the coast and the local seafood. As if it weren't bad enough that Katrina flooded the local oyster beds, which thrive in brackish water, with salty ocean water the retardants used to break up the surface oil sank the oil to the bottom, further decimating the delicate ecosystem that the oysters depend on. How can I go down if I can't eat the oysters?

In 2011, Fort Gaines was named in *Time* magazine's annual Most Endangered Historic Places list but I still didn't make it down.

When Uncle Bert, my father's brother, suddenly dropped dead in the fall of 2015, I debated skipping the memorial in Atlanta. But my parents were too ill to travel and Lisa convinced me to make the trip.

"Would someone please put Annabelle in the basement?" is the first thing I hear when I arrive at Bert's house. It's been so long since we've spoken, I didn't know that he had a dog named Annabelle. He was actually on the second dog he'd named Annabelle. No one will tell me if this is a coincidence or not, and it does cause some confusion. I can't tell if people want to go for a walk with the dog or me. But it makes sense; it's in keeping with one family tradition: big family, small pool of names. Bert, who has just died, was named for Great-Grandpa Bert Gurwitch, and my father, Harry, was named for Great-Grandpa Sugar. We've had a slew of Berts, Bert Larrys, Mayers, Meyers, and Annies. We've got Maxes, Cookies, Fannies, Bubbas (every Southern family does), multiple Robins and Mindys and cousins who are known only as Cousin, and one who went by Cousin Brother. "Cousin Brother" might have been the name on his birth certificate; I never once heard him referred to in any other way.

My sister asks to say a few words at the memorial. She tells a story I know well. It was winter of 1967. Our parents didn't have two pennies to rub together, as they say in the South, and we were about to move to Delaware. There wasn't even enough money to buy us winter coats. But there is a detail I didn't know. Uncle Bert bought mittens, scarves, and hats for us. The hats and scarves have been lost to time, but Lisa's taken those mittens with her everywhere she's ever lived. She produces the mittens from her pocket and holds them out for all of us to see. There isn't a dry eye in the house. Looking around, it dawns on me that we're not the next generation of the family: we're the elders now. Our parents are failing, if not dead already, and we will need to remember them to each other.

I tell the cousins about the land on Dauphin Island. No one, except the ones listed on the deed, knew our family still had property there. Wouldn't you know it? Everyone else's grandparents sold their parcels at the one brief moment between hurricanes when property values spiked.

"Let's go down. Let's do a cousins' trip," I suggest.

Maybe it's the carbohydrate rush from the bagels we've just in-haled, but we all get excited by the idea that this sandy lot could be our geographic connective tissue. It's hard to believe we're not in some Southern gothic novel and it's 2015 and not 1895 when cousin Robin says, "You have to go to the cemetery in Mobile. You'll love it, you know everyone there!"

We promise to arrange a trip and take photos, striking our best Becca poses. Our grandmother took annual buying trips to New York for the clothing store and considered herself extremely fashion forward. Every picture is carefully posed. Standing at a slimming angle, always making sure to keep her chin lifted, one foot forward, featuring her slender ankles. "She was ahead of her time" is the phrase I've heard since I was little.* At every gathering I can remember, someone has called out, "Do the Becca pose." And so we do.

We all return to our busy lives, and it's only after Cousin Bert Larry, the last of our Berts, passes away a month later that I spring into action. I check an Alabama seafood safety watch site. They've been testing the oysters, and they've been deemed clean enough to eat. It's tough to pin down a date, but it seems like January can work. I pull the trigger and send a group e-mail.

Responses start to come in: *Sounds great. Let me check on dates. Ike and Becca would have loved this. What a great idea. Let's get gumbo, y'all!*

---

* Becca claimed to have discovered Elvis Presley. She said that Elvis played at one of her annual store fashion galas, and the timing would have been pos-sible. Alas, no documentation exists.

Robin arranges for me to spend the night at her parents' home before heading to the island. Sandy, her mother, is one of the few remaining cousins in Mobile. Her husband, Billy, was Dad's cohort in the scrap metal and pool hustles.

A month out, the tide starts to turn: *I can't come because of my son's upcoming Bar Mitzvah. It's not looking good, but will check back in a few days. We're going to be on a cruise. I might have to be in Saipan.* All of the reasons people can't come are valid. Robin teaches at Duke and works with the CDC. She lectures all over the world, and she really does need to be in the Mariana Islands.

My sister is coming and Bert's son, Michael, is on board as well. He might even bring Annabelle, which seems fitting.

Hoping to get the legal issues resolved so we can make a decision about the future of the property, I tell Michael that my dad says his dad had the will and the deed to the land, but they hadn't spoken in the five years before Bert died. One owed the other money and wrote off the debt in a settlement with the IRS, but the other reported that debt on his tax returns as being a different amount. I am 100 percent certain that at some point in the past the situation was reversed and they were equally at fault.

Michael thinks he saw the will in a box somewhere. Having just been at his father's house, I can only imagine how hard it might be to locate it. I opened the microwave to heat up a bagel and it was stuffed with appliance manuals from the 1960s and photographs of Rebecca modeling outfits from Ike's Clothing Store.

Michael promises to look for the documents and get back to me.

When I hang up the phone, I feel so good that he and I have reconnected, but then it's the last week in December and I don't hear from him again. The week before our scheduled pilgrimage my sister e-mails *Would you hate me if I don't come?*

I am the only cousin in the cousins' club going home.

Fruit stand at the intersection of Hellfire and Legume.

massacre island, part II

It's a point of pride for natives that Mardi Gras originated in Mobile and not New Orleans, but it's only been since 1994 that Dauphin Island has held Krewe de la Dauphine, their own Carnival celebration. The idea was to boost visibility for the island, but it's a bit of a stretch. Mardi Gras is traditionally held on Fat Tuesday, the last hurrah before Ash Wednesday, so a Mardi Gras on January 9? Still, I have to give it up to the Dauphin Island city council for going for it, and I've planned my trip to coincide with the parade. Creepiness! History! Shellfish! And gumption!

On my way to the airport, I tell my Uber driver, Kanas, "I'm going home." It's an hour ride and I'm speaking so animatedly about my upcoming adventure that I'm afraid I'll get a bad customer rating, so I turn my attention to him. I learn he was born in Fairouzeh, a village two miles outside of Homs in Syria, a city that's been hit hard by war. Like our family, his people have worked to bring family members to America. Many from his village are re-lated through intermarriage, own liquor stores, and live in an old-world-style tightly knit community.*

"We used to go back every summer, but it's been five years since we've been home. It's good that you're going," he tells me, in the perfect send-off. I promise to get in touch when I return and we award each other five stars.

The trip to Mobile takes a full twelve hours of travel time, and I'm anxious the entire time. *What was I thinking? Will I recognize anything or anyone?* But when I head out of the parking lot of the Mobile airport, I am instantly flooded with nostalgia. The terminal has been given a face-lift, but the airfield is still bordered by a chain-link fence, just like when I was little. On Saturday nights, we parked on the patch of grass in front of the fence and watched the planes take off for entertainment.

On the way to my cousin Sandy's home, I pull my compact rental car up close to read a bumper sticker on the SUV in front of me. *I Miss Ronald Reagan.* There isn't a speck of dirt on the sticker. It looks new.

It's been thirty years since I've been here and I get lost on my way. "It's a left turn at the Mitchell Apartments," she tells me on the phone.

"Mitchell? As in our cousins the Mitchells?"

"Yep." I've spent my life passing through cities, a stranger in a strange land, and have returned to the only city on the planet where my family has left a visible trace.

Sandy, who's close to the same age as my mother, greets me with

---

* Over the last eighty years, five thousand villagers have been brought over. They hope to bring more.

a big hug. She's standing on a *Shalom Y'all* doormat, the calling card of my people. Hanging on the wall facing the door is a poster that reads *I Really, Really Miss Ronald Reagan.*

She's got a picture of Great-Grandma Rose on her fridge. Our sailor-mouthed, card-shark moonshiner of a great-grandmother is surrounded by a gaggle of little Gurwitches, including Sandy's daughters, my sister, and me. We are all holding hands. The same photo hangs in my home in Los Angeles.

There's a bowl of gumbo waiting for me on the kitchen table. Sandy's got my number. There have been few times in my life when there wasn't a container of my dad's gumbo in the freezer.* It's his trademark recipe and I am powerless to resist a bowl.

Recently, scientists at Emory University trained mice to fear the smell of cherry blossom by pairing the smell with a small electric shock. Despite never having encountered the smell, the offspring of these mice had the same fearful response. If associations with scents can be inherited, why not other senses, like taste? Clearly, I am genetically predisposed to associate seafood from the Gulf of Mexico with a warm family feeling.†

Sandy and I gab about this one's children, that one's divorce, and people in the media who dress like *nafkas* (that's Yiddish for "hookers"). We're "thick as thieves," as they say down here.

We go to bed to get an early start in the morning. Sandy is a member of the sisterhood of the shul, and they've arranged a morning coffee klatch for me. Though I've never met her, Manette, the

---

* Along with not liking children or pets, Mom wasn't a fan of cooking or Dad's gumbo. "It's too messy, too expensive, and too fattening!"

† I don't think it's an accident that the study was done at Emory, in the South.

president, has baked banana bread in my honor. Cousins show up, including the children of my pediatrician in Mobile, who was, of course, a relative. We who were pictured with Rose are reunited for the first time in over forty years. Bari, a cousin who lives in nearby Fairhope now, has created a family tree consisting of 291 descendants of Goldie and Sugar; he also has felt the pull of the ancestors, and we all search for ourselves on the tree. Manette shows me a framed tablecloth that hangs on the wall of the banquet room. The cloth was painstakingly hand-embroidered with Jewish stars by the Ladies Aid Society in 1952. Stitched alongside each angle of each star are the names of members of the congregation. I'm related to all of them. It's like a Gurwitch Shroud of Turin.

Our cousin Shirley arrives. My mother's grandfather and Shirley's grandfather were brothers, Jewish immigrants from Russia who came to America around the same time as my dad's family. One brother stayed in Philadelphia and the other went to Mobile. It was at Shirley's wedding that my parents met. My mom, Shirley Maisel from Philly, met my dad when Cousin Shirley, Shirley Maisel of Mobile, married his cousin. That's right, there are two Shirley Maisels who both married into the same family. Are you confused yet? I am.

Shirley and Sandy tell me stories about when my mother, whom it's clear they have great affection for, first came down to Mobile.

"Your father thought he was marrying into the movie business because your granddaddy was a projectionist, and your mother had no idea what she was getting into. Ike was on hard times when your parents got married," Sandy tells me. "But he showed up with three Cadillacs because he said he'd gotten a good deal."

Everybody not only knows your name in a small town, they also know how much money you have in your bank account. On the other hand, my mother was quickly folded into the hectic social scene. "When someone had a party, you didn't need to ask, you knew you were invited," Shirley says.

Everybody has a story about Rebecca.

"When she was the president of the Mobile Women's Business League, she took a class in Robert's Rules of Order to prepare. She was ahead of her time."

When I see the picture of Ike among the past presidents of the shul, which include cousins dating back to Meyer Mitchell, my namesake Annie's father, I can see how my mother thought the Gurwitches were pillars of the community. I tell them I like to think I resemble Rebecca and that I inherited some of her flair.

"Here's my favorite memory of your grandmother," Sandy says. "We were visiting my mother-in-law in the hospital and all of a sudden, this amazing smell is coming toward us. Rebecca bursts into the room carrying bags of mouthwatering food. She'd been cooking all day for us. She had her stuffed cabbages, her sweet-and-sour meatballs, her fried chicken and banana bread. She even brought plates and silverware with her."

"You know, I was Rebecca's favorite." Everyone laughs. "What?"

Becca told every single member of our family that they were her favorite. That might explain the puzzle of the steak knife in my care package. I picture her dividing her silverware up between all of the favorites on her mailing list.

I mention my conversation with my Uber driver and ask my family if they've heard that only three days before my arrival, Alabama senator Jeff Sessions sued the federal government to bar

Syrian refugees from settling in the state. A federal judge dismissed the case, but even my cousins are concerned about an influx of refugees because we don't know "their people."

"What if we had been turned away?" I ask. The question hangs in the air.

Over coffee, I talk to Shirley's son, Neal. He's a few years older than me, has a successful law practice, and has lived in Mobile for most of his life. He's also inherited his grandmother's land on Dauphin Island. Sisters Becca and Freda bought adjoining lots. He only learned about the property when he took control of his family's finances in 2005. Neal rarely goes down; he's got a house on the beach in nearby Gulf Shores, which has developed into the kind of vacation destination envisioned by the island boosters.

We calculate that we've paid more in property tax than our grandparents paid for the land. "We have to do something about it," I say enthusiastically. He looks at me like I've suggested we eat vegetables that aren't fried. Or vote Democratic. But he chivalrously agrees to come with me.

My next stop is to visit the relatives who couldn't make it to the coffee. Our shul's cemetery is located on the edge of town, past the historic garden district with its plantation-style houses and wide front porches—ghosts of the gracious Southern living that was built on slave labor, of course.

There's a joke that's got its own version in almost every religion. It's about how two Jews will build two different houses of worship on a desert island, and as relatively small a community as it was at the outset, that's exactly what the Jews of Mobile did. Our shul, Ahavas Chesed, "Love of Kindness," is the conservative synagogue, while the Springhill Avenue Temple attracted people who were less orthodox. The congregations insisted on two separate cemeteries as well.

Springhill's cemetery has a wide entrance, the graves are spread out over a sunny expanse, and there are some rather impressively large mausoleums. Not our hallowed ground. Our eternal resting place, established in 1898, has been padlocked due to a spate of vandalism a few years back; to be in possession of the code to the combination lock makes me feel like I'm a member of a secret society. Our plots are well maintained but a world away from our neighbors'. It's a narrow stretch of land. My people are buried as they lived, practically on top of each other. Even though many were extremely wealthy, they've re-created the shtetl of the old country and are in death as they were in life: thick as thieves.*

It's customary to leave a stone on top of a grave as a reminder that the person is not forgotten. It may be that the shul's Hebrew school kids place these markers randomly. I'll never know if it is by chance or on purpose that the headstone of one relative has a pair of dice on it and another is adorned with Mardi Gras beads.

I've always been wary of tribalism, but this is the tribe whose genetic markers I've inherited, along with a tendency toward moles, outsized earlobes, and the overshare.

In the presence of the ancestors I feel awed by the hardships they endured for a future they knew they wouldn't live to see. The day-to-day sacrifices made during their early years in this country are simply unfathomable to me. I find it intolerable when my

---

* Great-Grandpa Sugar was something of a mama's boy—he's buried next to his mother, Goldie, not his two wives.

browser takes longer than ten seconds to reveal the voluminous pleasures of the known universe in the comfort of my living room.

Both of my parents have told me in no uncertain terms, "Whatever happens, don't send me back to Mobile," and maybe it's the gumbo talking, but I lie down on the grass next to my grandparents and for the first time in my life, I want to rest in the bosom of my family.

It's time for Neal and me to hit the road, so I drive back to Sandy's. I'm following him down, so it's me in my rental car and Neal in his Olds as we head out of Mobile. They are expecting forty thousand, the mayor has told the local news station, and we're hoping to arrive before the Mardi Gras traffic hits. Neal and I haven't seen or spoken to each other since we were kids, but we strike up the kind of intimate conversation you can have with someone who shares your people's secrets. We talk on the phone as we drive.

"Neal, do you think it's just geography that held our family together?"

There's a long pause before he parses an answer: "Once the Jewish community here was able to integrate into the larger society, we could associate with people we weren't related to. We didn't have that luxury before." No wonder he has a successful law practice.

A hard rain begins to fall. If it really starts coming down, that's not going to help the crowds, and the island needs the business. There are currently twelve hundred full-time residents, with an average per capita income of $22,225, which is not much of an economic base on which to operate.

By the time we hit Rattlesnake Bayou, the rain is coming down in blinding sheets. I can't see more than a few feet ahead of me. I pull to the side and tell Neal I need to wait it out, as my car is sliding across the road.

We're on the corner of Hellfire and Legume. Those aren't really the names of the streets but there are three churches on one corner—Baptist, Christian, Christian Youth—and a fruit stand with a hand-painted sign that reads *Gloria's Hot Boiled Peanuts*. I have to get pictures. Dodging puddles, I hold a jacket over my head and dash across the street with my phone.

A woman in overalls, frizzy gray hair in a bun, waves me over to the stand.

"Hi, baby, I'm Gloria, what can I do for you?"

"Oh, I'm heading down to Dauphin Island for the night. I'm going to see my grandmother's land for the first time."

"Well, that's just great, baby, you gonna love it. And come on back, people stop at Gloria's from all over the world."

"I sure will."

We're in low country now. That riveting first season of the HBO series *True Detective*, with Woody Harrelson and Matthew McConaughey, was shot in Louisiana, and it looks a lot like Bayou Le Batre, the part of Alabama we're driving through now.* There's something dreamy about driving the flatness of the wetlands. The Dauphin Island Parkway is a two-lane highway that crosses low bridges over the Deer, the Fowl, and the Dog Rivers, but for the most part, you're on the same level as the water, gliding across the landscape: it's all sky and tall marsh grass. We pass through small fishing villages and spot a couple of roadside eateries that are exactly the kind of places you hope you'll find there. I stop to take a picture

---

* The second season was shot in a place called What the Hell Were They Thinking? The acting was over the top, the dialogue sounded phony, the "sex club" looked like outtakes from *Eyes Wide Shut*.

of the front of Uncle Dave's Sand Bar; the door has a large black sil-
houette of an absurdly curvy female painted on it, like the kind of
pneumatic blow-up doll you see on mud flaps, only the lady is a mer-
maid. It's the kind of place my dad would love. The menu includes
red beans and rice and crawfish. There are also turnoffs leading to
chemical and petroleum plants hidden behind the dense pines lining
the parkway, including Exxon/Mobile and Evonik. Gulf seafood,
when there is any, gets shipped all over the country and brings in the
tourists, but for as much as the BP oil spill devastated the economy,
six local mayors, two county commissioners, the Alabama governor,
and the director of the Alabama State Docks are haggling over sixty
million dollars in settlement money that they will use for environ-
mental rehabilitation and economic stimulus. Aerospace, chemicals,
and steel are the real engine of the economy down here.

Before I realize it, I'm on the bridge. Here's how I've pictured the
moment for the last ten years: I'm cruising in a Tesla roadster convertible. Sunlight is streaming down from the heavens, a warm gulf breeze
blows, and Joni Mitchell's "Both Sides Now" plays on the radio. In
reality: the downpour has lessened to a light drizzle, but the sky is
overcast and a dull gray. I'm gripping the wheel of a Chevy Spark and
a local radio host is advising an acolyte that it's okay to stop talking to
his brother because he's a homosexual, pronounced with a "T," as in
"homosextual," as I cross the bridge to Dauphin Island.

Directly ahead is the old-fashioned water tower that went up in
1955. A hand-painted sign welcomes me to America's Birdiest Island. It's so quaint! Then I spot a rinky-dink carnival that's been set
up in a parking lot. It's ten a.m. and already poundingly loud canned
music is blaring, and I can understand how Dauphin Island got its
current nickname: the Redneck Riviera.

The bridge takes you past the small harbor where fishing boats and the ferry from the mainland are docked and lets you off right on the main drag. Bienville Boulevard runs straight through from one side of the island to the other. Turn left on Bienville and you're on the east end, where there are homes, an RV park, the golf course, Indian Mound Park, the Sea Lab and Estuarium, and Fort Gaines. To the right and you're on the west end, with the schoolhouse; the public beach; the priciest vacation homes; lots that were lost to Katrina, now underwater; and a four-mile thin strip of privately owned beach.

Our lots are on the east end, the less desirable area, wouldn't you know it. We slow down by the turnoff into Indian Mound Park, with its shell mounds and the famous "goat trees"—ancient live oaks dripping with Spanish moss that wild goats used to climb up and sleep in to evade the local gators*—but I can't wait to see our land, so we take a second turnoff onto Hernando. There are modest homes amidst the empty lots and *For Sale* signs every few feet. We turn at the sign that reads *Hunley Place*. A second notice affixed to the post reads *Dead End*.

As if it weren't ominous enough to have earned the moniker Massacre Island, the committee that formed the original trust picked street names that held significance to Southerners. Some pay homage to local tribes, the Pascagoula, the Natchez, but not our street; no, Hunley Place is named for a submarine that played a small role in the Civil War. The *Hunley* successfully fired upon a Union warship, becoming the first combat submarine in history to

---

* When my son was five years old, we took a road trip to the Everglades with my dad. He was elated that Ezra tried fried alligator, which, you guessed it, tastes just like chicken.

sink an enemy vessel, but the entire crew was lost in the battle. Did that stop the Confederate Army from deploying the sub again? Nope, they launched it three more times. A total of twenty-one men, every sailor who ever manned the vessel, including Horace Hunley, the designer, met a watery grave aboard the *Hunley*.

Neal and I pull our cars to the end of the paved road, where Hunley Place dead-ends into pine trees, waist-high ferns, and Mexican fan palms. Across the street from our lots is the one house on our block. It's a neat, freshly painted cottage built to post-Katrina code, on high pilings. Neal steps out of his car and does a slow hand pan, like he's dumped out a very large load of laundry in front of the smallest washing machine in the world, as if to say, "Now, what are you going to do with this mess?"

The lots are packed thick with dense foliage. This land looks much the same as when my grandparents purchased it and probably not all that different from when the Mound Builders first began visiting the island. I look down and sure enough, I'm standing on oyster shells. I pocket one for me and one for my sister.

The grass on my lawn in Los Angeles, natch, is fashionably brown, so it's a relief to be standing in such lushness. Our lots look like the set of *Gilligan's Island*, only more improbable—it's like the cartoony prehistoric landscape in Sid and Marty Krofft's *Land of the Lost*.

"No way am I going in," Neal states flatly when I suggest we make our way into the interior of the property. "It's snake season."

It does seem daunting, but I'm wearing tall boots and it took me ten years to make it here, so I head straight into the color green. I have to touch the ferns to make sure they're not plastic. There's a pathway that's been cut through the property and I can just make out another structure toward the back of the lot. I yell to Neal, "It's probably their meth lab!" but he's returned to the safety of his car. I pivot, clearing underbrush with my hands, and find myself standing on scrubby sand dunes, gulf water sparkling just a few hundred yards away. It's official: I am madly in love with our land.

Why? Why did I insist on that Cyndi Lauper hairstyle in 1983? The amount of hair spray I used in one day alone is probably responsible for a measurable amount of the depletion of the ozone layer!

Why? Why didn't Becca and Ike buy directly on the beach? That land might be worth something to a climate-change denier with deep pockets. Still . . . We're *walking* distance to the beach. I start pricing in my head: How much could it possibly cost to build a place? I could build a small cabin, or better yet, an artists' colony! *Gurwitch Grove.* I imagine switching on the lights at the grand opening by plugging in the extension cord sent to me by Rebecca in 1991. The Grove will be a Gulf Coast version of the MacDowell Colony. That is, except for not having MacDowell's thirty-five million dollars of assets, four hundred acres, and inaccessibility to the majority of the artists working in North America, and for the fact that every year from June 1 to November 30, hurricane season in the Atlantic, I'll be holding my breath hoping that the Grove doesn't flood. Other than that, it's exactly like MacDowell.

Neal is amused by my excitement, but not so much that he wants to stay a single minute longer. We kiss good-bye, and I tell him, "I'm going to try and meet the neighbors. If you never hear from me again, bury me next to one of the other Annes in the family, and you better put Mardi Gras beads on my tombstone when you come to visit me."

Our neighbors aren't running a meth lab, but they did clear the path to the house on the next block, which is occupied by a reclusive, retired scientist. The neighbors are also responsible for the

path to the beach. Sandy,* the woman who answered the door, is a
retired teacher from Minnesota. "We like how quiet it is here," she
tells me, not opening the door more than an inch. Is it because she's
in a bathrobe that she doesn't open the door or is it that they really,
really appreciate a quiet existence, the kind that doesn't include
welcoming a potential neighbor? Maybe she's pegged me as one of
the island's many absentee landowners and can't be bothered. Or
she thinks I'm serious about coming down and is imagining easy
access to the beach disappearing. I sense I've overstayed my welcome on her porch and make a mental note that when I build the
Grove I shouldn't expect to be borrowing a cup of sugar from
Sandy.

I head toward Bienville, where the Mardi Gras will take place,
and spot another neighbor. He's a lanky guy, maybe late fifties, in
jeans and a cowboy hat, and he's staked out a prime viewing spot
on his front lawn. He's a bit early—it isn't scheduled to start for
another two hours—but he's already sitting, day-drinking under a
Confederate flag. I'm not sure what he and the other folks down
there are going to think of my *I'm the liberal, pro-choice feminist you
were warned about* T-shirt. I will need to wear a Crimson Tide jersey
and keep a stockpile to issue to the artists staying at Gurwitch
Grove to don when they go off campus. In the meantime, I cover
my T-shirt with a vest.†

I make my way toward a white clapboard building with a wide

---

* Yes, that's the second Sandy in this chapter; this is a story about a group of
people with the same names.

† There are, to be fair, progressive people and artsy communities like Fairhope, on the eastern shore of Mobile Bay, so it's not a monolith.

front porch and a miniature red-and-white-striped lighthouse that is oozing with old-timey Gulf Coast charm. It turns out to be a small complex composed of a gift shop and an art gallery in which most of the paintings are of ibises—one of the birds that make this the birdiest patch of sand in the USA—and the lighthouse is a coffee joint. I amble up the few steps and peer into the coffeehouse. A piece of paper has been taped to the inside of the window, and a single word is printed on the sign: *CLOSED* in all caps. *PERMANENTLY* has been scrawled in pencil and underlined several times, in case the absence of furnishings and the fact that the lights are off doesn't fully communicate the finality implied in *CLOSED*. I stop in the gift shop, purchase a leather necklace with a shark's tooth, and tell the owner that I'm looking for a great cup of coffee. She is the mother of the barista who had the shop next door. "He has abandoned ship," she tells me, "but you can get a good cup of drip coffee at the Quik Mart, the convenience store next to the gas station." This does not bode well for me. I am on a strict regimen of espresso that must be administered twice daily. Her son, who was born and raised on the island, has moved to Los Angeles to become an actor and producer and find people he has more in common with.*

As the Mardi Gras revelers park their cars, I realize I have made numerous mistakes. First: never, ever, ever go to a Mardi Gras alone. There are families, couples on dates, students from the Sea Lab, all outfitted in colorful tutus and wigs, and not another lone

---

* There is a bakery on the island, but it's closed for termite control. I will call her son when I get back to L.A. He calls it Mirage Island, because it seems like you should be able to make a go of it, but with only a three-month season in which to make your money for the year, success was elusive for him.

straggler. Even my neighbor, the day-drinking Confederate, has a posse. I'm also the only person carrying a reusable water bottle. I stick out like a sore thumb. A Yankee sore thumb. Second: it's all about infrastructure. Most folks are driving SUVs and trucks: they've got portable barbecues and are grilling up chicken and burgers within minutes, popping cans of beer, setting up stadium seats and boom boxes.

I am so little of a football fan that it takes me a half an hour to realize that I'm at my first tailgate party. There's a group who've come in a motorized covered wagon decorated with University of Alabama banners. My father attended the law school for a year and never misses a game, but I haven't inherited the Roll Tide gene. The covered wagon has a wide-screen TV tuned to the game and is pulling its own porta-potty on a small trailer. The bathroom has been covered in aged wood so that it resembles an outdoor latrine. These folks know how to *laissez les bons temps rouler* and then some. I have been plotting my trip down for the last ten years and I didn't even pack an umbrella.

I stroll past the town square, where the town hall, visitor center, and police station look like those friendly forest ranger stations you see at national parks. Kids coast lazily on scooters and bicycling moms pedal right down the middle of the main street. Vendors hawking cotton candy and ice cream from pushcarts make their way toward me as the parade starts, led by the Mobile Police Department Mounted Unit, and it makes perfect sense that in an e-mail the mayor called the town Mayberry by the Sea.*

---

* The department just had a contest to name a new horse; names submitted included "Cotton," "Moonpie," and my favorite choice: "Clotilde," after the

If you've ever been to a Fourth of July parade in a small American town, it's a lot like Mardi Gras on Dauphin Island, except for the beads that are being hurled at your head, which will one day wind up, best-case scenario, I know now, on a gravestone. It doesn't have that undercurrent of sexuality that infuses Mardi Gras in New Orleans. Instead, there are Shriners: old guys in fez hats perilously perched on an even older convertible with a toilet seat hanging off the back, the sagging trunk of the car scraping the asphalt. There are floats with the casts of the local school productions of musicals: *Cats*, *Annie Get Your Gun*, and *The Wizard of Oz*. *Hamilton*, the hip-hop smash-hit musical, hasn't made it down here, and it seems doubtful it will be premiering in this zip code anytime soon.

Interspersed between themed floats, local bands like Mud Bucket and MT Pockets are advertising their hard-rockin' sounds by offering up musical entertainment as they travel down the parade route on small platforms pulled by Ford Raptors. The musicians seem to have attended training seminars that recommend dressing for the job you want, because they are uniformly outfitted in a manner that screams, "I am in a band from south of the Mason-Dixon Line." They sport mullets of varying lengths, a fair number of cowboy hats, sleeveless black T-shirts, jeans, and at least one bandana tied around an arm or ankle or worn do-rag style.

The Mardi Gras parade is over in maybe forty-five minutes and the crowd thins out quickly. I jump into my car and drive past Hunley Place, just beyond the trailer park to Fort Gaines. The fort overlooks the water at the far east end of the island. Before arriving, I

---

ship carrying would-be slaves that was abandoned in Mobile Bay in 1859. "Merlin" is the name that was chosen.

studied maps, plotting out routes for my visit, and I understand why Neal looked at me like I'd grown a second head when I pressed him for exact directions to each of the island's points of interest. The minuteness of the island was inconceivable to me.

I'm the only visitor. As I make my way inside the Civil War–era fort, I picture the starry nights when Boy Scout Troop 484 pitches their tents in the grassy courtyard, and I think on how my son probably wouldn't have dyed his hair pink when he was fourteen if he'd grown up in Mayberry by the Sea. I stroll through the empty barracks built in 1851, shoes echoing loudly on the stone floor. It's impossible not to feel like there's been a zombie apocalypse and I'm the last person left on Earth. From the cannon bay atop the brick wall surrounding the fort, I've got an unobstructed view of both Mobile Bay and the Gulf of Mexico.*

During my youth in Miami Beach, entire neighborhoods were blighted by boarded-up kosher hotels. When the art deco district was first revitalized, one could leisurely enjoy stylishly restored low-rise elegance. Now towering condos rise out of the sand and nightclubs crank out pulsing electronic music 24/7. Here, there is nothing to mar the view between sea and sky and I'm so glad the island hasn't been overdeveloped.

There is an invigorating majesty one can experience on the steep white cliffs of Dover, a sweeping epicness that rouses the soul. The flatness of the gulf shoreline has a different kind of beauty. It's a relaxing mellowness that inspires kicking back and cranking up the Jimmy

---

* Okay, that's not exactly true—there are oil rigs—but you can find views that are completely unobstructed.

Buffett.* Coupled with that low Alabama minimum wage, it's under-
standable why day-drinking in a lawn chair—not under the Confederate flag, but drinking a beer at eleven a.m.—might seem like a
reasonable way to pass an afternoon.† I've never been much of a beer
drinker, so when I explore the brick-lined ammunition storage areas
carved deep into the cool earth, I can't help but think that the fort
would make a great wine cave. If I've traveled twelve hours to get
somewhere, I would like to have a really good glass of wine waiting
for me, and there is nary a wine bar on Dauphin Island. There is one
sit-down restaurant outside of the numerous self-identified dive bars.

I wander into the original blacksmith shop, a small brick enclave
at the base of the fort, where a blacksmith, costumed in a style worn
in the 1800s, is sweating through his cotton smock as he hammers
out an iron cross on a steel anvil. This part of Alabama *is* really
churchy. I can just make out something penciled onto the wall above
his head. Is that his name? "Ivan?" I ask in a total tourist move.

"No, I'm Ralph. That's the mark where the water got up to
during Hurricane Ivan in 2004," he says, instantly snapping me
back to just how precarious life is on a barrier island. I introduce
myself as a landowner, and when I say that I'm meeting the mayor
for dinner, Ralph asks me to tell him that it's the dredging of Mobile
Bay that's the real problem for the island. Like everyone I meet, he
has strong opinions about the potential fate of the island. He's so
worked up that I don't mention I'm aware of the issue. The bay is
shallow; that's why the island had such a great value in the early

---

* Like me, Buffett spent part of his childhood in Mobile.

† The minimum wage in Alabama has been stuck at the federal minimum of
$7.25 an hour since 2009.

part of the last century. Large ships would dock and unload at Dauphin Island and then the cargo would be moved by smaller barges across the bay to Mobile. Now dredging allows shipping to come directly to Mobile, but it's robbing the island of sand, as if storms and sea-level rise weren't enough! I nod, compliment him on his ironwork, and express my disbelief that the fort is empty; it's so well preserved. The museum has a collection of letters written by Confederate soldiers while stationed at the fort. The stories of their laboring with no soap and no pay, chronic hunger, and the unrelenting heat make for fascinating and terrifying reading. You'll never be more grateful for modern plumbing than when reading the soldiers' accounts of the dysentery epidemic at Fort Gaines. But when you live near a historical site, you don't stop in on a regular basis, unless maybe they're serving a chilled rosé.*

It's time for my scheduled dinner with the mayor but the island recently won the right to call itself "the Sunset Capital of Alabama," another ploy to attract vacationers, and I have to check it out.

The sun is large and low on the horizon and the sky ribbons into bands of red, orange, and purple, right on cue. It is one of the most vivid sunsets I've seen in Alabama or elsewhere. I'm reading a sign along the beach about how the ibis was once endangered but thanks to the Audubon Society is making a comeback, when a baby bird scampers over to the water's edge.

I snap a shot of the sprightly ibis and text it to my husband. *Looks great!* he writes. To get a dramatic close-up of three ancient

---

* Prior to this trip, I was in Edinburgh, where you quickly get used to the improbable sight of a fast-food joint in an anteroom of a castle. Businesses have been integrated into the ancient structure, ensuring that it remains a central and vibrant part of life in the city.

tree stumps in the water, I zoom in on the smooth, bleached-out grooves. Widening my view, I notice water lapping at the roots of several live trees on the shoreline. Wait a minute. We're on the *ocean side* of the island. These stumps aren't ancient; they are recent casualties of the salt water. This is that beach erosion coupled with the sea-level rise that I've read about: the two to three feet that are lost each year, taking the trees and other vegetation with them. The island is only 1¾ miles wide; you can do the math. I look back toward the fort and try to imagine how different it would look with an added seven hundred feet of beachfront. That's how much has been lost to date.

JEFF COLLIER is wearing khakis and a polo shirt, wardrobe left over from his former career as a golf pro. With his easy, friendly manner he's every bit the mayor of Mayberry. I tell him that my cousins in Mobile knew his dad. "Isn't he oyster people?" cousin Shirley had asked.

"That's right, there's a seafood business that's been in the family for eighty years." My people know his people. Over plates of blackened gulf shrimp, I gush that I've fallen for the island and I can see his problem: the very thing that gives the island its charm, its refusal to enter the twenty-first century, is the same thing that is threatening its economic future.

"When I added the one traffic light on the island a few years back, people were angry. They don't like change."

He just approved a building that is six stories high, making it the tallest building in town, and people are really pissed off.

"But is there a place for Mayberry in the future?" I ask. It's a

Mayberry that is expensive to maintain.* They are not only trying to hold back time, they are literally trying to hold back the tide. He has successfully funded beach renourishment for Fort Gaines and hopes to do the same for the west end, but it seems like a long shot. Hank Caddell, secretary and treasurer of the Alabama Coastal Heritage Trust, has called such interventions in nature's plans "folly," even invoking Joni Mitchell: "We've paved paradise and put up a parking lot!"

"Hey, if a hurricane takes out the west end, will that make my east end land more valuable?" We both laugh. He tells me my land is probably worth now just a bit more than what my grandparents paid for it. Or not. He has land there as well. Who wants to buy now, anyway, when the sea is rising? We're in the same boat.

There's the briefest pause in our conversation. We're exactly the same age. If I had stayed in Alabama it's likely we would have met years before. We are both invested in and enamored with the island's history, appreciate its natural beauty, and my people know his people. I admire his advocacy and he's a good-looking guy. Am I Reese Witherspoon in *Sweet Home Alabama*?

In that rom-com, Reese, who has been living the high life in New York City, comes back home to Alabama to resolve some

---

* The Gold Coast in Louisiana is able to attract beach renourishment funding because tourism brings in big bucks, making investment seem worthwhile. Some environmentalists are up in arms that reparation funds are also being spent on tourist attractions, but a compelling argument can be made that if environmentally fragile areas have greater economic value, it's more likely they will get preserved.

unfinished relationship business. Essentially Reese must choose between her childhood love, who flies a crop duster, Pilot McSix-Pack, played by hunky Josh Lucas, and her big-city boyfriend, played by Patrick Dempsey, aka Dr. McDreamy. Both are blessed with shiny white teeth and are great-heads-of-hair-over-heels in love with her. Decisions, decisions! In the end, Reese chooses Pilot McSixPack, who conveniently is able to pick up and move to NYC, successfully merging her past with her present and future.

The check comes and we're informed that a local businessman at the bar is paying the tab. Damn, they take that Southern hospitality seriously. Only it turns out that it's just the mayor's check that's being picked up, not mine, and Jeff doesn't offer to pick up my tab. I'm no Reese; he's more interested in how I'm going to portray his beloved home than getting into my pants. When I say, "Can't you guys just have one wine bar?" he shrugs it off dismissively. He knows that "wine bar" is code for someone who does hot yoga, marches in gay pride parades, thinks her kid looks great with pink hair, and will ultimately find the slow pace and solitude of the Gulf Coast oppressive.

I'm emotionally exhausted from the day, so I skip the local nightlife—trivia game and darts night at Fins Bar—and head for the Willow Tree Cottage.*

Bill Harper built and owns the cottage, which is adjacent to and is a twin of his own. The cottages, on nine-foot pilings, overlook the marshland on the bay side of the island. Bill is a little younger

---

* I forgot something. Mr. Mayor also said it wasn't snake season, a relief, but tick season, which is even worse! Maybe he was making it up to keep me away.

than my dad but went to Murphy High School in Mobile with my cousins. Mobile really is a small town.

Bill is retired but has worked all over the world with the Red Cross and Red Crescent and met his wife in Montenegro. Bill and Slavica welcome me into their home and promise to make me an espresso in the morning with their Jura Giga 5, one of the best machines in the world. I settle in, and just as I'm wondering how they occupy themselves, Bill's knocking on my door to tell me that he needs to move my car; the tide is surging and there might be flooding. Residents must be vigilant at all times. It's not even hurricane season. Is this nature's way of reminding me how expensive flood insurance is going to be for Gurwitch Grove Writers' Retreat?

I'm not exaggerating when I say that I sleep that night the kind of satisfying sleep you have when you've been away for a long time and you're so glad to be home.* In the morning, I enjoy an exquisitely tight espresso with Bill and Slavica, but how many mornings in a row can I stop in before I wear out my welcome and a *PERMANENTLY CLOSED* notice goes up on their front door? I send my sister a shot of the view of the marshes. *Don't you want to move down with me?* She writes back, *Sister, I hate to break it to you, but it's going to be you and fifty cats, you know that, right?*

On the drive back to Mobile, I'm the only car on the road. I stop when I see the *Hot Boiled Peanuts* sign.

"Hi, baby, did you like your gamma's land?" Gloria has remembered me!

---

* The Inuit language is famous for having fifty words for snow. We should have more vocabulary for types of sleep. I'd call this: *the slumber upon returning home: slhombering.*

"I loved it, I really loved it." I buy some blueberries and we chat about how healing the beaches are here.

"Of course you love it. I lost my husband to mesothelioma, and my girlfriend and I, we walk the beach every morning. It helps. I just had surgery on my leg." She shows me the scar and we commiserate about getting older and talk about our kids.

"My granddaughter is twenty-three and she still has her purity ring," she tells me, beaming with pride.

It seems like a good time to make my exit.

"It really brings them in," she adds, pointing to the *Hot Boiled Peanuts* sign. I nod in agreement, but I know that "them" means the tourists and that "them" includes me.

Sandy's got a bowl of gumbo waiting for me in her kitchen. My plane leaves in a few hours, so I eat slowly. I want to return to Los Angeles with the taste still in my mouth.

I ask her if she knows why my family left Mobile. "Of course. Your daddy didn't have two pennies to rub together. He had an idea to sell health insurance for pets and open a pet cemetery. He went to everyone in the family to raise money but he'd gotten the reputation, like his daddy, of being someone who wanted to make a fast dollar. Leaving was tough on your mother; she loved it here. We all felt badly; Billy wanted to help, but I said no. We were just starting out."

Pet cemeteries and pet insurance? Just like Rebecca, he was always ahead of his time.* Even though we're talking about something that happened more than forty years ago, I can see how much it still pains her.

---

* In 2014, people spent $870 million on pet insurance in America alone.

"Maybe it was all for the best. The bosom of your family can be comforting but it can also be smothering," I tell her, wondering if she considers me to be one of those people who work in the media and dress like a *nafka*.

"Sometimes your family can know too much about you," she says, and we kiss each other good-bye on the *Shalom Y'all* doormat.

I call my dad on the drive to the airport and ask him to fill in the blanks of the story.

He and a business partner were funding a small housing development in Toulminville. Dad's partner discovered that my grandfather Ike, who also had a stake in the business, was funneling a considerable amount of supplies and workers to make improvements on his home. You might call it embezzling. It's so horrible that I try to make up a clever axiom about this, but I can't think of any word that rhymes with "embezzling."

Mobile was burned for him. No wonder he said, "Whatever happens, don't send me back."

When he tells me this, I remember that someone, maybe my mother, once told me how just after Dad graduated from Vanderbilt, where he made money by leasing pinball machines to his fraternity, he started law school at the University of Alabama. He received a call from Becca. Ike had suffered a heart attack and he needed to come home and help his family.*

"I didn't know you were in business with Ike," I say, and he explains that he'd always been in business with his dad in Mobile. Ike

---

* Ike had a heart attack during a liasion with a lady of the evening, I will later learn from a cousin. Mobile is a really, really small town.

had raked up so many debts that when he turned sixteen, all of his father's assets had to be put in his name.

Our cousins climbed that crooked ladder, but my dad had gotten stuck with his father on a lower rung.

I tell him that I learned that I wasn't Rebecca's favorite. "You know, Rebecca wasn't exactly anyone's favorite," he says. "People thought she was putting on airs. Uncle Sam felt responsible for taking care of his baby sister, Rebecca, the youngest of his siblings, who'd been left behind in Russia all those years before. They'd underwritten Ike's business for years, ponied up for her fashion sprees in New York. They even paid for the membership to the Standard Club in Atlanta. After they died, she tried to cash a check from them for three thousand dollars but the family wouldn't honor it. She carried that check in her purse for years after that, hoping they'd change their minds."

I tell my father that everyone was kind to me, that I might have even experienced that elusive "sense of place," that I love him and I will call him soon. I return my rental car and pull up the picture of Rebecca, the one my cousin Michael and I found in Bert's microwave, on my phone, only she doesn't look eccentric and glamorously dramatic. All I can see is the damage. Ahead of her time? More like behind the times, caught between the old world and new. A Blanche DuBois who depended on the kindness of family.

It takes me all of three minutes to clear airport security, so I send shots of Dauphin Island to the cousins who couldn't make it down. I think of how proud I am of all of us who emerged from a small town on the Gulf of Mexico. My sister and cousins are do-gooders who work for charitable organizations, the majority of us are on speaking terms, and none of us have served time. Yet. Having gone into showbiz and with a proclivity for putting on airs, I have the most in common with our huckster ancestors. I'm the black sheep of my generation!

Waiting to board, I get a text from my husband: *Are we moving to Dauphin Island?*

I text back: *Only the ibis can go home again.*

Huh? he writes.

I'll explain when I get home, I dash off before the plane takes flight.

A FEW DAYS LATER, Kanas and eight others, representing three generations of his family, and I are digging into homemade Syrian delicacies at his townhouse in Burbank.* Fadwa, Kanas's sister-in-law, explains that her family and Kanas's are intermarried in as confusing a configuration as my own family. Most of the family lives close by, except for a few of the first generation of American-born who have moved to Northern California. Nahla, his wife, explains how to make her signature dish; it's intestines stuffed with ground beef, tomatoes, and rice, and is not unlike the stuffed cabbages Rebecca regularly sent to my dorm in New York City.

"I love *masareen*," Amanda says. She's Kanas's niece, one of the first generation in the family to be born in America. She's twenty-one, impeccably groomed, and between bites is sucking on a hookah filled with strawberry-flavored tobacco. When Nahla explains

---

* Leaving the house, Ezra had yelled, "You do know someone was murdered by their Uber driver this week, Mom."

"If that's how I'm going to go, I'm fine with that!" I called back, hoping those wouldn't be my last words to my son.

that it takes four hours to prepare the dish, Amanda sheepishly protests, "But you know, I'm studying to become a dentist. I'll never make it myself." Another of the aunties pipes in, "No, you can do it! You'll come home at night . . ." and as she talks through the preparation of the rice and beef, Amanda listens and nods with a smile frozen on her face and I realize that for all my claiming to love gumbo, I've never once attempted to make Dad's recipe. *She's never making that masareen,* I think as I smile and nod assurances.

Things move slowly in the South and even slower in my family. It's hard to imagine that we'll ever get that will probated. Wouldn't that be just like my family, if I passed on to my son property taxes for a piece of land he'll never visit? Maybe it will be the ocean that ultimately brings resolution.*

Meanwhile, there are second- and third-generation things to attend to. Sandy's grandsons are becoming B'nai Mitzvah in a month in Las Vegas, and the descendants of Goldie and Sugar, Rebecca's favorites, all of us, will be there to witness the occasion.

---

* As I write this, the Isle de Jean Charles, an island in Louisiana just four hours away from Dauphin Island, is preparing to relocate all of its residents. Only a 320-acre strip remains of what was once a 22,400-acre island. The water level is expected to rise between two and six feet by the end of the century.

> A Pet
> Dog
> Furry cute
> Wallks barks, jumps
> Likes to be petted
> Petey

What would those intrepid souls who crossed the Plains in covered wagons make of a world where you can purchase half-million-dollar canine compounds equipped with temperature-controlled daybeds and quick-drying doggie nail polish?

outward hound

I will never dance at Callie's wedding. I will not cheer at Tucker's college graduation. I won't meet Mia's children or enjoy a girls' night out with Mary, but I will be expected to mourn them when they shuffle off this mortal coil, because they are the four-legged family members of people I love. Some days, it appears a pet genocide is taking place on my social media feeds. There are not only pictures of adorable antics but pleas for intercessory prayers and news of the impending demise, precipitous decline, and inevitable deaths of Copernicus Q. Cutiepie, Mr. McMugglepuss, and Sir Barks-a-Lot.

Their departures will unleash an outpouring of emotion from their caretakers. *I'm bereft. Heart is broken. We've lost our angel.* This will be followed by a collective grieving that I am not keen to participate in because I am an unfeeling cad. I can find a depth of feeling for your human family even if I've never met them, but I have a hard time summoning that same emotion for your fur babies.

I'm all for the humane treatment of all animals. I've committed to eating lower on the food chain. I rarely eat red meat, gave up veal, and am foie gras free, but I wear leather, wool, and cashmere. Even worse: I subject the cats that live with me to baby talk, silly nicknames, and stream-of-consciousness musings about their cuteness. I also force them to submit to hours of merciless petting and then confine them to the crook of my arm.

To the purest adherents of the tenets promoted by the Pets Are People Too movement and PETA, my conduct is unenlightened and tantamount to the enslavement of animals.*

It wasn't always this way, this sentimentalized relationship with animals. Looking out over the San Gabriel Mountains from my bedroom window, I often contemplate the steeliness of those intrepid souls who crossed the Plains in covered wagons, most of them accompanied by working dogs pulling sleds loaded with wood and other goods, in addition to performing their hunting duties. What would those settlers make of a world where you can purchase half-million-dollar canine compounds equipped with temperature-controlled daybeds or quick-drying doggie nail polish, or open your home to a potbellied pig without bacon on the brain?

A conspiracy nut might even suggest that videos of telegenic mammals doing the darnedest things have replaced religion as the opiate of the masses, allowing governments and corporations greater

---

* PETA's latest focus is educating the public on abusive practices employed during the harvesting of wool and cashmere, but they believe that the use of comfort animals in the military is also questionable. They also object to using the word "pet."

control over our lives while we're home oohing and ahhing over a kitten nestled in the arms of a gorilla. But what's landed me in the doghouse with many of the folks I share my life with is that I don't consider animal companions to be family members. They are *like* family but aren't actually family. In the same way that carob, with its dry, lintlike texture, is not even a distant cousin once removed to chocolate.

The depth of the interspecies familial bonding was brought home when Lauren, a family friend, showed up at my sister Lisa's formal Thanksgiving dinner "wearing" her Chihuahua, Mia, in a dog carrier modeled on a baby sling. Lauren neglected to mention she was bringing the pooch and didn't seem to register the look on my perfectionista sister's face that I know means: *This is mildly amusing but you are dead to me now.* Mia, not surprisingly, looks a lot like her "mommy," Lauren. Both are petite, are fine boned, and have the same hair/fur color. Mia was dressed in a Mondrian-patterned nylon number that had more ruffles but was otherwise identical to Mommy's outfit. We all giggled upon learning the sling was made by a company called Outward Hound—pet people are so clever with wordplay*—but I thought Lisa was going to have a stroke when Lauren seated baby Mia at the dining room table and served her on our grandmother Rebecca's Royal Crown Derby china. That dinner is now affectionately referred to as the Mama Mia Incident by our clan.

But it wasn't until my friend Craig waxed poetic about his Labrador retriever at a dinner party that I considered I might be the

---

* A doggie-day-care center opened up down the street from my office called Bone Sweet Bone, a local pig rescue group is called Lil' Orphan Hammies, and it just goes on!

problem. Craig announced that Boo's presence in his life had convinced him that everything in the universe happens for a reason.

"Why?" I asked.

"Because the videos I make with Boo have helped raise money for children who have cancer."

"That's funny, Craig," I said, "because children who have cancer are why I'm convinced that nothing in the universe happens for a reason." Our dinner companions looked at me like I'd just stabbed Craig in the eye with my fork. Was I undervaluing the bond between my friends and their pets? I'm always saying my friends are my chosen family, so shouldn't I accept their chosen family members unconditionally? I resolved that night to forge relationships with my friends' fur-bound children with the same enthusiasm and sincerity with which I celebrate their human offspring.

1. CALLIE'S BITCHY RESTING FELINE FACE™

Dinah is my age, is single, and has a wicked sense of humor, five sisters who live in Pennsylvania, and an adorable daughter whose favorite color is purple. She shares her home with Calico, a cat with whom I've never taken the time to establish a meaningful rapport. Until now.

When I show up at her place, Dinah launches into her list. She loves cats and has shared her life with a lot of them. "Fluffy, Daisy, Dandy, Dave, Dusty, Stan, Roger, Fluffy Muffin, and Flutter Nutter." The list is so long, it's possible that Flutter Nutter and Fluffy Muffin were the same cat, but when I ask for clarification, even she's not sure anymore. She can't imagine a life without cats, a determination that precipitated the dissolution of her marriage. She tells me that she and Callie have "an understanding."

"We spend hours staring deeply into each other's eyes."

I too have lost hours gazing into those mysterious marbles, imagining a connection of sorts, but what does a cat (average human IQ equivalent: negative 25) think about when staring us down? Perhaps it's similar to an experience I had binge-watching *The Walking Dead*. After three episodes, I wasn't sure I even liked the show, but I felt compelled to watch the next five seasons to find out if Rick makes it out of that town, that church, that cannibal compound, and that pair of pants. With a captive feline, we're the only channel they've got, so there's a good chance they're tuning in to see how long it will take until we stop moving and they can feast on our eyeballs.

Callie is three years old, so I brought gifts just like I would when visiting a friend's toddler. The cat eyes me warily as we attempt to get her into the brown cotton vest with rabbit ears, which looks very much like the bear and tiger getups I put my son in when he was Calico's age, except that my son was much more compliant.* Is Callie unhappy to be wearing a garment that transforms her into another species, or is it that brown isn't her color? There might be a scowl on her face, but do cats have facial expressions? Internet sensation Grumpy Cat is actually frowning. He suffers from feline dwarfism and has a severe underbite. Callie's scowl might be her

---

* Cats don't like to be clothed, which is why it was so brilliant when the citizens of Brussels tweeted out cats in outrageous getups while police searched for the Paris bombers. Nothing says both "Fuck you!" and "We're fucked!" more than cats in costumes.

Bitchy Resting Feline Face.™ What is undeniable is that she wriggles out of the vest, scampers off, and hides under Dinah's bed.

I suggest a little one-on-one playtime with Callie. As I dangle a faux mouse on a plastic fishing pole over the edge of the mattress, trying to lure her out, I feel like I'm on *To Catch a Predator* and any minute Chris Hansen will emerge from a hallway to arrest me. I don't even score a pity pet. It takes a lot of time to develop "an understanding" with a cat you're not sleeping with, though I am confident that every cat person reading this sentence will think, *You would instantly fall in love with my cat if you met them*, myself included.

2. THE REAL HOUSE DOG OF STUDIO CITY

My friend Gia's terrier, Tucker, appears so frequently on her Instagram account, it seems like the dog's exploits are being documented as a reality TV show. There's Tucker eating dinner. There he is getting groomed. I'm certain the day will come when he'll be filmed tossing a glass of wine in another canine's face. So when I show up at her home in Hollywood, I'm flabbergasted to discover that she's got another dog. "Who is this?" I ask, like I caught her cheating on her husband. "Bailey is my heart," she tells me. It turns out that the Rottweiler is so precious to her that she prefers to keep that relationship private. Also, Bailey is elderly while Tucker is young and spry, so there's that.

Bailey has been with her for fifteen years, and Gia's favorite thing about him is that he's an enthusiastic licker. "He licks everything—people, silverware, the floor, shoes, even furniture!" I know right then that we will not be BFFs. I've never understood the appeal of a doggy sponge bath. The dampness reminds me of reaching for a handhold on public transportation and encountering moisture of unknown provenance. With dogs you can pretty well assume that tongue has been surveying his own genitals, if not the genitals of most neighboring canines, before giving you a good shellacking. Seeing Bailey lying listless at her feet reminds me of when Stinky, my cat who lived twenty-one years, began spending her days stretched out in pools of sunlight. Our family accepted that she'd retired to Florida and we prepared for the end. I might have come too late in the game to get to know Bailey, so I focus back on Tucker.

Tucker joined the family as an unofficial comfort animal for her husband, Dan, who was in a traumatizing car accident. "People like Tuck's photos so much that even total strangers ask me to post more," Gia says. I was planning to accompany Gia on a walk with Tucker and then build a relationship over a series of visits, but she doesn't want to leave Bailey today, so we cut the visit short and she proposes I stop in next week. There is something different about Tucker in person from his public persona, but I can't put my finger on it. I also can't stop myself from inquiring about it.

"I Photoshop his fur. I make it just a bit whiter. I'm really not sure why," she confesses. When I tell her that he looks cuter in pictures, Gia glares at me like I've suggested her child is ugly.

"I'm kidding! Kidding!" I assure her as she ushers me out the door.

By the time I get home, she has already posted on Instagram that someone said her dog wasn't as cute in person. Commenters posit that this insensitive infidel should be drawn and quartered. Thank goodness she didn't mention my name or a lynch mob might have gathered outside my home. Two weeks later I receive an e-mail informing me that not only do I owe her an apology but I won't be granted another playdate with the Tuckster.

3. ALONG CAME MARY

"We're not those people!" Glenn exclaims as I enter the home he shares with his husband, Mark; Mary, a cocker spaniel; and Mr. Mooney, a pug; and I instantly know that not only are they "those people," but I've gone upriver.

During the ten years of our acquaintance I've never been to Glenn's home. We take a quick tour of the house. "Don't mind the mess, we didn't clean up because you're *family*!"*

Glenn is Mommy and Mark is Daddy to the pooches, and every surface is a testament to their parental devotion. Sofas and chairs are covered with sheets to protect them from dog hair. Mark is particularly proud of the sliding kitchen shelving he had designed for dog food and medications. They're a blended family, so there are framed photos of the dogs in both yarmulkes and Easter bonnets. I see what unmistakably appear to be two containers of ashes on a shelf, one labeled *Lorna* and the other *Doris*. "Your mothers?"

---

* For some people "family" means people who you don't mind seeing your dirty dishes and unmade beds. In my family, it means you must scour your home for days before inviting them in or they will embarrass you by cleaning it themselves in front of you.

"Doris was Mark's mother and Lorna was one of our dogs, but she was even more maternal than Doris."

The monikers Glenn and Mark have given their dogs, besides being a total hoot, serve as a testament to the utterly pointless ridiculousness of gay conversion therapy. Glenn's dogs have included Lucy (Ball), Ricky (Ricardo), Judy (Garland), Liza (Minnelli), Lorna (Luft, Liza's well-known sibling), and Joey (Luft, Liza's sibling that nobody likes all that much, which also went for the dog named for him). Currently, they share their home with Mr. Mooney, named for the president of the local bank frequented by Lucy Carmichael on *The Lucy Show*, and a male dog named Mary. Mary?

"We have a neighbor who is homophobic but he loves dogs, so we get a kick out of the fact that in order to greet our dog, he has to yell, 'Hi, Mary.'"* I rest my case. There is simply no kind of therapy that could knock the gay out of these guys. Electroshock therapy might rob them of their short-term memories, but Mark and Glenn would probably still be deliciously Mary.

The question of whether these dogs are "family" seems moot; these pups are more like royal family. Glenn was awarded the dogs in his divorce, for which he engaged a pricey attorney who specializes in pet custody disputes.† There is little in the way of services and care Glenn and their new stepfather, Mark, haven't lavished upon their boys—Mary is particularly keen on doggie acupuncture, at

---

* "Mary" is a name that people have disparagingly called gay men but was embraced by those same gay men it was meant to insult.

† My dad really was ahead of his time with his idea of pet insurance and pet cemeteries in 1967. If he'd been able to finish law school, he'd have had a field day with this kind of thing.

fifty dollars a pop—but even their parents have been shocked by the lengths they've gone to.

"Lorna needed to wear adult diapers and we could only keep them on her with Glenn's man Spanx. Getting her into them was daunting, but we did it. We also tried to find a rabbi to preside over a shiva for her when she died, but no rabbi would do it.* We would have paid anything. If we were younger, we'd have had kids, but we're old-school gay. We've spent enough to send all of our dogs through private school in Los Angeles." But when Mr. Mooney was experiencing vision problems and they consulted with a Beverly Hills canine ophthalmologist who offered to fit the dog with a false eye—you know, not so he could *see* better, but to *look* better—they couldn't bring themselves to go that far. They had hit their limit.

I admit that I too have gone to extreme measures and recall administering subcutaneous fluids three times a day to my cat Stinky when her kidneys started to fail. But, recently, I hit my limit, and I tell them the story of why my cats are not family members.

We were contentedly allowing our cats, Anthony Perkins and Alexander Pushkin, to travel in and out of our home, at their leisure, through a cat door. That is, until they began chasing rodents inside, turning our house into a small animal killing field. The tipping point was when the cats invited a particularly stealthy varmint into our household and promptly lost interest when the clever scoundrel wedged itself inside the bench of our breakfast nook.

---

* The official party line in Judaism is that dogs don't have souls, hence no ritual observances like sitting shiva.

We hired a humane pest control service to try to coax him out. Nada. We hired the exterminator with the plastic rat strapped on top of the truck to set decapitating traps. More nada. We could hear our new roomie scratching and scurrying beneath us as we gathered for meals. Still, we honored our Schengen policy. Then *el ratón* ate through the wiring in our refrigerator. Then he ate through the wiring in the washing machine. Long story to thousands of dollars spent on new kitchen appliances, we nailed the cat door shut. Sometimes the kitties get stuck outside for hours at a time, even entire nights. I wouldn't do that to our son, who has brought equally questionable living beings into our home, but that's the difference between him and the other two males living under our roof.

I can't say I'm surprised when Glenn and Mark announce that Mr. Mooney can speak actual words, but it does render me speechless. We lean forward, craning our necks, heads tilting slightly.

"Hey, you? Heeeey, yoooouuu?" Slowly and deliberately, Mark speaks in the way you do when teaching children to sound out a new word.

One of the reasons that it's hard for some people to accept Darwin's theory of evolution is that it's difficult to picture the vast amount of time it takes for species to evolve. Numerous institutes of higher learning have taken to dramatizing the passage of time by unfurling rolls of toilet paper and marking landmark dates in the history of our planet on the individual squares—it's called a Toilet Paper Geologic Timeline. A standard roll contains approximately four hundred squares. If square 400 represents the formation of Earth, five billion years ago, square 394 sees you at 65 million years ago, with the mass extinction of the dinosaurs; the first proto-humans appear 100,000 years ago, at the tip of the last square, square one; recorded human history begins. One millimeter from the end of square one. Yet so many of us are convinced that we might take part in the first interspecies chitchat that you can find videos similar to the scene we are playing out in Glenn and Mark's house in thousands of videos on the Internet.* I nod and smile, but honestly, Mr. Mooney's response sounds a lot like someone gargling salt water.

It would be hard to say whether I bonded with Glenn and Mark's dogs, but I felt unmistakably moved by the capacity for love I witnessed. "Could I feel unconditional love for a dog if I wasn't so fond of his owner?" I ask the guys. Glenn and Mark tell me they adopted their dogs from a rescue group called the Brittany Foundation and they urge me to go and visit.

I've never visited one of these organizations; I've always been a bit dubious of the priorities of animal-rescue types. I know these folks have only the best intentions when they post on social media: *Found an adorable terrier on the corner of Highland and Hollywood Boulevard, no tags! House trained, loves treats, and so sweet, needs a forever home.*

But, just once, I'd love to see this: *Found a homeless vet on the corner of Highland and Hollywood Boulevard, tags! Not exactly house-broken, loves opioids, and so sweet, needs a forever home.*

Not only do they have an open house coming up, there is one

---

* For about a month, my husband was convinced our cat could talk, and that was the first time I suggested that he might want to consider getting his real estate license. The cat never spoke, but six words formed in my mind: *Too much time on his hands.*

volunteer spot that's available, so they invite me to participate in their annual A Day in Their Paws fund-raiser.

4. STRAIGHT OUTTA KENNEL

The instant I post on social media that I am spending the day at a dog rescue, messages appear from people I never hear from. They write: *I love you* and *YOU ARE MY HERO.*

I've supported a lot of worthy causes, including a stint escorting women into Planned Parenthood clinics. People get shot doing that, but nothing I've ever done has garnered a response so affirming of my saintliness. I explain that volunteers commit to spending the day cooped up inside the individual kennels with the "residents"—their word, not mine—during which time the foundation is open to the public. The public is invited to pledge money to "liberate"—their word, not mine—the volunteers at the rate of a dollar per minute of freedom from the kennels. Pledges start rolling in.

The sanctuary is located off a freeway north of Lake Casitas, which is an hour north of Los Angeles, where the sea of Priuses trickles down to a stream of four-wheel-drive SUVs.* It makes sense that a place housing sixty dogs at any given time would be off the beaten path, but I start to wonder if I've been snookered into some kind of black-market organ-harvesting scheme. Surely most of the people who would willingly spend a day cooped up in a dog

---

* In February of 2011, Toyota announced that the official plural of "Prius" is "Prii," but you can't write that or say it out loud without feeling like a pretentious idiot, so I'm pretending I don't know that.

kennel must be single and childless? I phone my husband for what might be our last communication with both my kidneys intact as I turn off into a dirt gulch. "If you don't hear from me in four hours . . ." I say, about to give him the address, when my phone service cuts out. The high desert winds propel a large tumbleweed into my windshield and I'm about to turn around and pack it in when I spot a ranch-style hacienda on a rocky plateau just ahead.

Entering the rambling structure that serves as both the foundation's headquarters and the home of Nancy, its founder, it seems unlikely that I'll encounter bathtubs filled with ice. Well-worn chintz couches and doggie beds fill the living room. A long corridor leading to the bathroom and bedrooms is lined with Nancy's ancestors in antique frames. "Photos of my humans," she allows, but points out that hanging directly opposite are her other family members, ancestral dogs, in the same antique frames. There are black-and-white photos, yellowed with age; some of the pooches are posed in the same formal settings as human matriarchs and patriarchs.

The bake sale offerings are an indication that these folks are not vegan, hemp-wearing, anti-wool-and-leather, PETA animal advocates. Luncheon meats in neat white-bread sandwiches are set out for the volunteers.

I'm also wrong about the pool of volunteers; not all of them are childless, but there is a common theme of "I prefer dogs to people." I ask LeeAnn in what way she prefers them. "A dog has never lied to me," she says with a finality that makes further inquiry seem ill advised.

Before heading outside to my kennel, I visit the garage, where racks of doggie outfits are hanging for sale. There are the ubiquitous (knitted sweater vests, raincoats) and the more niche (leather coats with chain mail), and then there's the sexy Santa suit. It's strappy, and the red felt halter top has an underwire push-up bra built in. The skirt is adorned with S & M–type sharp metal spikes. Now, how's a pooch gonna roll over and get his stomach scratched in that getup? A close inspection reveals it's not a one-off, hand-made item. The stitching is uniform and professional, clearly factory made. How many were made this year? How many sold? Has someone mistakenly put a human costume on the rack? That would be worse, because that would mean it was made for a child. I try to banish the thought from my brain as Yvonne leads me to my kennel.

Yvonne, who's in her fifties, is a mortgage banker, single, child-free, who devotes time each weekend to the dogs. She'd like to phase out of banking and hand make soap, which she's learned to do on DIY Internet sites. She's selling her first batch today, which is why I am able to step in and take her place.

We pass row after row of kennels manned by volunteers quietly communing with their kennelmates. My new haunt is at the far end of the row of adjoining pens. Because I'm the newbie, it's like I've been assigned the seat on the plane directly in front of the bathroom. At some point during the day, every sitter will stroll past to make deposits in the poop cans in front of my kennel.

Kennel housing varies by the size of the dog. I'm in a condo, eight feet by twelve feet, but the big dogs get bungalows, ten feet by twelve feet, which is approximately the size of my college dorm room. Each pen has an igloo with soft bedding inside and an army-style doggie cot. The accommodations are comfy if Spartan, with cooling misters for hot days and a perfectly unobstructed view of the mountains surrounding us. It jogs a memory of the first apartment I looked at in New York in 1981. It was a basement room with a dirt floor. There were tiny windows, air vents, really, that treated you to a spectacular view of shoe leather and authentic West Village detritus. Price tag: nine hundred dollars a month in 1981 dollars. The super took in my stunned expression, shook his head, and muttered, "Location, location, location." We're under a big sky in the open air and the sun is shining directly upon us, so as locations go, there are worse spots to be a human or canine in this world.

Bright Eyes and Simba, my kennelmates, were rescued from a hoarder's apartment along with two hundred other dogs. It was so crowded they were burrowing into the walls. An additional forty dead animals were discovered when the police came in. Not having socialized with humans early enough in their lives, these tiny dogs with big sad eyes will never be placed. They've been at the foundation for fourteen years. Simba's legs bow slightly and he's got the same kind of arthritis in his joints as me. I am rooting for him as he attempts, over and over, to jump the two inches to reach his camp bed. I reach out to help, but he yelps, recoiling from my touch, and withdraws into the igloo.

Having had no experience with feral dogs, I assumed the term implied a ferocity of sorts and imagined I was risking being torn to pieces by them. I've confused feral and rabid. "With a lot of patience," Yvonne tells me, "they might come to you." She's known as the Hot Dog Lady around the joint. When Mr. Bojangles arrived, she held hot dogs in her hand outside his igloo for five hours each Saturday and Sunday for four months until he developed enough trust to come out and take them from her. She leaves me alone with the dogs as I reflect on how five hours is four hours and fifty-five minutes longer than the amount of time I ever waited for my son, as an infant, to eat applesauce from a spoon, and that Yvonne is really well suited for long hours of stirring soap over a hot stove.

After hearing of Simba and Bright Eyes's plight, I am filled with purpose and the good feeling that comes with being of service. We are doing important work here. I am also ready to go home. I check my watch. Exactly twenty-nine minutes have passed.

Visitors begin arriving at the foundation and stop by my kennel. They draw close as the dogs, with their wounded fragility, pull at their heartstrings, but most drift off quickly because Simba and Bright Eyes don't want to interact and everybody wants to be with the friendly dogs.* Possessed by the desire to make my dogs more popular, I turn into a carnival barker, hitting those headlines hard. "Hoarder! Two hundred dogs! Can't be adopted! Here for life!" A woman steps close, fixes me with watery eyes, grabs hold of my hand through the chain link, and says, "Thank you so much for what you're doing." I feel like a fraud. She doesn't know I'm not a regular volunteer and I know what I must do.

I've been given a bag of treats for the dogs. I was told that the day after these open houses the dogs get diarrhea because the sitters offer them too many snacks, so I will need to be prudent, but I'm determined to give Hot Dog Lady a run for her money. I hold a few biscuits out in my hand. Simba edges forward but I have to drop

---

* It's just a natural reaction. The same holds true for babies. When my son was born with medical issues and had to spend time in the NICU, I learned from the nurses that research has shown that babies who are cuter and less fussy get held more, so they're trained to resist that example of natural selection in action.

them on the ground before he'll take them. Bright Eyes doesn't even try. This standoff continues for at least an hour. Finally, Simba lurches toward me. Grabbing at the bite-sized morsel with his teeth, he accidentally licks me in the process. I'm so excited that I yell out, "Simba ate from my hand!" which sends the dogs cowering into the corner of the kennel. Still, I depart elated but also terrified. Is this how it starts? Is a lick the gateway fluid exchange that leads to Photoshopping your dog's fur? Next stop: hot dog ladydom.

I am still getting props on social media days later and I start fantasizing about inviting Simba and Bright Eyes to live with us. My time at the rescue has affirmed what screenwriters and novelists understand: when you know someone's backstory, even an animal's, it elicits compassion. And when someone exhibits empathy for animals, we're really rooting for them.

In September of 2015, news of the Syrian couple, the al-Kadris, who crossed the Mediterranean with their kitten in tow captured almost as much of the public's attention as the family who lost their son on the treacherous journey to Greece. After all, they loved their darling kitten, Zaytouna—"Olive"—so much that they must be good people. Lest we forget, Lenin was famously a cat lover. Not one report speculated that they'd put the cat's life in danger or might have used precious resources that could have helped another refugee make the crossing. Update: little Olive was quarantined and reunited with his owners, who felt certain that the cat recognized them instantly.* I find that hard to believe. I'll see one of our

---

* Moner and Nadia al-Kadri seem like great people, and I wish them all the best. Note: they brought the tabby in a baby sling, much like the one Lauren toted Mia around in.

cats across the street from our house less than ten minutes after he left my lap, call out to him, and he'll look right through me. But I hope, for Moner and Nadia al-Kadri's sake, that it is true.*

Three things happen in quick succession.

First, Mia the Chihuahua's mommy, Lauren, stops by my home wearing the newest addition to her family, her infant human daughter, Tara, in a baby sling. I take an embarrassing amount of pleasure in holding little Tara and teasing Lauren about having traded her Outward Hound for a BabyBjörn.

Then Glenn's beloved Mary dies. I call to make sure he shouldn't be put on suicide watch.

"This was a tough one. Just don't tell me Mary is waiting for me at that fucking Rainbow Bridge."

I've lived my entire life unaware of the Rainbow Bridge until this moment. Glenn explains that it's a mythical place described in a popular pet-grief poem. To summarize: It's a place where "pets who have been especially close to someone" go when they die. They are happily enjoying all the food they want and playing, but "there is just one thing missing: us. They wait there to be reunited with us so we can cross over the Rainbow Bridge together."

It's hard to make sense of the conundrum that is the Rainbow Bridge. Is there some other place for those pets we haven't been especially close to? Or do all the pets we've had during our entire lifetime wind up there? As a child, I had turtles, Bagels and Lox, that smelled funny and I'd be happy never to see them again. What's *under* the Rainbow Bridge? Also, who gets to decide who

---

* A recent study showed that cats can understand a limited number of words, it's just that they don't care enough to acknowledge us.

crosses the bridge with whom? Last year, we got a call from a family down the street. Anthony Perkins, who has figured out how to take off his collar, was showing up at their home for a second breakfast and late lunch so often that they assumed he was their cat, until he turned up one day wearing his collar. We live so close by that when the big earthquake finally hits, it could take us all out at the same time. Who gets to cross that Rainbow Bridge with Perkins? What if I live until I'm a hundred? Will I be leaving all of my deceased pets in a state of suspended unhappiness? How selfish of me. I should stop washing my hands. What about those forty dead dogs from the hoarder's apartment? They deserve a Rainbow fucking Causeway!

"It's a pet purgatory animal-geddon!" Glenn adds, and I'm so glad that though he's got a broken heart, he's still got his talking dog, Mr. Mooney, and his sense of humor.

That same week, Gia's Bailey leaves the building. The day Bailey dies is November 13, 2015, and as news of the massacre in Paris begins to make its way around the world, there are condolences on Gia's social media that include speculative musings on whether it feels worse to lose a dog or to lose 130 people in Paris. One person writes, "Maybe Bailey died to escort all those souls in Paris to heaven."

> *Dear Gia,*
>
> *Isn't it unbelievable that in this 24/7-news-cycle world we're so overloaded with catastrophes that we've lost the ability to distinguish between the global tragedy of terrorism and the very real but still minor-in-comparison unfortunate death of your doggie?*

No. No one wants to hear that at this time.

I am an insensitive jerk. I am also wearing wool and eating a carne asada burrito. I should be sent to PETA prison.

> *Dear Gia,*
>
> *I'm glad I had a chance to meet Bailey when I came over to see Tucker. I left that day thinking about how we are so eager to put our best selves out into the world that we are sending our pets, more lovable versions of ourselves, to stand in for us. Our pets have become our avatars. That is the reason why you are Photoshopping Tucker's fur. And so sorry Bailey is dead.*

I am an asshole.

> *Dear Gia,*
>
> *I'm so sorry for your loss. It's heartbreaking. I know how hard it will be to carry on without your angel. I'm sure he's waiting for you at the Rainbow Bridge.*

I pick up Alexander Pushkin and cradle him in my arms, hoping that I won't be saying good-bye to him anytime soon. Looking deeply into his blank feline eyes, I whisper, "You are my booboo, Pushikins."

My grandmother Frances would be turning over in her grave. She never had the patience for nineteenth-century poetry. Frances also never had pets. What was she going to do with a cat or dog in her row-house apartment? With two daughters to raise, no hired help, a clerical job at the welfare department, and her husband,

Johnny, working nights as a movie projectionist, who was going to walk a dog or change the kitty litter? There were letters to write and care packages to send to her brothers fighting overseas in World War II. Her parents, grandmother, and sister lived nearby, and someone was always getting sick and needing her patented leaden matzoh ball soup. Plus, spinster aunt Bea, the garment factory seamstress, who might have liked girls, was always showing up with her dirty laundry that had to be hand-washed and dried on a line. Later there would be grandchildren to babysit and Johnny with his early-onset Alzheimer's. She would no sooner cradle a cat than a boot.

Me? I just wasted half an hour scratching my cat's chin today and I'm looking forward to a nice long skin-to-fur cuddle tonight.

"I wuv you," I say, kissing the mouth that hunts more vermin than I'll ever know. For the briefest moment, I contemplate what it would be like to breast-feed a cat, but of course, I don't. Everybody knows that cats' tongues are like sandpaper. Right?

For Girls and Boys
BLUE STAR CAMPS
A Summer
"In the Blue Ridge Mountains"
Hendersonville, North Carolina
CAMPING ADVENTURE
Water-front activities are featured along with all camping activities at this privately-owned summer camp located in the Blue Ridge WITH A PURPOSE
Mountains.

Dear Folks:
Arrived safely. Will write letter later. In the meantime, please send all mail to me as follows:
CABIN No. P-12-R
c/o BLUE STAR CAMPS
POST OFFICE BOX 1029
HENDERSONVILLE, N. C. 28739

Will write as often as I can — Please do the same.

Love to one and all,
Anne

P.S.—Camp is nice—they even write our cards for us.

Post Card

Dear Mom & Dad, Hi! As usual they put me in a cabin that everyone is a year younger, if you had said you wanted me in a cabin with people of my age I would enjoy camp more # I HATE YOU

Ice-cream cones in hand, we'd sing as the wind rushed through
the pines, blowing tangles through our virgin hair.

welcome home,
sunshine

I've flown north and am speeding through winding mountain passes, past sun-dappled vineyards. Three hours into the drive, I'm deep in the redwood forest. I'm sure I've missed the turnoff when I spot the hand-painted signs tacked onto the tallest trees on Earth. *Not All Those Who Wander Are Lost.* I've always hated that aphorism, because isn't it a lot like that saying about paranoids? But I *Hurry Up and Slow Down* and *Yield to the Present* because a bearded fellow with a mischievous smile and rainbow clown wig is making the universal motion for me to pull to the side of the road. He roller-skates over and introduces himself as Huggy Bear. It looks like Huggy Bear has been hitting the honey jar; a roll of hairy fat spills over the top of his low-rider bell-bottoms. He's giggling as he asks me to get out of the car. I leave the safety of my rented vehicle and he invites me to howl with him. It doesn't seem like he is going to take no for an answer. He lets loose a piercing coyote howl and I produce a noise that sounds like a ferret being strangled.

Looking down, I notice that his watch face is covered by a strip of masking tape: the words *Right meow* are printed on it. That's unexpected. He hands me a brown paper bag, into which I am to deposit my computer and phone. Huggy Bear leans in and whispers two words that shake me to my core: "Welcome home."

Twenty-four hours earlier I was on a street corner near my home in Los Angeles. I had gotten a ticket for jaywalking on my way to a yoga class. I was stressed out because our health insurance premium was skyrocketing. Now my blood pressure was skyrocketing, I'd missed the class, and I had a $174 ticket to boot. Standing there, seething, ticket in my hand, I noticed a poster advertising a summer camp for adults in the window of my local haunt, the Dandelion Cafe. The food isn't very good at the Dandelion, but the calico tablecloths and triple-layer coconut cake under glass remind me of a joint my husband and I frequented on getaways to Big Sur before parenthood turned our vacation budget into braces, math tutoring, and twelve-panel at-home drug test kits. The Camp Lazydaze poster was a warm mustard yellow. The list of activities included crafts, a talent show, and archery. You can find craft centers in just about any city, and every living room in Los Angeles is a stage for a talent show, but archery, that's something you only do at summer camp or a Renaissance Pleasure Faire.

In the mid-1970s, my sister and I were sent to Camp Blue Star, nestled deep in the Blue Ridge Mountains outside of Hendersonville, North Carolina. Blue Star has been owned and operated by one family since its inception. As of 2015, the Popkin family is on its fourth generation of continuous commitment to being the summer "home away from home" for Jewish children from all over, but primarily the Southern states of the U.S. The camp website exhorts would-be campers to join the "Blue Star family," and that's exactly how we thought of it.*

We played sports, stitched lanyards, swam in the great outdoors, and participated in a "living Judaism program." This consisted mostly of Israeli dancing and singing songs commemorating the Holocaust.

My fondest memory is of our ice-cream runs into town. Piled onto an old flatbed farm truck, only a rickety wooden fence penning us in, we'd careen around the hairpin switchbacks of the moonlit mountain roads. On the drive back, ice-cream cones in hand, we'd sing as the wind rushed through the pines, blowing tangles through our virgin hair.

On a wagon bound for market, there's a calf [think: Jewish person] *with a mournful eye. High above him there's a swallow* [think: Nazi!] *winging swiftly across the sky. How the winds* [think: the world!] *are laughing. They laugh with all their might. Laugh and laugh the whole day through and half the summer's night.*†

You might think that the sheer weight of these sorrowful songs would bring us to our knees, but it didn't. We'd return to pull off some prank like filling someone's underwear with shaving cream, short-sheeting a bed, or locking an unsuspecting bunkmate out of the cabin while they were nude. And somewhere in a box of

---

* My sister and I were second-generation campers; our father was a counselor and taught riflery, a skill he picked up at his military high school.

† Both Joan Baez and Patty Duke recorded versions of this traditional song; it's called "Dona Dona."

memorabilia, I have a certificate from the last of my summers at Blue Star, during which time I was recognized, in a ceremony witnessed by the entire camp, for having scored the most hickies for my age group, second session.

Summer camp was something of a distant memory until I was hit with a bout of crippling anxiety at auditions. I consulted a hypnotherapist, who asked me to fork over two hundred dollars and told me to close my eyes and go to a "happy place."* What popped into my mind was the infirmary at Blue Star. At least once during each summer, I pretended to be sick so I could spend a solitary day lying about, lost in whatever Kurt Vonnegut novel I was reading. Once refreshed, I returned to plot when Bunk 4 of Pioneer Girls should untie Jeannette Weinberg's bathing suit top so as to cause her the most embarrassment. That's how camp became my "happy place," and that's exactly what I needed now.

I went home and Googled Camp Lazydaze. A cursory look at the website showed the kind of pictures you might expect: adult campers wading into a stream, racing across an athletic field, chowing down in a mess hall.

A notice on the site flashed the news that the next and last session of the summer was starting in less than twenty-four hours, and in the way that the Internet allows you to do things so quickly that before you know it you've posted a tweet that ends a friendship or any chance of future employment, I was going to camp. And because I'm a creature of the twenty-first century, I put the news of my upcoming adventure on all of my social media feeds.

---

* There might have been more to the therapy, but I was hypnotized and can't remember.

It wasn't until after I clicked the nonrefundable purchase that I noticed the camp wasn't local to me. It was in Northern California, near San Francisco. That was a plane ticket. Scrolling farther down, I learned it was actually three hours north of the city. That meant I'd need to rent a car, but I'd paid for camp and announced it on Twitter, and once you've put something on Twitter, you can't take it back.

I didn't bother to read the lengthy camp handbook that downloaded into my e-mail because I had to pack, and besides, I'd gone to camp. I got this. I mean, it's camp.

"You're going to an ass-ram?" my father asked when I called to let my parents know of my plan.

"It's 'ashram,' Dad, and no, I'm going to summer camp."

"You hated camp," my mother called out. "Blue Star made you write letters home every Friday night before Shabbat dinner and you always wrote that you hated it."

"Don't be ridiculous, all kids say that," I told them. I hung up and told my husband.

"You're what?"

"I'm going to summer camp."

"Are you seeing someone?" he asked.

"No."

"Well, if I ever tell you I'm going to camp, you'll know I'm seeing someone."

If howling with Huggy Bear could be considered "seeing someone," then he was right.

After parking my car, I am issued my very own camp tin water cup by a young man with a handlebar mustache painted on his face, wearing shorts and a cape. His name tag reads *Sir Racha*. Mr. Hot

Sauce informs me I have been assigned to Hawk Village and hands me a name tag on which to write my nickname.

"No thanks, I'm not really a nickname person."

"We don't use names at camp, just nicknames. There's no talk of 'W,' work; no technology; no mention of your age; no clocks; and no alcohol or drugs are allowed on the grounds." I really should have read that handbook. There are members of my family who call me Sergeant, and I've heard myself referred to as "cranky" or "an acquired taste," but I decide to go for irony and christen myself Sunshine.

I set off for my village, stopping in at the camp store along the path. Located as we are in the Anderson Valley, this outpost could be renamed the Wes Anderson Valley, as someone appears to have indulged in repeated viewings of *Moonrise Kingdom*. The store is stocked with items that seem to have come from the movie's prop department and have no value other than kitsch. There is a collection of portable record players, small valises covered with vintage travel stickers, classic aluminum scouting canteens, and scratchy army blankets. Next to the store is the infirmary, which is manned by a young woman dressed in old-fashioned nurse's whites complete with a starched cap. She's reclining on an ancient wooden wheelchair, knitting a sweater, and she looks to be at least five months pregnant. I'm unclear as to whether or not she is an actual medical professional because the red cross on her cap has been hand-drawn with a Sharpie.

At Hawk Village, I meet my counselor, Popcorn. She's a hearty gal with a mane of golden, curly tresses and extremely approachable, which makes sense because everyone likes popcorn, right?

The twenty women who make up our kettle gather around

Popcorn for our initiation rites into Hawk Village.* We put on neckerchiefs festooned with the image of our avian namesake and feather earrings. We're taught the official Hawk greeting and encouraged to use it when we encounter our brethren. Our "cry" turns out to be a two-syllable piercing shriek accompanied by a gesture that resembles a bird's wings flapping, which technically isn't correct, because as I understand it, hawks glide, they don't flap. I do it anyway.

Popcorn takes us on a short tour of the village. There's a bathhouse a half a mile away with running water, but when she announces with some pride, "We've got our very own outdoor latrine," I know I won't be getting much use out of that official camp tin cup.

Our bunks turn out to be more crèche than cabin. The shallow open-air structures bring to mind the kind of tableaus typically associated with Christmas nativity scenes. Children's bunk beds have been hastily placed inside them. But where is the fourth wall? I walk around the side of what I will learn is called an Adirondack shelter to see if there's a hinged barn door that we'll close at night, but there's not even mosquito netting.

I whisper to another Hawk that my most recent camping experience, with my kid's school, was at a state park where the cabins had Jacuzzis and margaritas with crushed ice were served with dinner.

"That's not camping, Sunshine, that's glamping," she says in a voice dripping with contempt.

Popcorn invites us to circle up and say what we hope to accomplish at camp in one word, and the consensus of the group is that they want to be more social. When it's my turn, I say, "Chillax."

---

* "Kettle" is the scientific term for a group of hawks.

Chillax? I've never said that word, except to make fun of it. Is that a word that Sunshine regularly uses?

We learn that "in the amount of time it takes to boil seven consecutive eggs," we'll be heading down to the costume parade. This is the first time this weekend, but not the last, that I hear time referred to in this way. The thing is, I hosted a TV show for six years that was equal parts comedy and cooking, but I still can't remember how long it takes to boil an egg. Is it three minutes or ten minutes? And are we talking about hard- or soft-boiled eggs? What about the time it takes to heat the water to boil the eggs and the time it takes to let the eggs cool down? Over the next two days, I will find that adapting to the technology ban is surprisingly easy, but clocks are what I miss the most, not only because I can't figure out how to plan my day, but because I am continually offered references to things that hold no meaning for me. A meal will be happening in the time it takes for MDMA to kick in, to pasteurize goat cheese, to get a tattoo removed, or to watch an episode of *Your Pretty Face Is Going to Hell*, to which I have to repeatedly inquire, "How many *Seinfeld*s is that?"

"Before we head to the athletic field for the opening ceremony," Popcorn says, "we're going to do a little download. Talk to the person sitting closest to you and tell them how you're feeling." Oh, no, I'm sitting next to the same bird of prey who introduced me to the term "glamping." Her name tag reads *Serene*. Serene is lanky with a boyish haircut, and has the unmistakable drawl and countenance of a Midwesterner, but in less than the time it takes to pull a shot of espresso, I find out that she and I have something in common. We're the only campers who have chosen ironic nicknames.

Serene is anything but. She was a convoy driver in the army who served in Baghdad before the tanks even had armor. She's been through firefights and lived in war zones, but nothing is as terrifying to her as the emotional pain she's in right now. "I'm only here because a friend brought me; she's worried because I haven't been eating and I'm so depressed." Her husband, also former military, has fallen out of love with her and Serene told him to decide what he wants to do by the time she gets back from camp. I listen to her, wishing that we were just a bit further up the coast at the Esalen Institute, a new age retreat center that is staffed by trained professionals, because the only person in charge here is a counselor who has named herself after a buttery snack food and I'm afraid that I'm out of my depth. "I feel like a failure," she blurts out. I'd like to tell her I was fired from my own comedy act once, so I know a lot about failures. I'd like to know her age, because that seems like an important factor when talking about big life transitions. I could tell her that because of my relatively advanced age, I've learned that it's possible to live through monumental disappointments, but I want to observe the rules of the camp. On the other hand, she could be suffering from PTSD, so what can I say that will be meaningful? I listen to her catalogue of woes until it's time to go to the athletic field.

The grassy expanse is teeming with two hundred funsters, a colorful bunch ranging from Plushies to people on stilts or wielding puppets. It's like a cultural exchange program where the masked meet the caped. I grab hold of Serene's hand and we execute a passable limbo down the center of the parade.

Huggy Bear jumps onstage and announces, "We're going to raise the camp flag to show we're in session. To see who will get the honor, we're going to play rock, paper, scissors." All of us. At the same time. We're told to turn to our right and play the person next

to us, and then whoever wins turns to their right and plays that
person, until we have a winner. I've heard the term "clusterfuck"—
in fact, I've used the term "clusterfuck"—but I've never actually
been in one until right now. In an instant, there's a rush of sound
and movement and jostling for position that I suspect is not unlike
the Soviet bread lines of the 1970s. I'm eliminated in the amount of
time it would take to pour the glass of pinot noir I'd like to be
drinking if alcohol were permitted. The winner raises the flag and
the crowd goes wild.

We head into the mess hall, and I'm so disoriented I can barely
down my quinoa kale loaf. Tables full of campers are yelling chal-
lenges to adjoining tables over who has more "spirit" and a rumor
circulates that the flag has been captured. As a camper with a flag
stuffed down her shiny spandex catsuit dashes out of the mess hall,
Huggy Bear appears with a megaphone and announces the imminent arrival of Gummy Bear, the camp director. Huggy and
Gummy are brothers. Like Blue Star, this is a family enterprise.

Gummy Bear's entrance is heralded in a manner befitting the
second coming of Christ. My fellow campers worshipfully chant his
name. This will be repeated whenever he materializes during the
weekend. The camp is unmistakably his brainchild. He is dressed
in a 1950s scoutmaster uniform, sports a comically oversized handlebar mustache, and carries a clipboard.*

The crowd is so enthralled, I flash on images of Spahn Ranch
and worry this "family" might have some things in common with
Charles Manson's Family. On his orders, the campers commit a

---

* A handlebar mustache takes several months to grow; obviously, he didn't
plan to come on a whim, as I did.

rock-and-roll felony. They butcher the lyrics of Tom Petty's classic "Free Fallin'" by altering "I'm free . . . free fallin'" to "I'm free . . . free balling."

Gummy Bear explains his vision for our time together but it's so loud I can barely hear him. From what I can make out, we're going to create a kind of utopia. We're making up our own traditions and rituals, we'll form lasting friendships, and most important, we're going to have fun. Fun! FUN! (He didn't add, "Or else!" But I definitely heard it in my head.)

After dinner, I witness the first of numerous signs that portend the coming of the end of civilization and give insight into what we can expect in the event of a major disruption of our power grid, beginning with a stop at the Tea House. It's a yurt lined with rugs and furnished with a piano, near which small tea stations have been set up. Campers are sitting on the floor while Sir Racha bangs out tunes on the piano. They're your basic show tunes and classic rock songs, only these young people can't remember all of the lyrics, so songs trail off into a jumble of chords and speculative endings.

"They paved paradise and put up a . . . what?" What did they put up? Who knows? Maybe another Walmart, or maybe it's a store that sells all-natural, organically farmed, hand-packed artisanal pickles. These campers may never know. I want to say, "I know what they put up!" and appoint myself choirmaster, but that might lead to a discussion of age, which is a violation of camp rules, so I only stay for the time it takes to get a mammogram before heading up to Hawk Village to try to sleep off the day.

Our hutch is freezing and pitch-black. Serene is already asleep in the bunk above mine. There's no electricity and I am shivering as I change my clothes in the open air. I'm not changing my clothes so much as adding layers. I put on two T-shirts, a sweater, another pair of pants, and two pairs of socks. I pull on a hat, don a pair of gloves, hang my towels around the bunk bed to block the wind that's picked up, and dive inside my sleeping bag.

Go to your happy place, I tell myself, but the cold has intensified the arthritis in my hands, which are now curled into angry fists. I know I shouldn't complain, because Serene slept standing up in a tank in Kandahar, but every bone in my body aches with stiffness.

I can't make it through this night. I will die. I will die and no one will claim my body for weeks. Everyone at the camp knows me only as Sunshine, and when the story hits the news that a camper has died of exposure, no one will suspect that it's me, because no one who has spent five minutes in my company would associate me with the name Sunshine. If somehow I live through the night, I will be humiliated after talking the camp up and spending so much money to get here. Is it possible that I really did hate camp? Can it be that I am a fully grown independent adult, the mother of a teenager, and my parents know me better than I know myself? It would be preferable to expire right now! I'll never live this down. Why did I put it on Twitter? My husband will need to fly up because I will be stuck in this contorted position and require assistance to be removed from this bunk. I'll need to be airlifted out in a medical transport plane, and that will cost a small fortune, and no way is that going to be covered by our new insurance plan. I am definitely not in my happy place.

After the sun rises, it's warm enough for me to stumble down to the mess hall and look for my counselor.

"Popcorn, I can't do this. I need to leave."

"We all love you and we're all so happy you're here."

"I don't fit in here and I'm freezing."

"We all love you and we're so happy that you're here."

"And so tired."

"We all—"

"Quinoa tastes like sand."

"How about we try getting you into a tent?"

It feels like Manson Family talk. There is no fighting it. I ask if I can stay in the infirmary, but she insists that the infirmary is colder than the lean-to. I have no idea what time it is, no way to reach the outside world, and I don't really want to abandon Serene. I buy three scratchy blankets at the camp store and lie down in the sunniest spot I can find, right smack in the middle of the athletic field. I manage to nap for the amount of time it takes to have the colonoscopy that I'd prefer to be receiving, because at least you get the good drugs.

I'm feeling a little better when I rouse myself, but I've slept right through archery. I spot Serene at a picnic table. When I ask her how she's feeling, she rests her head on my shoulder and cries. Screw the rules of the camp.

"How old are you?" I ask.

"Twenty-six."

"You're so young! You have your whole life ahead of you. Anything that happens to you during the next four years you can write off as 'things I did in my twenties.'"

Serene describes her financially strapped childhood in the heartland and how the military helped her get an education, and now, with a possible divorce, she's worried about her finances. We chart out her student loans, her mortgage, and her other monthly expenses, how much she's saved in her 401(k). Without disclosing where she "W's," she explains that, like most of the campers, she spends her days in front of a computer, and that she and her husband work on projects as part of the same team. I've watched enough episodes of HBO's *Silicon Valley* to recognize this as tech sector talk.* I should have known, given the camp's close proximity to Mountain View, I have wandered into a tribe of techie geeks. That explains why Serene was unfazed by the stilt-walkers in tutus and the Furries.

"Techies place a high value on weirdness. My 'W' isn't a haven for cosplaying types, but we have a 'play space' with foosball, darts, and pool tables—they want to distract you from the long hours they expect you to put in. Sometimes my husband and I are on campus for eighteen hours a day," she explains.

"Apply for a transfer. You need to get some space. 'Familiarity breeds contempt' is a well-known axiom because it's true."

I am tempted to tell her that I know something about this because I've seen casts of plays devolve into bickering kindergartners, but Serene is convinced that I "W" as a therapist and I'm afraid if I reveal that although I am not a therapist, I've been in a lot of therapy, she won't take my advice to heart.

"You're going to be fine," I tell her.

"But I've been with my husband since we were in high school. How will I meet people to date?" We make a list of her hobbies.

"I've got a dog."

"Great, you can go to dog parks."

---

* Months later, watching *Veep*, I will sympathize with Julia Louis-Dreyfus's aide Amy, who turns down a job at a fictional tech start-up called Clovis because she doesn't want to work with people who play with Legos.

She bikes. "That's another good way to meet people," I tell her. In the amount of time it takes to get your teeth cleaned, including X-rays, we've sketched out a possible exit plan for her.

Huggy Bear skates over with the news that my tent is being put up and a survival skills workshop is starting in the amount of time it takes to boil a cup of tea. I decide to give it a try. Serene is going back to the nest for a nap. He points me in the direction of Bobcat Village and says I'll probably find it, adding, "But does it really matter if you get there? Isn't it the journey that counts, not the destination?" As he skates away, I imagine Huggy Bear's hair catching on fire and how I will point the firefighters only in his general vicinity.

The path leads past Bobcat Village to a clearing in the woods where three structures have been set up. They are labeled: *This, That,* and *The Other Teepee.* I have to give it up to the cleverness of the staff of the camp, and even chuckle until I notice that there are couches inside and the teepees are lined with rugs. Wait a minute. I spent the night in a shipping crate while there were actual enclosures? I curse this, that, and the other counselors who failed to inform me of Teepee Village.

I spot a rocky plateau just beyond the teepees and join a group awaiting the arrival of the survival skills instructor. Of those assembled, I recognize only one person I've seen elsewhere at the camp, Hug Me, a petite boho goddess.

Hug Me is frustrated. "I intended for people to say, 'Hug Me,' out loud so I could offer hugs, but everyone who reads my name tag thinks *I* need a hug, so now I'm telling people to call me 'Hug You,' which isn't working out either." She's got daggers in her eyes when I suggest that she make "Hug Me" her surname and "WouldYa" her first name. I mentally add "suggesting that someone might be taking the camp too seriously" to the list of topics that are off-limits at camp.

Mellow Out shows up, apologizing that he lost track of the time. I notice his watch face is masked with a piece of tape that reads *Love*. He intended to teach us a series of knots and snares and how to make a fire with the dowel-and-bow method—skills that might be useful in an emergency—but alas, because of the tardiness, he'll skip that. "Besides," he says, "if things ever get so bad that you need to be making a fire by rubbing sticks together, your best hope is to run for help." I'm not sure if this was Mellow Out's intention, but so far I have learned something: the most important survival technique is to never cover your watch face when in the wilderness.*

Mellow points to a dome-shaped hut a few feet away. It's a sweat lodge built by the group from the last session, but before we consider going in, he wants to share the wisdom of the forest people with us. "Don't believe the timeline you've been told. Two-legged has been walking on Turtle Island since the time of the dinosaurs."

"Excuse me," I say. "So you're saying that the fossil records, as interpreted through radiometric dating, a scientific practice accepted across the globe, are incorrect?"

"Yes," he answers. "Now, who would like to participate in a sweat lodge?"†

This will entail all fifteen of us squeezing inside a muddy, pitch-

---

* I also learned that the premise of every dystopian futuristic movie is flawed. If there is a catastrophic event, the entire population of Earth will just be running for help.

† It might be worth noting here that Mellow Out was not of Native American descent.

black twelve-by-nine-foot enclosure with temperatures reaching 180 degrees, facilitated by someone who won't be keeping track of time, to experience a purification ritual so fraught with danger that it recently caused the death of several people in Arizona.

"Did you say the temperature might reach a hundred eighty degrees?"

"Yes," he answers.

I'm the first person to put her hand up.

We enter on our knees, crawling across the dirt floor in a clockwise direction, as instructed, each of us calling out, in Lakota Sioux, "*Mitakuye oyasin*," or its English translation, "All my relations." Mellow asks who feels they can handle sitting in the inner ring of the lodge. I scurry over to the spot closest to the fire pit. I've shvitzed in my fair share of saunas. Finally, my glamping background will come in handy.

One by one, he totes fire-heated volcanic rocks into the lodge on a broken shovel held together with duct tape. Mellow calls the rocks "grandpas," because "rocks are our ancestors." As the temperature rises, I am hoping that Florence Nightingale is an actual medical professional, because I'm seated only six inches from the sacred fire and one of our grandpas is rolling dangerously close to my bare toes.

Mellow pours water on the rocks and invokes the spirit world, and the sound of drums, flute, and chanting fills the lodge. Two *Seinfeld*s into the ceremony, we've sweated into each other's skin, puffed from the same pipe, and drunk from the same water jug, and our numbers have halved. He praises our warrior-like endurance and invites us to share a prayer or song. Hug Me/You warbles a tune she picked up in Papua New Guinea, someone sings a Sikh melody, another fellow traveler leads a call-and-response in what might be Klingon or binary code. As a drum is passed to me, signaling my turn to make an offering, the mud sticks my thighs to the ground, the smell of mugwort chokes my lungs, and I am gripped with an intense desire to fit into this tribe. I'll sing something that shows that I occasionally eat low on the food chain and read McSweeney's; okay, I don't read it, but I can spell it correctly. But when I open my mouth, what comes out is "Hava Nagila," the most clichéd, overused folk song that was sung at Blue Star, at Bar Mitzvahs and weddings the world over, by my parents and their parents, by all my relations, perhaps for thousands of years, but probably not all the way back to the time of dinosaurs. And the hipsters, even the ones who are completely naked by this point but who don't want to make eye contact with me because I remind them of their mothers, all sing with me. For the time it takes a piece of Bazooka bubble gum to lose its taste, I am someone who can legitimately answer to the name Sunshine.

We emerge from the lodge and the people who haven't already shed their clothing strip down to wade into the nearby stream. I smile but decline the invitation to join them. I've gotten naked with plenty of people whose names I never knew, but I know in my heart that I'll never be joining a tribe that takes itself so seriously, or believes that dinosaurs and humans coexisted, and I don't want to traumatize the younger campers by treating them to a glimpse of the inevitable future of all flesh.* Also, I can't risk lowering my core temperature with the coming nightfall.

---

* Getting naked with strangers is a bit too much like "W" for me. Working in theater and even on movie sets, actors regularly disrobe in front of crew and

On my way back to Hawkville, I stumble into the camp's color war. There are some things that you can never unsee. When the Internet was young, before easy access to fetish porn got same old, same old, my husband insisted that I check out a woman getting up close and personal with a Coke bottle. That image is seared into my mind, as is this: a raucous bunch covered in body paint is cheering as their teammates receive haircuts and fistfuls of shorn hair being glued onto the naked bodies of their fellow teammates. Why? I do not and will never know, but it's a camp tradition, two years running, making the hickey competition at my summer camp seem like a Victorian parlor game.

Gummy Bear is taking in the scene dressed in flannel pajamas and fuzzy bedroom slippers, but still clutching that clipboard.

"Last session the campers acted like twelve-year-olds. This session they seem to be nine," he noted before tipping his scout's hat and sauntering off.

"Are you okay? You look like you're about to have a stroke." Two kindred spirits have bounded toward me from across the athletic field. We're similarly costumed in cloaks of irritability. They're also surprised to discover themselves at campy camp, but being locals, they've spent most of their time comfortably holed up in the insulated tent they brought from home.

"I'm not sure how I'll make it through the night," I tell them, and one slips a folded note into my hand.

"Open it in your tent."

Back at Hawk Village my tent has been set up. I am thrilled to

---

cast members; that becomes something very easy for us. Getting to know people with your clothes on, that's a challenge.

discover that inside the rolled-up paper is half an Ambien. Between the multiple layers of clothing, the three blankets, the knowledge I am leaving in the morning, and the drugs kicking in, I'm almost cozy.

My mind drifts to earlier in the year, when I acted in a Subaru commercial directed by Wes Anderson. I played the mother of six children. The spot opens on a slow pan of the interior of my home, which is decorated in the director's preferred palate of muted yellows. A moment of quintessentially Andersonian chaos is unfolding. All the kids are costumed: one little girl is playing dress-up in what is ostensibly my wardrobe, a gown and long strands of drapey pearls; another child is in a bear suit; another is playing a set of drums; and yet another is dressed as a mad scientist and is standing over an erupting volcano in the living room. My husband is in the kitchen cooking dinner, pots are boiling over, and he's balancing a baby on his hip. We hear me talking him through the steps of a recipe, but I am unseen. I'm explaining that I am stuck in traffic, but the shot continues to the exterior of the home, and the viewer sees that I'm actually relaxing in my car, which is parked in the driveway. Another of my children, wearing a shark-themed wet suit and carrying a surfboard, wanders outside, and I whisper, "Shhhh!" and close my eyes. Show business is an industry fraught with randomness, but somehow, I was perfectly cast as a woman who relishes her alone time.

In the morning, I hastily pack my bag and the entire Hawk Village claps and flaps for me. They were sure I was going to bail. I tell Serene I'm coming back up north soon.

"Come stay with me," she says.

"I will," I promise, because we've made a deep and lasting connection.

"See you next year!" Huggy Bear yells as I roar out of the parking lot, but I take off my Hawk earrings in the airport security line and leave them in the white plastic container on the conveyor belt.

In earlier eras on Turtle Island, assimilation into another tribe wasn't the norm. Upon encountering an "other," either in wartime or through a chance meeting, an outsider might have been accepted into the fold, but more likely they'd have been killed on the spot or turned into a slave.* I have to hand it to Gummy Bear for his commitment to that handlebar mustache and his utopian idealism, but when stripped of preconceived notions associated with work, age, and status, we still don't unconditionally accept everyone into our chosen families. Even toddlers, long before developing childhood alliances and notions of popularity, choose preferred playmates, excluding others. In the Let Your Freak Flag Fly Clan of Cultivated Weirdness, you have to drink the Kool-Aid, or in this case, kombucha, to fit in. To be fair, the age difference might have been a big part of it. Spending your precious vacation with someone older than your parents might be similar to arriving at your dorm room at college, only to discover an octogenarian roommate. An interesting sociological experiment, but not really the BFF you'd hoped for.

"We all love you," Popcorn said, but for all that talk, Sunshine is

---

* We know now that there was interspecies mating between Neanderthals and Homo sapiens. The temperature can drop to −40 degrees in the Altai Mountains in Central Asia, where proof of the species coexisting concurrently has been discovered, and any old hominid can look pretty good to cuddle up to at that temperature.

not featured in a single one of the hundreds of pictures the camp posted in the online photo album. Neither is Serene, nor Our Ladies of Ambien, or the other campers who didn't fit into the confederacy of cultivated weirdness.

I never heard from Serene. It can be hard to make those long-lasting friendships envisioned by Gummy Bear, though the anonymity of the nickname might have been the very thing that allowed her to confide in me, like a seatmate on a transatlantic flight who tells you about their torrid affair with their best friend's spouse.

Back in Los Angeles, I recount the events of the weekend for my husband. Jeff politely intimates that I must have been dehydrated or hallucinating when I describe Sir Racha gluing another camper's hair onto Popcorn's areolas. But then, he's still convinced I was shacked up with someone at a motel in Big Sur.

I'm a sucker for sisterhood.

what price
sisterhood now?

Someone has traced *Wash Me* on the windshield of the station wagon that's parked in the driveway of a single-story house in a middle-class neighborhood of Los Angeles. Stickers on the car's bumper include a peace sign subtly doubling as the letter O in *One Earth* and an unambiguous *Unfuck the World!* There's a poster for a benefit to save Darfur, circa 2009, resting against a pot of what once were daisies on the front porch. Whoever these people are, they seem like people I would know.

I'm here because of an invitation from Funny E-mail Name. Funny E-mail Name is one of those cute addresses left over from that time when the arrival of an e-mail was reason for giddy celebration and novel enough to inspire the Hollywood blockbuster *You've Got Mail*. I was so sure that I'd never forget who'd thought up this hilarious moniker that I neglected to enter their contact information into my address book. Nowadays, I ignore half the e-mails that clog my inbox, but I couldn't resist opening this one because the subject line read: *Help a Sister Out*. In a nutshell, it read: "Most of you know what I'm going through and might even be sick of hearing about it. I'm tired of shaking the can and I am starting my own health and wellness business to raise money for my son's medical expenses. Please consider doing your shopping with my family." Above a glossy shot of a young man with gravity-defying checkbones in a wheelchair were the words "This is my son." "This is my store" was printed above the logo for a skin care company that rhymes with the words "far gone." It was signed *Love, Cindy*.

I can think of a number of Cindys who this might be. There's a casting director, the former girlfriend of a former boyfriend, two Cindys who were administrators of a theater company I worked with twenty years ago, and four Cindys on my list of Facebook friends whom I can't remember if I know personally or are friends of friends. But a sister in need? How could I refuse her invitation?

I'm a sucker for the sisterhood. I was one of those girls whose mothers subscribed to *Ms.* magazine, even if they themselves weren't living examples of Gloria Steinem's brand of feminism. Unless she shacks up with Ann Coulter, Steinem will always be my leader, and I'm pleased that signs of sisterly solidarity abound in ways less enervating than *leaning in*.

I was kicking my antidepressant before trying to get pregnant and my husband was out of town. Nauseous and shaking uncontrollably, I was curled up in the fetal position on the cold bathroom tiles by the time my friend Juel made it over.* She fed me soup, got

---

* Bonobo chimpanzee females leave home and form societies based on sororal bonds. It sounds like a painful gum disease, but it's a model for human

me into the shower, and tucked me into bed. You could call it *lean on* feminism.

When my son was born with medical problems, my Los Angeles girlfriends pumped milk for him. My sisters have provided shelter, lent jewelry and shoulders to cry on, and made middle-of-the-night fried chicken runs for me. So when Cindy invoked the call to "help a sister out," she was speaking my language. Whichever Cindy she might have been.

The door opens and Cindy, late fifties, looks familiar but I still can't place her. She's got dream catchers hanging from the ceiling and her bookshelves are crammed full of books, a positive sign.* A patio leads to a yard with rows of vegetables. When I see chicken coops, I know I've never been to this house, because I would have remembered chickens.

Cindy's sponsor in this new venture is a smartly dressed, square-shaped matron with matching everything, impeccably manicured nails, and bold sculptural jewelry. She's an Anna Wintour-esque blonde who seems a bit out of place in Cindy's hippy-dippy abode. She asks the ten or so of us who have answered the call to introduce ourselves. I will come to learn that in the Fargone lingo (as well as that of other multilevel marketing companies), this is something called your WHY. The majority of us have come to support Cindy, but one or two say they're looking to get into the wellness business.

---

sisterhood. Like our bonobo cousins, and like many of my female friends, Juel and I met long after we left home. Unlike our bonobo cousins, I've never turned a twig into a French tickler, but I admire their inventiveness.

* Books have been replaced by wicker and rattan decorative balls in many homes. What the hell do they signify, other than a great way to measure how much dust is in your air?

Sponsor Blonde tells us that she is using her business (no one ever calls this a sales job) to fund charitable pursuits. She's interested in cancer research, and it's with great pride that she announces that the company's nutrition line has been endorsed by the Mayo Clinic. We all clap. The Mayo Clinic endorsement *is* impressive.*

Sponsor Blonde launches into an overview of our amazing opportunity to get into the thirty-four-billion-dollar skin care business. It's an industry, we learn, *we are already in.*

"Every time we recommend a movie or a product we like, we're in the network marketing business. The only difference between you and me is that I'm getting a check for recommending products I personally use. It's the future! Everyone needs toothpaste. Everyone needs shampoo, right?"

She's right about that. Everyone *does* need toothpaste and shampoo. Now we're all nodding our heads. The promise of extra income "without affecting our focus on our artistic pursuits" is tantalizing. More clapping.

Sponsor Blonde turns the floor over to Cindy. Cindy is a whiskey-voiced earth mother, with bare feet, a caftan, a glorious mess of long hair, and those same gravity-defying cheekbones as the young man in the e-mail. She wears little makeup and radiates warmth. She tells us her WHY, which includes her son's motorcycle accident the year before and how hard life is for him, being paralyzed from the waist down, how much effort is involved and how expensive his care is for the family. When she says that work has

---

* Fargone specifically forbids consultants to say this. The Mayo Clinic is mentioned on the site, but there's no endorsement; however, you can find consultants' blogs touting this claim all over the Internet.

dried up in nonprofits, I'm able to place her as one of the theater Cindys. She says at her age, late fifties, she doesn't think it possible that she'll find full-time work again. She's been working as a personal assistant and organizer. We nod in agreement. Everyone in the room is either a freelancer or looking for a midlife reinvention. We share her economic insecurity. She's so genuinely unaffected, she admits to not really knowing what she's doing with Fargone, but she's using the "yummy" anti-aging creams and swears that the food supplements are keeping her son alive.

Sponsor Blonde tops her moving endorsement with the news that Cindy, who has been in the business less than two months, is already moving up to the next level, where she'll get even higher commissions on everything we purchase, and is poised to get all kinds of great benefits, including a free white Mercedes.*

"I am?" Cindy asks.

"Yes!" says Sponsor Blonde. "The health and wellness business is *booming* and Cindy's success is assured because everybody needs toothpaste and shampoo." Even more clapping. It's very intoxicating in a "You go, girl" way.

One of the women, already a customer, shares that she keeps a bag of Fargone caramel snacks in her purse. They are delicious, she tells us, but she wants to know how many she can safely take per day. Sponsor Blonde fields the question of caramel snack dosage with a practiced authority that suggests she is prescribing a course of antibiotics.

---

* Later I will learn that Fargone offers an eight-hundred-dollar monthly Mercedes car allowance as a sales bonus, but you lease or buy it in your own name, so if you miss your sales number or quit the biz, tough titties, you still have to pony up for the car.

"As part of your healthy diet, you should keep them in your purse and take five or six daily as quick pick-me-ups."

I do a quick Google search of the snack's ingredients on my phone and find I have to agree with Dr. Blonde. Candy really does provide a quick pick-me-up.*

We're invited to check out the products catalogue and Sponsor Blonde breezes through an enticing but completely confusing set of commission percentages that represent the financial freedom we will enjoy as we attain various levels within the company. For a multilevel marketing company, it's a relatively inexpensive buy-in, with a $79 annual fee to become a consultant, but both the company and consultants recommend that you personally try everything, so most will end up investing more. One attendee says she's ready to sign up and plunks down $1,300 for the anti-aging line on the spot.

The Fargone name seems familiar, but I can't figure out why, so I ask Cindy how she got connected to the biz. Sponsor Blonde and Blondie's sponsor, a dynamo of the local Fargone ranks with an impressive array of university degrees, got wind of her son's condition and they took the time to meet with her at a bar on New Year's Day, no less. Cindy was touched by their concern and offer to help.

Me too, I want to help too. But the last thing I need is another product. I carefully stretch thimbleful applications of a less expensive skin care line that I purchase from Karen, another local mom and a licensed aesthetician, who works out of her converted garage/

---

* Each Fit Chew (the size of a typical Tootsie Roll) contains four grams of sugar, which is roughly a teaspoon of sugar. They contain brown rice syrup, dried cane syrup, sugar, and palm oil, which, according to a study featured on NPR, raises LDL cholesterol—that's the bad kind.

studio. I've been a customer for seven years, and Karen's income supports her middle schooler and her husband, who is working on his contractor's license. I buy toothpaste and shampoo from Anonymous Sales Associate with Chalky Pink Lipstick at my local CVS, and she might have children and a husband with a fledgling business to support as well. But when Cindy's son wheels by, pokes his head in, and sheepishly waves, I feel compelled to buy a product, and not the cheapest one like I planned before showing up.

When I go home, I check out the company website. "The Fargone family is made up of thousands of individuals working to make their dreams come true." There's no mistaking that message: we're in this together. The site features testimonials from consultants. Their WHYs are variations of needing to make money and craving flexible hours. Former nurses and teachers testify to all the quality time they have with their families now that Fargone has freed them from the yoke of their former employment. It sounds ideal, except when you stop to consider what the world would look like if everyone followed this model. We'd all be spending quality time homeschooling our children and learning how to perform appendectomies in our kitchens because schools and hospitals would be completely understaffed.*

Then I realize why the Fargone name sounds familiar. Sure enough, I've got a flyer with the company logo, a colorful mash-up of a daisy chain and the McDonald's logo, crumpled up in my

---

* Not to diminish the real need to fix problems in these workplaces and relieve people from crushing student debt.

purse.* Earlier in the week, I saw a play and went for drinks afterward with Lara, one of the actresses, and her cheering posse, all members of her "downline." That's multilevel marketing lingo for Lara's "team," people she's recruited to sell the products and from whose earnings she collects a percentage. The flyer is an invitation to an introductory meet-up at a private club in Beverly Hills. I'd stuffed it into my purse and completely forgotten about it. That's two friends in one week inviting me to join up.

I'd always associated these schemes with bored housewives peddling Mary Kay cosmetics to their neighbors for mad money in the mid-twentieth century. But it makes sense that this model has made it to Hollywood. Productions now shoot in far-flung cities where producers hire cheaper crews and local performers in supporting roles, leaving actors and crew members who for decades earned solidly middle-class wages, not to mention the dry cleaners, caterers, gardeners, and even dog walkers that depend on their trickle-down dollars, in the dust.

Over lunch, I ask my inner circle if they've been recruited. Mishna, an actress, says she's been bombarded with exhortations to host parties for friends' multilevel marketing launches. Barbara, a designer, has been deluged with invitations to attend trunk parties for Cabi, an MLM (acronym for "multilevel marketing") clothing line. Kendall, a writer, is dodging calls from someone who wants her to come to a Stella and Dot—yet another MLM company—costume jewelry trunk party.

"One of the selling points is that you get a big discount on

---

* I don't need to point out the irony in the daisy-chainish logo, do I?

costume jewelry, but how much costume jewelry does one person need?" Kendall asks.

"But if someone makes the product themselves, that's different," Mishna adds. "I'm more likely to spend money."

"Me too," I agree, "but are we punishing people for not being crafty?"

"I was given the hard sell by a friend who told me I need to be using the Fargone lipsticks because I'm ingesting chemicals with the brand I wear," Kendall tells us. "Meanwhile, she's got a face full of fillers and Botox."

"Okay, but what if she had a job at a department store and was selling to strangers—is that better or worse?" I ask.

No one has an answer.

Christine, who works at a nonprofit, tells of an out-of-touch acquaintance who kept suggesting they catch up. Plans were eventually made, but when she showed up for what she thought was a dinner date, she was handed a sign-in sheet. It was a recruiting party for Nerium, another skin care product MLM. She gets nervous now when she hears from someone who wants to "catch up."

At the same time, each of us has been feeling so pinched that we've given an MLM real consideration. Mishna is making ends meet by renting out her home on Airbnb. When a good offer comes in, she and her partner, daughter, and two dogs move into a lower-priced short-term rental and pocket the difference.

These franchapreneurial opportunities* are not just sweeping

---

* There's a lot of controversy over whether it's entrepreneurial, which is what MLMs like to say about themselves, or whether this is akin to opening a franchise; hence the term "franchapreneur."

through my Hollywood-adjacent community; over 18 million people are working in multilevel marketing in the U.S. alone, up from 15.6 million in 2011. Women make up 78 percent of the sales force, so MLMs know who they are marketing to. Network marketing, as it's also referred to, is experiencing a resurgence in what's being called the gig economy. Women over fifty have some of the highest rates of underemployment in the U.S., so coupled with the ability to cast a wide net on social media, it's a perfect storm.

I'm so shaken by this window into the fragility of both the economy and the sisterhood that I e-mail former labor secretary Robert Reich, who is a friend, to ask if he is worried about the trend.

"The gig economy plays a role here. It's all a rip-off, as far as I can tell. Have you looked at Amazon's Mechanical Turk? We're back to the piecework of the late nineteenth century."

Reading his e-mail, I realize that I have very limited personal experience with the gig economy, other than being an Uber customer. I thought I was in the gig economy, but as I earn my living in something I've trained to do, I'm technically a freelancer. The gig economy generally refers to juggling part-time jobs as an independent contractor, often in unrelated fields, and I've never even heard of Amazon Mechanical Turk.

The Turk is a crowdsourcing Internet marketplace where employers, referred to as "requesters," advertise to workers, called "providers." The tasks to be performed are called HITs, Human Intelligence Tasks, and are primarily writing product descriptions or transcription services. Turk is named for a chess-playing "computer machine." It was an elaborate hoax designed to impress Empress Maria Theresa of Austria in the late eighteenth century, in which a human chess master hid inside a contraption—sort of a precursor to the IBM Deep Blue challenge matches.

Providers test into a ratings system to qualify for the highest-paying jobs. Whatever else you've done in your life counts for nothing in this system. It is essentially an equal playing field open for workers around the globe, which means you're competing for jobs with people whose expectation of wages might be significantly lower than yours. Another way to move up in the system is to do jobs in exchange for ratings—essentially a stint in the world's most unglamorous, faceless, soul-sucking internship program. Here is an example of the kind of employment an entry-level provider can vie for: filling out a survey on the People's Party of Spain's position on minimum wage. The estimated time in which to complete the task is one hour. The compensation: three dollars.*

Out of the 656,848 HITs advertised, one of the few I am qualified to even apply for is a transcription gig. Thinking I am one clever provider, I decide to cut out the middleman and go straight to the website of Speechpad; that's the requester. The rates are exactly the same as the ones advertised on Amazon. Oh, well. There is a project requiring the transcription of twenty-two minutes of audio. The time allotted is two hours and five minutes, and the pay is 25 cents a minute with no overtime. That translates into an hourly wage of roughly fifteen dollars, provided that you can complete the task in the time allotted.

I sign up for the online qualifying test. First, I slog through a lengthy set of instructions illustrating acceptable standards of every

---

* I am now wary of the report I recently heard on the BBC about Spain's economy improving.

imaginable configuration of grammar. It includes a collection of the most provocative grouping of sentences I've seen in one place. I am not making these up:

Felix was a lonely, young boy. Not lonelier than I am as I sit here at my "workstation."

Merchant owes vendor 13,656,000. If you've ever wondered what incites others to want to overthrow a government or turn to a life of crime, I can offer some insight. I feel stirrings of violence as I try to calculate how many hours of work at 25 cents a minute I'd have to make to earn 13,656,000. It's simply irresponsible to include a number that ginormous on a practice test for low-wage providers.

51% of people voted but only 6% were counted. The instructions warn over and over that you are not to contact Speechpad's clients, but I am willing to risk my 25 cents a minute to find out what election these percentages were culled from, who collected this statistic, and how the "requesting" organization feels about what appears to be a documented case of voter fraud.

I start transcribing my five-sentence test paragraph, estimated to take two minutes, at nine p.m. I'm not a millennial, so I have trouble working the link and the sound keeps cutting out, and it takes me about ten minutes to get the playback to work. I play the text over and over. It's challenging to focus my brain on a subject I am unfamiliar with, some kind of technical description of a telescope. Here is my transcription:

The James Web [How many B's?] Space Telescope is a project of NASA, the space agency [Is there another NASA? Do I really need to include "the space agency"?], with international cooperation from the European and Canadian space agencies. [Had to listen to that three times; is there really a Canadian space agency? With Trudeau in office, who'd want to leave the planet? LOL.]

James Webb features a 21 feet diameter SOME-THING and a primary mirror that will orbit the planet in tandem from a perch of SOMEWHERE at SOME DISTANCE for SOME AMOUNT OF TIME at an ASTRONOMICAL COST. [Can I just put that, because it's kind of funny, right?]

At 9:36 p.m., I submit my sample, and in less than the time it takes for me to hit the submit button, I get rejected for a 25-cent-a-minute gig.

But the majority of people who are doing this work live in countries where the money they are being paid is much more valuable, right? But no. The latest published numbers indicate that 80 percent of HITs were performed in America. A little searching on the Web leads me to Krazy Coupon Lady's blog site. This blogger claims to have earned $26.80 by completing a HIT in two hours. She calculates anticipated earnings of $800 a week, but it's such a fragmented way to earn a living, I'm dubious. I wouldn't be surprised to learn that she was Coupon Lady before her two-hour tenure at the Mechanical Turk drove her crazy with a capital K.

After less than an hour of "piecework," I feel ready to hit up my friends, neighbors, and entire social network to try to sell them my spleen.

That's when a Far-bomb goes off in my own home. First, my friend Yvonne shows up to my holiday potluck with her new BFF.

Tiny in stature, her new BFF turns out to be the local bigwig who tag-teamed with Sponsor Blonde to recruit Cindy on New Year's Day. She's enlisted both Yvonne and Becky, yet another of my inner circle of girlfriends. The Diminutive Dynamo brought a tub of Fargone face cream to the potluck, which is a lovely offering, but it doesn't make a great dip for crudités. Still, she might become my new BFF, because she generously invites me to her home to attend a presentation for a college counseling service.

During the presentation, she serves Fargone Fizz, a flavored "energy" drink mix whose taste evokes a remembrance of sodas past. The packaging is helpfully placed well within the guests' view.* Her dining room china cabinet displays the entire Fargone line, which feels a bit like a hard sell, but I'm charmed by her gracious inclusion of me into her parenting community, impressed by her elegant home, her refined bone structure and stylish wardrobe. Why do I have to be such a killjoy? She just wants to support her friends, which I seem to be one of now, and the college adviser proves to be invaluable to our son's college application process.

A few days later, I am at the weekly exercise class that I attend with Becky, the other new recruit. I quiz her about her Fargone experience. She's someone whose integrity I admire, and if she can do it, maybe I can too. She is a singer who teaches yoga, but neither of those is providing a steady income for her anymore.

"I really need the money," she gushes. "There's always somewhere to go and I've met so many spectacular women."

I need money. I like to go places. I am always looking to meet

---

* Like many products advertised as "energy drinks," one of the reasons it provides "energy" is that it contains caffeine.

more spectacular women. I know very few people who wouldn't agree.

MLMs know how isolating the gig economy is and have been happy to step in to fill the gap. Daria M. Brezinski, PhD, a practicing psychologist and former marketing director for a multilevel marketing magazine, echoed this sentiment in a Forbes.com interview: "Multi-level marketing companies are successful because they help people satisfy a number of important human needs, 'I'm doing this because I'm meeting amazing people . . . making so many connections . . . and I feel so good about myself.'" Amen to that, sister Brezinski. Every picture on the Fargone site features smiling women locking arms, toasting each other in convivial groupings in pastoral settings. A few men dot the landscape, but it's mainly sisters helping sisters.*

Becky is a closer friend than Cindy, so I feel like I have to order something from her. I order a mud mask that costs six times what I paid for the one I already own. I stop for coffee on my way home and I'm stunned to see Cindy's son wheeling down the sidewalk across the street from the coffee shop. I'm sure he doesn't recognize me, but my face is burning with shame and I avert my eyes. My ordering from Becky is stealing money from his care. I'm also cheating Karen's family out of my business. And the Fargone products I bought mean lower revenues for CVS. It's a tiny drop in the bucket, but what if everyone in my neighborhood switches over? That could impact Anonymous Sales Associate with Chalky Pink

---

* Sara Horowitz, founder of the not-for-profit Freelancers Union, knows the loneliness of the gig economy. What started as an organizing tool for health insurance now offers meet-ups and drinks nights for connecting with other freelancers. Membership in the FU is free.

Lipstick's ability to earn a living, and even those whose WHYs are unknown to us need toothpaste and shampoo, right?

Later in the week, I hear that another friend, Morgan, has joined Cindy's downline. Cindy's son is in a wheelchair, but Morgan has Parkinson's and she's a rung closer to my inner circle. If anything, I should be purchasing from Morgan, although Anonymous Sales Associate could be putting on that chalky lipstick to cover up some horribly disfiguring skin condition.

I meet up with Morgan and I'm shocked to see how much her condition has deteriorated since I saw her last. She's in constant motion, her spine twisting, and even her speech is difficult to understand.

"Do you really think that Fargone is a good fit, honey?" I ask.

"I'm so lonely."

She describes how there are calls to listen to and support groups, and Sponsor Blonde has been so encouraging; she's accompanying her to meet prospects for coffee dates.

"You should really check out that Beverly Hills soiree," she tells me.

When I walk into the Beverly Hills Country Club, the room is buzzing with a Bel Air–spirational vibe. Everyone is dressed to the nines. It's a heady combination of social and business networking that you don't often get as a freelancer.* I've come as Becky's guest and I try to ingratiate myself into a group that is worshipfully hovering around Becky's sponsor.

---

* The good feeling in the air is for real. A recent study at UCLA showed that when groups of women get together it releases oxytocin, which is a stress reducer; the same hormone is not triggered in male groupings.

As each woman shares WHY she is here, I learn that we are schoolteachers, psychologists, physical therapists, and artists. No one is looking to underwrite an expensive coke habit or spa vacation; a good three-quarters of us are saddled with student loans.

A fragile, birdlike figure, Carly, gazes reverentially as Becky's sponsor, No-Nonsense Networker, presents her WHY. No-Nonsense announces that she's not interested in being in the skin care business, and that's convenient, because the real money isn't in selling products, it's in building that downline. She also wants a "willable" business that she can leave to her young children should anything happen to her.* Carly is completely enthralled by No-Nonsense. Carly is in her early twenties, recently dropped out of community college, and is struggling.

"It's my second go-round with Fargone," she says. "My family wasn't supportive of me, but this time it's going to be different."

"What will make a difference this time?" I ask gingerly.

"I turned my life over to the care of Jesus Christ. Jesus is my business partner now."†

I'm not a biblical scholar, but I vaguely recall Jesus instructing his followers to eschew material possessions, which presumably includes exfoliating scrubs. I pray Carly has deep pockets and I wish that she'd go back to school, where Jesus could be her study

---

* Fargone's website makes it clear that only heirs over eighteen can inherit your business, but I doubt that she's aware that what she's saying is a partial truth at best.

† There's been some pushback on MLMs in churches. Amanda Edmondson of Sojourn Community Church in Louisville, Kentucky, says in *Christianity Today*: "If we aren't careful, people can quickly become an opportunity for our financial gain instead of a brother or sister in Christ."

partner, but I don't say anything and neither does No-Nonsense or anyone else.

A few of the assembled have hit high sales levels and are being anointed national vice presidents tonight, to rousing applause and cheering. "This is so much better than making some CEO rich" (a line I've also heard repeatedly), someone next to me gushes. I lean over and whisper, "Yes, but I'm sure that Fargone's CEO really, really hopes we will make a ton of dough, but we don't have to worry about her if we don't, because unlike everyone here, she's a salaried employee." In fact, not a single one of the company's executives or board of directors has come up through the sales force, so you're not actually a national vice president of anything but your own sales team, but I just think that part.

Another shiny, happy person steps ups and announces to tremendous applause, "It's hard to believe that only a year ago, we were just a few and now there are over two hundred of us here tonight!" I want to say, "Do you think someone will mention how great it is for them because they got in early, but that there are so many of us only underscores how hard it's going to be to start out in a market that might be oversaturated?" but I'm afraid I might get lynched.

The difficulty of earning a sustainable income in an already crowded market is noted on the website, buried deep in the legalese that governs a consultancy with the company; however, none of the consultants I speak to have read the impenetrable agreement. But then, has anyone ever read their phone company's terms of usage? I'm positive that everyone there has the best intentions of uplifting the sisterhood and the few straggler gentlemen in their ranks. I'm sure many of the consultants genuinely love the products as well. I also feel confident that the actual leadership at the company, as well as other MLMs, are grateful they don't need to offer health insurance, paid maternal leave, or the kind of severance packages that would typically go along with a national vice presidency of a multinational corporation.

A select group including No-Nonsense and Diminutive Dynamo are lavished with praise and rewarded with designer purses and David Yurman jewelry. "Next month, we'll be having a Mercedes presentation for Unintelligible Name!" The tacit acceptance that these are the trappings of female success turns my stomach in the same way that I found Mel Gibson nauseating in the movie *What Women Want*, and that was even before he referred to a female cop as Sugar Tits.* But I'm alone in this sentiment, because the crowd gets whipped into a frenzy of allegiance to Fargone and to network marketing in general.

"We're in a thirty-four-billion-dollar business!" crows one of the golden ones.†

The newly appointed national vice president Diminutive Dynamo spots me in the crowd. As she moves toward me, fixing me with a determined look, it's clear she's heard through the grapevine that I've been asking the wrong questions. The only question we're supposed to ask is, "How soon can I get started?" She all but demands I exit the premises with a stern, "What. Are. You. Doing.

---

* In that movie, he develops telepathic powers that allow him to bond with women by cloyingly saying things like, "Let's take this relationship slow."

† Showbiz, like cosmetics, is also a thirty-four-billion-dollar industry, but that doesn't mean you and I are going to see any of it. I prefer the showbiz anti-recruitment ethos—even the most successful people will go to any lengths to try to talk you out of getting into the biz.

Here?" I laugh nervously but quickly head for the door. I can still hear the roar of the crowd as I hop into my car.

"You're in business for yourself, but you're never in it by your-self," touts the Fargone website, but only if you're the kind of person who shows promising results and thrills at the mention of cruises and Hawaiian vacations. Okay, I admit it, the Hawaii trip does sound appealing.

Why do I have to ask so many questions? Why did I have to find out that only 13 percent of consultants in the U.S. are making money on a monthly basis and the average annual income of 59 percent of consultants is $674*? *I want to believe.* I want to be an Agent Mulder, but I'm a natural-born Scully.

I'm reminded of the olestra potato chip introduced by Frito-Lay in 1996. I was intrigued but never ran out and bought a bag. It promised to be a chip that didn't make you fat, but wouldn't you know it, there was an unexpected downside: anal leakage. A protest was mounted when it was taken off the market. Protesters argued that everyone should get to decide for themselves if they want to wear Depends while scarfing down chips. So guess what? Frito-Lay reintroduced the chips a few years ago under a different name. Most people didn't even notice it has the olestra and it's a big seller. Clearly, I don't understand marketing or sales.†

---

* According to my read of a 2015 compensation chart laden with squishy lan-guage suggesting that only consultants who earn every month are factored into averages, so the possibility exists that some sister made $34 billion during one month and then sailed off into the sunset. (Retail profits are also excluded from compensation.)

† I've received messages on Facebook from women offering sponsorship in It Works, a weight-loss body wrap; Terra essential oils; Rodan + Fields; Nerium;

In the case of Fargone, it helps if you have a well-appointed home, good-looking spouse and offspring, and enviable wardrobe. It doesn't matter if those things are the vestiges of a former career; it's an aspirational lifestyle business, which is why the women in my circle who are succeeding are doing so by promoting Fargone with FOMO-inducing pictures and updates on their social media feeds.*

One of the presenters at the Beverly Hills event, a dapper British gentleman, told us he liked that he could be his "authentic self," but I suspect that Cindy's genuineness may not translate into a white Mercedes anytime soon. She has so much on her plate with her son's health care that she can't keep up with all of the outreach required, and "owning a business" starts looking a lot like "shaking the can." At Cindy's launch Sponsor Blonde said we could reap the rewards of a forty-hour workweek if we put in ten hours and outsourced the other thirty hours to three other teammates. But the recorded coaching calls I listen in on exhort consultants to text and call at least three people a day, get their product in front of thirty people a month, attend Impact Training workshops (which carry a fee), try as many products as they can (there are no free samples), offer samples to their kids' coaches and teachers (you could go broke investing in these outreach tools), keep samples in their car to give away to open-minded strangers (it must be nice for Fargone to get all of this free advertising), and above all, build relationships. "Date your prospects slowly," they advise. "Take them for coffee

___

and a company whose name couldn't be revealed unless I made a phone date with a complete stranger to hear the pitch.

* The Fargone grapevine touts success stories like a former bus driver who is now a millionaire. None of those who repeated this example recognized this as marketing and not a vetted news story.

dates." (Let's assume you are paying for them.) "Attend launches, throw parties, throw more parties, go DEEP and WIDE."*

It sounds tiring, so it's not a surprise when Cindy's next e-mail announces that she is *EXHAUSTED* and isn't there anything we can please, please order so she can get to the next level and qualify for a Caribbean cruise? She reminds us that the wellness business is *BOOMING* and it's just that she has dropped the ball: "I suck at it, but what if I told you that I could show you a way to earn big bucks?" *I wouldn't believe you*, I think to myself, feeling pangs of something I learn is referred to as "compassion fatigue" in marketing speak.

I'm not the sister I aspire to be. I'm stretched thin. My sisterhood already includes Wendi, who's going through chemo; Liz, who needs meals delivered as she recovers from surgery; and Toni, who would like help in writing a book proposal. Cindy is going to have to go deeper and wider, but doesn't everyone need toothpaste and shampoo?

Over the next months, I check in with Cindy and inquire how it's going. She's not sure exactly how much she is making because she's a "terrible bookkeeper," and it's her own fault, her son has been doing poorly and she hasn't been able to focus on the business. She tells me her sponsors couldn't be more supportive. But there was no meet-up at the local bar this New Year's Day to celebrate the anniversary of her induction into the Fargone sisterhood. Her friend who bought $1,300 of products? She stopped returning her phone calls. Carly's church is sending her to Wales, which might be

---

* "Deep and wide" is marketing speak. Go deep into your phone book, hitting up family and friends and their contacts, then people you've lost touch with. "Going wide" means networking with people in regions that are less saturated: fresh territory.

fresh, untapped territory—at least I hope so, for her sake, because when I inquire if she's moved up any levels, I get no response, and it seems unlikely that if the news was good, it wouldn't be shared. Morgan had two friends hang up on her with the admonition to never call them again. After amiably assisting at several outreach coffees, Sponsor Blonde seemed frustrated by her lack of progress and Morgan feels she let her down. She's embarrassed to call for more support and is using the products she invested in herself. The money I spent on products is a loss I can afford to absorb, but for Morgan, the three hundred she spent is going to hurt this month.

It breaks my heart to hear my girlfriends say it's their fault that they aren't doing better in the biz. None of them wants to accept or acknowledge that the odds are against them. An officially sanctioned Fargone video advises, "Instead of asking yourself what if it doesn't work, ask yourself what if it does?" If it doesn't work, you're not doing it right, is the unspoken message. This is another example of that dark side of positive thinking that Barbara Ehrenreich wrote about in her book *Bright-Sided* and part of the insidious flatness of our brave new Internet world, where facts seem fungible. I fully expect to be having a conversation one day soon and have someone say, "Gravity? Oh, that doesn't work for me."

"It's the future." I heard that over and over, because every consultant recites the same talking points.* Actually, it's the past. It's not just the long line of Tupperware, Mary Kay, and Xocai chocolate network sales forces. My great-grandfather, the peddler who

---

* I also heard the word "yummy" used to describe face creams by many consultants. I'd never heard that word used in that context, but it may explain why a consultant brought face cream to my potluck. Fargone consultants are encouraged to stick to the scripts that are circulated among them.

sold pots and pans from a swaybacked mule traveling from shtetl to shtetl? He sold to customers culled from his network of family and friends, only he didn't need to convince anyone else to load up a mule and hit the road. "The future" is being pioneered by Grace Choi, a thirty-year-old techie who has innovated a 3-D printer that will allow you to make your own customized cosmetic products at home, which should retire that old phrase "I can't believe they discontinued my favorite lipstick!" But until that time, "social sales," as Sponsor Blonde referred to it, is our inescapable present.

What price sisterhood now? I wonder, mentally bastardizing the most quoted line from George Bernard Shaw's play *Major Barbara*, when I learn that the Fargone sisterhood has made more money off of me than I'd even realized. Five percent of the college counseling fee I ponied up after attending the presentation at Diminutive Dynamo's home was commissionable. I thought that I was attending a gathering of local parents, peers, friends, even. My father shared some of his hard-won poker wisdom with me once: "If you look around a room and you don't know who the mark is, you're the mark." Not only was I the mark, I was encouraged to invite other parents as well, so I was both a mark and a shill. This blurring of the lines between friendship and business is symptomatic of how we're able to connect with more people, but we're left with shallower relationships. But Diminutive Dynamo is probably close to two hundred in the hierarchy of my acquaintances, and I'm surely way outside of her Dunbar's number.

In the late 1990s, Robin Dunbar, a British anthropologist, posited a theory that, given our neocortex size, humans can only comfortably maintain stable interpersonal relationships with between one hundred and two hundred fifty people at most. You have people on the periphery who include past relationships, colleagues, people you grew up with, and people you do business with. You can switch people into closer connection, but you can't expect real friendships with more than Dunbar's number. I made the mistake of thinking that my sisterhood was deeper and wider than it was. "The only difference between you and me is that when I recommend something I use, I get a check," Sponsor Blonde said, untroubled by the monetizing of social capital, but it depresses me. How long before I am inviting acquaintances to catch up over coffee when what I really want is to sell them skin care products that I may or may not actually use, because I will never be able to be honest again? Who will answer my call on that inevitable day when I need to ditch my current antidepressant for a more powerful remedy? If only I had a stronger constitution. The consultants shall inherit the earth.

A few weeks later, I make an appointment for a facial. Karen's garden, normally verdant, looks a bit ragged, and the curtains are drawn in her husband's home office, aka the guest bedroom of the house. Is her husband sleeping during the day? Could it be that her marriage is in trouble? Has his business gone belly-up? Maybe her WHY is more urgent than I realized? I quickly shut that train of thought down. The last thing I want to know is another WHY. I prefer to remain blissfully unaware and enjoy what is a completely satisfactory business transaction, hoping she'll go both deep and wide as she exfoliates my face.

My mother is making the great leap backward.

going tribal

Why didn't I see it coming? I'm someone who views the future with a modicum of sobriety. When I saw a photo of Johnny Depp's *Winona Forever* tattoo, I knew it should've read *Winona for the amount of time actors typically spend together, which ranges between two and a half hours and the last day of shooting on the film we fell in love working on.* I'm always thinking ahead! That's why I don't have tattoos!

For some, the parental role reversal is heralded with the first changing of the adult diapers; for me, it was a phone call announcing, "We're broke." When you grow up helping your parents avoid phone calls from the IRS, a call like this isn't totally unexpected. Despite a deficit of income and a lot of creative bookkeeping, they

---

* Depp chose to have the tattoo reworked into *Wino Forever*, but I prefer my idea; it's evergreen and a teachable moment for your offspring. He's just changed his tattoo of ex Amber Heard's nickname from *SLIM* to *SCUM*; I think *SLUMP* is a better choice.

had managed to get by, often with considerable panache. How they afforded this panache was something of a mystery. The sale of their remaining asset, my childhood home, revealed that much of their lifestyle was underwritten by multiple mortgages. Now that they've paid off the three remaining loans on the property and chipped away at the mountain of credit card debt, lines of credit, and outstanding taxes, there's not much money left over and decisions must be made.

My sister, Lisa, and I have been called in to mediate the stalemate over where they'll live next, a decision that has reduced my parents to squabbling children. The choice has been narrowed down to two residences that are within their budget.

When push comes to shove, people go tribal. Some ancient longing to *go home* stirs inside us; maybe it's coded in our DNA, though in earlier centuries, when life spans were much shorter, you might have been thirty-three and toothless when you felt the call to return to your place of origin and be surrounded by your people. For most, that place would have been a few minutes or a few steps away, if not in the same house/teepee/hutch/lean-to/and before that, cave.

But where is home? The intoxicating concept of manifest destiny, uprooting for jobs, relocating as a sign of economic mobility— it all adds up to America's singular identity as a modern society on the move. When Bruce told Wendy, "We gotta get out while we're young, 'cause tramps like us, baby we were born to run," you knew Springsteen was urging her to flee from Asbury Park with an urgency that no one has ever used to suggest hightailing it out of the Fifth Arrondissement in Paris.*

---

* Okay, for Bruce aficionados the example is fraught, as Bruce's main residence is only 12.5 miles from where he grew up.

The year I left home to become a New Yorker and find my theater tribe, 1980, was the apex of internal migration in American
history. Over the next years, both my sister and I moved further
from our family. Our grandmother Rebecca lamented this uprooting, characterizing our "traipsing" from city to city in the most dis-
paraging way she could think of: "Y'all are like two Gypsies!"
Which just goes to show that members of one marginalized group
can always find another, more marginalized group to feel superior
toward.

Since the late 1980s, the trend has reversed. When we do pack
up, it's to move closer to our blood relations. The combination of
stagnant wages and a soaring housing market is resulting in more
intergenerational households.

Baby boomers are purchasing granny pods, something akin to a
Barbie's Malibu Dream Hospice, in record numbers. Prefab units
can be plunked right down in your daughter-in-law's backyard.
The more luxurious models come equipped with sensors that alert
for emergencies, video monitoring, and even a trolley suspended
from the rafters that transports you from bed to bath, a geriatric
twist on a sex swing.*

Our children are also coming back home at unprecedented rates.
My neighbor's son left college to take a gap year that lasted for
three. The biggest determinant of whether you'll live near your
family is not unsurprising: money. That college-educated professionals, the highest earners, are able to move further from home

---

* The cottages are also referred to with the libido-killing moniker "med-
homes." I prefer the granny pod made from a cargo container—it's stream-
lined and very mid-century. Someone please let my son know, in case
early-onset dementia prevents my telling him.

can be useful information if you're the parent of a teenager who is slacking off.

"You don't like listening to my opinions? Fine, study more. People with lower incomes, on average, live only eighteen miles from their mothers, so crack a fucking book if you want to get away from me!"

My parents have missed this window of opportunity. They're unable to move closer to either my sister or me because they need to stay in Florida to be near their doctors.

My mother wants to return to "her people," only she doesn't mean our family. Between cherished long-standing grudges and more recent perceived slights, she is on speaking terms with only a handful of family members. No, she's making the great leap backward, aligning herself with our ancestors.

My grandfather's family, the Maisels, were teachers and rabbis. We would like to believe that the namesake of the Maisel Synagogue in Prague, a mayor who held office during the sixteenth century in the Jewish ghetto, was a relative. That's about as much as we know about them, but we do know a lot about my grandmother Frances's lineage.

Menasha Lidinsky, later Anglicized to Moshe, and then Morris Laden, my grandmother's father, fled the Ukraine with his wife, Sarah, when my grandmother Frances was five years old. Fleeing the pogroms, they came over on the *Prinz Oscar*, having made their way to Germany from Russia in 1913. Moshe's profession was listed as dry goods salesman. My great-grandfather was what villagers referred to as a "swaybacked-mule junk dealer," or peddler, trudging from town to town earning a meager living selling goods off of an ancient animal's back. If we had a family crest it would feature a donkey, a potato, the one pot we had to piss in, and the family motto: "My feet are killing me!"*

Bubbie Sarah and Zayda Moshe opened a dry goods store across the street from the famous *Jewish Exponent* newspaper on Pine Street in downtown Philadelphia. They had an apartment above their store, like many shopkeepers at the time. They never ventured far from their community, spoke mostly Yiddish, and lived in fear of that multitasking God who had enough time to concern himself with not only the workings of the entire universe but with whether a tiny subset of a single species on a spinning blue ball in the outer suburbs of the Milky Way dared to defy his grand plans by mixing dairy and meat.

This is why the Tel Aviv Gardens is on our list of senior living facilities to visit this weekend. It's on a twenty-five-acre campus with housing options that range from independent-living apartments to hospice care. My mother imagines that her mother, Frances, our nanny, would have felt at home there.

Nanny never spoke of spirituality, but she did believe that Jews were a kind of chosen people—the tribe entrusted with the responsibility of keeping the planet spic-and-span. Cleanliness was not just next to godliness for her, it was a devout calling. In the same way that nuns see themselves as brides of Christ, Nanny pledged herself to Ajax, lord of germs, whose dominion covered the expanse of surfaces in her home and the domiciles of her offspring. Her idea

---

* Moshe and I actually have a lot in common, as the day-to-day life of a swaybacked-mule junk dealer is much like being an author on a book tour. I've sold books from the trunk of my car.

of keeping a kosher kitchen entailed producing flavor-free food; at least that's how it seemed to us grandchildren.

A typical meal at Nanny's might include iceberg lettuce, meat, and a starchy vegetable. Lettuce was scoured and scrubbed with so much vigor that each lifeless leaf emerged from these interrogation sessions virtually translucent. These were the years when lima beans were the most exotic item offered on dinner tables in suburban America. Not only was it a punishment to eat them, Frances seemed to want the beans to suffer for their own failure to be more appetizing. The legumes would be liberated from a can, only to be subjected to a pressurized moisture-extraction process that included several rounds of squeeze-drying in layers of paper towels. Chalky and granular; eating them sucked the moisture from your mouth.

Beef was purchased only from a kosher butcher, but you could never trust people entirely, so it was subjected to repeated rinsing and salting and then would be secreted into paper towels for additional dehydration.* Biting into it was like gnawing on particleboard.

My mother never showed any interest in keeping kosher, but she's pining for Nanny, whose personality she experienced as exacting. Death has conferred an almost saintly quality on her memory. My mother has adopted Nanny's mercurial housekeeping habits and is reaching further back to Bubbie's dutiful observation of holidays. My mother wants to attend the weekly religious services at the Gardens. She has started lighting Sabbath candles. She pictures

---

* The number of trees sacrificed for meals prepared in Nanny's kitchen is unfathomable. I hope those quarters we collected in the ubiquitous tree-planting campaigns for Israel in the 1970s added to the aggregate number of trees in the world enough to balance it out.

her grandmother's hands gently resting over her own as she mouths the words to the prayers recited in a language that she herself never bothered to learn.

She's also taken to needlepointing mezuzah covers and prayer shawl holders, which in my secular household become makeup bags. I have so many of these that my makeup bags have their own makeup bags. During my childhood, she crafted intricate Japanese designs, but her lotus flowers and white cranes have given way to mournful scenes of Eastern European village life. It's all Chagall, all the time. The way she churns these things out, you'd think she was commissioned by an army of nomadic zealots who need carrying cases for their talismans. I tried to convince my son to take his lunch to school in a sack decorated with a forlorn goat wrapped in a prayer shawl playing the violin. He looked at me like I'd suggested he pack his sandwich in a moldy sneaker.*

Mom rarely attended services during her childhood, and although my parents insisted on a Jewish education for us, after my sister and I left home, neither she nor my dad went back to temple. Not even once. Suddenly, forty years of secular life are immaterial to her newfound identification.

What we are witnessing could be a sign of dementia, although it is also plausible that the impending reality of death is pushing her toward religion. Anyone who's had even a small brush with health problems knows the comfort and sense of purpose that religion can offer. My friend Killian, who is on the road to recovery after receiving an

---

* Why wouldn't that goat look pained? Inner monologue of Chagall goat: *Why do I have to play the violin and wear this schmata? The Bible is like a goat genocide, can't I catch a break? It's really hard for a goat to keep a scarf on.*

early-diagnosed case of pancreatic cancer, believes that God or the Universe gave him just enough of the disease to serve as a wake-up call. I would like this Universe to give me just enough collagen to return my skin to its former buoyancy, but I'm not holding my breath. I don't have much faith in the Universe's disease-measuring skills since it gave my friends David, Susan, Robin, Jane, Conrad, Jim, Kathy, Taylor, and Steve just enough cancer to kill them.

But Mom's desire to return to the fold is convenient because the majority of care facilities in the U.S. receive financial backing from religious groups. It's a challenge to find a place that isn't funded by or associated with one sect or another. Even the Motion Picture and Television Fund retirement home, catering to members of the showbiz family, is affiliated with the Episcopal Church.

One of the appealing things about Judaism is that if your mother was Jewish, you're in. You want to become Jewish? Study with a rabbi and you're in. And unlike, say, Mormonism, we happily welcome back those who've strayed, no questions asked. You haven't been to temple in forty years? No problem. She hopes to claim her rightful place as a Jewish mother and grandmother.

Both she and my father have been warm in-laws and devoted grandparents, flying across the country for baseball games and music recitals. Big Daddy never fails to come up with WAM, pronounced WHAM, walking-around money—cash that he palms into the hands of each of his grandchildren. Despite failed attempts to convince my husband to write a TV pilot about a female lawyer who moonlights as a dominatrix, Dad has been an attentive father-in-law. My mother is particularly enamored of Jeff because he's got better housekeeping skills than me. Come to think of it, we should have seen my mother's longing to return to her roots when she leapt at the chance to have her grandchildren call her Bubbie, as she called her grandmother.

Sebastian Junger argues in his book *Tribe* that "modern society has gravely disrupted the social bonds that have always characterized the human experience." He cites examples of early American settlers who assimilated into Native American tribes, whose way of life offered a glimpse into the cohesive communities that sustained our earliest ancestors. Many of these folks didn't want to return to "civilization" because the communal lifestyle fostered self-esteem, a feeling of usefulness, and a sense of belonging. "Women in particular," Junger tells us, "have high levels of depression in (contemporary) Western culture, with our emphasis on extrinsic, not intrinsic, values." My mother is the poster child for this research. It's not hard to picture her enthusiastically sweeping a teepee with a broom made of sticks.

Junger also offers the military as a model of a strongly bonded non-filial community, but he makes a serious omission by leaving out musicians. Even would-be musicians. My husband was in a band in high school called No Exit. The members pledged allegiance to cigarettes, Jean-Paul Sartre, and each other. To this day, he refers to the guys as his bandmates. Present tense.

What's most bewildering is that my mother was never a joiner. She wasn't in the PTA, nor a member of the local Hadassah chapter. Shades of this latent personality trait surfaced a few years back, when she helped found a women's empowerment group, WOMB: Womyn of Miami Beach. Members of WOMB advocated for women in crisis. My mother claims to never have been happier than in the WOMB, but the group disbanded after only a short time. Mom still wears the T-shirt with their catchphrase: "Uppity Womyn Unite."

In another surprising and possibly contradictory development, my mother's vocabulary is now generously sprinkled with expletives. "She's a royal bitch!" is one of her favorite sayings. "What an asshole" and "fucking this" or "fucking that" are tossed around frequently and wielded with glee. Who is this new potty-mouthed mother? I have no idea. Neither does my father, but that hasn't stopped him from throwing down the gauntlet on where they'll land next.

My father has an entirely different scenario in mind for where they should spend the last chapter of their lives. Dad's choice is a senior living residence called the Imperial Club, or the Ambassador Club, or maybe it's the Commodores' Club? I keep mixing it up. It's something vaguely nautical that implies luxury and first-class treatment befitting the tribe he most identifies with: the wealthy country club set.

The deal that brought our family to Miami and ushered in our country club years was one in a series of ambitious financial schemes that were sure to make a fast dollar. Not surprisingly, most of my father's associates were disbarred attorneys or CPAs who'd lost their licenses. If you were looking to my father to raise capital, it meant you'd probably exhausted all other options. This first deal, somewhat appropriately, was an opportunity for him to build a fast-food empire. Dad was hired to fold a restaurant franchise called Jamie's Great Hamburgers into another chain with forty-five outlets called Burger Castle. Jamie's had a few joints scattered across the South and their hook was that they offered a hundred different dressings for your burger. Burger Castle's hook was that people who'd had too much to drink might confuse them with Burger King. Burger Castle was sued by Burger King. I wouldn't know if the brands were, in fact, too similar, but as someone who has worked in food service, I think those hundred dressings sound like a *side work* nightmare.

The failed burger merger was followed by a multitude of gold-plated opportunities. There was the renovation of Union Station in St. Louis, a worthwhile project, but despite their best efforts, the train never left the station, so to speak.*

Next, Dad lit upon an idea for *H. R. Pufnstuf* creators Sid and Marty Krofft to create a puppet theme park that went up in a puff with, sadly, no stuff. A foray into distributing lithographs by famous artists like Peter Max brought in boatloads of cash that wealthy people were trying to hide until the IRS decided to shut down this kind of art tax shelter.

In the mid-1970s, Dad got back in business with another cousin from Mobile. Cousin Meyer, who went by Mike, was an entrepreneur who had a reputation not dissimilar from my dad's but had the benefit of being born into the part of family that not only liked to spend money but had money to spend. Mike bought a few movie theaters in Alabama and New Orleans, but his American dream was to be a big-shot film producer. Mike sank his own money into a low-rent *Deliverance* type of story starring Peter Graves. He tried to get the schlocky "King of the B's" movie producer Roger Corman to distribute it. Corman declined and warned him of the dangers of self-funding: "You're going to end up poor white trash." Mike promptly changed the name of the film to *Poor White Trash* and it made enough dough to provide entry into the film distribution racket. There was even a *Poor White Trash* part deux.†

---

* In 2014, the station finally opened. It was only disastrous financially for us; other investors made millions of dollars.

† Years later, I landed a role playing poor white trash in a Roger Corman production titled *Not Like Us*, a film that was not very good.

It helps to sigh, "It was the seventies," when noting my dad was able to buy the film rights to unrepentant Watergate burglar and CIA operative E. Howard Hunt's life, because Hunt was the Eglin Air Force Base cellmate of Dad's best friend, who was serving time for embezzling money from nursing homes. After Hunt was released, a dinner was scheduled. The night before he was expected at our home, Hunt phoned to say he was worried our house might be bugged. My father assured him he knew people who could handle it. I was assigned to do the "sweep." I did what any teenager who'd watched *Mission Impossible* religiously would do. I raced around, peering into light sockets and unscrewing telephone receivers. "All clear," I reported back to my father. Hunt had both the appearance and charisma of a wax figure and the movie never got made. The company went bankrupt distributing *The Silent Partner*, a thriller starring Elliott Gould and Christopher Plummer. It was the one decent film they ever acquired.

Having a sophisticated or at least a satiated palate has always played an essential role in my father's life. Every family story involves a meal or food group. During World War II, chewing gum was a luxury. To stretch the life of his Dubble Bubble, Dad would take a worked-over, flavorless wad of gum, sprinkle it with sugar, wrap it in wax paper, and freeze it. It's unfathomable to imagine an eight-year-old today going to that kind of trouble.* Stories about his time in military school in northern Florida revolve around hunting possum (not kosher) and making turtle soup (even less kosher) or eating alligator (don't even ask) in the Okefenokee Swamp. His gumbo recipe (which

---

* Dad also sold his double-duty Dubble to his classmates for a tidy profit.

has not only every kind of shellfish imaginable but bacon, ham, and pork sausage to boot) is famous in several counties.

Our family vacations were planned around food. We went to Boston, ostensibly, to visit historical sites. Pictures show us walking the Freedom Trail, but I don't remember it at all. The only vivid memory I have of that trip is climbing the narrow, dimly lit staircase leading to the century-old dining room of the Durgin-Park restaurant, where we ordered Flintstone-sized slabs of prime rib.

The Jockey Club offered tennis, dockage for yachts, disco dancing, casual access to the wealthiest locals, and over-the-top Sunday buffets. This combination of access to the monied class and marbled meats was irresistible to my father. A towering presence in his younger days, six foot four and 250-ish pounds, my dad had an insatiable appetite for money and food equally.

At the end of each week, the nouveau riche and the faux riche, like us, gathered at the club, where the gluten was free flowing and diners engaged in a competition to see who could raise their cholesterol level quickest. I was my father's daughter, buying into his financial alchemy and sharing in his passion for movies and meats of all kinds, so Sundays were special to me as well. Dressed in our matching shiny polyester shirts and bell-bottoms, we'd load into my dad's copper Mercedes 450 or my mother's powder blue 280 and take the causeway connecting our gated island community in Biscayne Bay to the private drive of the swanky club, located a bit further north on the water. I'm certain these were some of the happiest moments of his life. At least the ones that don't involve hookers or poker.

To this day, I've never seen so much food in one place in my life as I did at those Sunday brunches. Table after table of silver platters overflowing with eggs Benedict, eggs Florentine, sausage, bacon, ham, and lamb. The meats were laid out like the stations of the cross and manned by a corpulent server in chef whites and *toque blanche* who carved roast beefs the size of beach balls. These were the days before veganism displaced hedonism as the preferred ism of the moneyed classes and patrons gazed rapturously as the beef fat glistened in the Florida sunlight.

The clubbing days are long gone for my parents.

Dad's last high-profile venture was a relaunching of the Embers Restaurant, a Miami Beach institution famous for its thick-cut steaks cooked over an open fire pit that had fallen into disrepair. I'd just started college when the renovation was completed. I flew down and warbled Shirelles songs at the reopening-night party. Luckily, the acoustics were terrible and my singing didn't spoil the festivities. As with many of his ventures, business was booming at first, but very quickly graft became rampant, steaks were flying out the back door, and Dad couldn't hold on to staff.

Word got to our cousins in Mobile, who knew people who knew "Sam the Plumber," a bagman for the mob. Sam DeCavalcante was a member of the New Jersey Mafia who did a little moonlighting for mobster Meyer Lansky, who'd retired to Miami. I was home for the holidays when Sam brought a brown paper Winn-Dixie grocery store bag containing two hundred and fifty thousand dollars to our home. I stared at it on the kitchen counter, too frightened to peer inside but tempted by its contents nonetheless.

"Dad, you should keep it!" I advised with an eighteen-year-old's naïve enthusiasm. He didn't. In hindsight, with the benefit of re-peated viewings of *Goodfellas*, I understand that a bagman collects ill-gotten gains that the mob launders in a way that has nothing to do with washing machines, and there's never just one bag. Plumbing is always a good business to be in.

The restaurant went under and became a seedy nightclub. Five years later, my grandmother Rebecca would call to ask, "What is my grandbaby doing on the television looking like a *nafka?*"

"Becca, I'm playing a hooker." I was showing Detective Sonny Crockett on *Miami Vice* where I'd been "cut" on my neck by my pimp Choo Choo, while standing right where I'd sung "Dedicated to the One I Love." It's impossible to say what was more surreal, trying to convincingly portray a scarred-up streetwalker or filming at the location of the restaurant whose demise contributed to altering the course of my life.

Not long after the Embers closed, a massage table at the spa of another exclusive haunt, the Cricket Club, collapsed under my father's weight. Even though this turned out to be rather fortuitous, as my parents successfully sued and lived on that insurance settlement for several years, they were blacklisted from clubs and spas around town.

So, what kind of food the facility serves, whether the address will connote wealth, and whether it will be close to the casinos are the questions of the utmost importance to my father.

My mother rode that roller coaster for fifty-eight years, but that e-ticket to a cushy landing never materialized and she wants off. She's made her decision. She wants to be the one who gets to decide where they will live next, but my father isn't budging.

I'd like to recuse myself and turn this over to Lisa, but I can't. We made a pact.

After our grandfather Johnny received a diagnosis of Alzheimer's, my mom visited only a few times during the decade-long decline before his death. The caregiving fell to Gloria, Mom's older sister, and Nanny, who carried out her duty with her signature stoicism. When Gloria stopped recognizing my mother's voice, it was just too much for her. "I know my limitations," my mother would repeat. We begged her to go to Delaware, offered to pay for tickets, even to accompany her. When Gloria died in 2011, it had been ten years since my mother had spoken to her sister. Lisa and I promised each other that no matter what, we'd never stop speaking to each other and we'd try to divide the caregiving as equally as possible. This has required some stepping up on my part because I've enjoyed and, frankly, benefited from being the little sister.

In pictures from my early childhood, Lisa's arms wrap protectively around me. Lisa's leading us through a dance routine or comforting me because I'm bawling my eyes out on bumper cars at Six Flags Over Georgia. Impervious to the laughter that greeted our deep Southern accents, she spoke for me when we moved from Alabama to Delaware. In our Shari Lewis–inspired puppet shows, she was Lamb Chop and I was Lamby's less memorable sidekick Hush Puppy.*

Our parents still marvel at how on our Mexican vacation Lisa happily gobbled down ceviche and spoke perfect Spanish while I managed to get raw sewage dumped on my head and got hysterical when a guide instructed our tour group to throw me into a cenote, a deep well where the Mayans sacrificed virgins at the Chichen Itza pyramids. To be fair, the guide was kidding, but he sounded awfully convincing to this twelve-year-old.

Growing up in the shadow of her excellence was trying but in no

---

* Think about it: a children's puppet named for a cut of meat? Trigger alert! Shari Lewis would be filleted for that now.

way justified my cutting a rickrack pattern into her bangs the night before middle school picture day. This unfortunate incident was memorialized in the school portrait that still graces my mother's coffee table as a testament to my immaturity. When I headed into the arts and Lisa became an attorney, our roles in the family were solidified. She was organized and prompt. I was messy and possibly unreliable.*

I've managed to raise a kid and remain marginally employable, and have never left my house pantsless, but Lisa is my emotional rock. She reminds me when our parents' birthdays and anniversary are coming up and she can be counted on to host holiday dinners. But everything changed the year Lisa showed up to crash on my couch.

I was commuting between my home in Los Angeles and a one-bedroom apartment in NYC, rented by the television network I was working for, when Lisa called to say she and her husband of twenty-five years had separated, she was leaving the job she'd held for nineteen years and was setting off in a new direction, and wouldn't it be fun if we were roomies? My shooting days lasted between twelve and seventeen hours on location and the show's budget was minimal, so the apartment also served as our wardrobe, hair and makeup, and prop department, but I'd camped out at her place so many times, it was impossible to refuse. It seemed odd when she showed up with four large suitcases, scuffing the hallway wall on her way in, and odder still when she collapsed a clothing rack in the closet and shrugged it off. When she knocked over an illuminated sculpture, I was sure I was in the presence of a pod person and we were in a scene from a remake of the remake of *Invasion of the Body Snatchers*.

The next morning, I awoke to find Lisa in her pajamas, another

---

* Hence The Little Man; see chapter 1.

foreboding sign, as normally she's biking by dawn or heading out to solve the world's problems. Really, that's what she does for a living. She leads organizations dedicated to solving issues of global importance. But no. Recalling that I once cohosted a TV show called *The Dream Team* alongside a psychic–*cum*–dream counselor, she invited me to interpret her dreams from the previous night.

Here's something I learned as the host of a TV show about dreams: no one wants to hear about your dreams. We can't see "the turreted golden mansion with secret passageways leading to chambers filled with treasures," and that "when you tried climbing to the top of the tower, the steps of the staircase multiplied," and how "suddenly, you were driving a car and it turned into an egg and you soared into the stratosphere." But I comply.

"The mansion represents your talents that have gone unrealized, you are moving in the right direction but it will take more time than you anticipated, and your life is going to take you on a new journey across the globe." I was flying blind on the egg, so I suggested that her new life might involve dairy.*

"You're amazing."

"I learned from an expert," I said, neglecting to mention that the dream interpreter predicted our program would last for three years. We shot two hundred episodes and the network canceled us after airing only ten, but Lisa didn't need to know that.

Over the next days she announced that she was considering becoming a rabbi, a salsa dancer, or a salsa-dancing rabbi. "Let's take early morning walks," she suggested, even though my mornings

---

* Eggs aren't dairy, but that's all I could think of at five a.m. and precaffeination. That she didn't correct my mistake was also a bad sign.

already started at five thirty a.m. I was pulling the covers over my head on my one day off when she opened the door with, "Can you make a lecture at the Frick on humanitarian efforts in China?" Did she say "humidifying Crock-Pots for the vagina"? "Rain check," I mumbled.

I craved solitude when I wasn't working. She was networking with strangers in elevators. She traded contact information in our apartment building elevator with a guy who plays the "sad" clown in the Big Apple Circus and I prayed that she wouldn't run away with him on my watch, because I knew that our parents would blame it on me.*

Things came to a head after she treated herself to a haircut from Didier, a New York hair guru. Didier worked his magic and Lisa's hair was chicer than I'd ever seen, but as is inevitable with these celebrity hairstylists, once she got home, re-creating the magic proved impossible. After one washing, it looked like Lisa had bedazzled a Prada. I sat her down in the bathroom and called up the only measurable skill I've acquired from acting in low-budget films: proficiency with a blow-dryer. "You're pulling your hair in the wrong direction and you need a smaller brush." I caught sight of us in the mirror. My big sister looked so vulnerable and trusting. She seemed to have completely forgotten that I was the sister of rickrack-bangs infamy, and a wave of warm feelings spread across my chest. It turned out to be a hot flash, but still. I was filled with love for her and the satisfying largesse of the Big Sister.

---

* That clown turned out to be a great guy. As usual, my big sister has flawless instincts.

We started going on walks and enjoying late-night drinks, and I even made "I'm listening intently" sounds while she read to me from her journals. She regained her equilibrium, got the sculpture repaired, and went on a salsa immersion trip to Cuba. Within three months, she accepted a new position, relocated across the country, and forged a rewarding new relationship. My sister never fails. That visit marked my graduation out of little sisterhood.

Since the "we're broke" phone call, we've been taking turns, flying in for several days at a time. Lisa has taken the lead, as per usual, with financial and legal matters, but she is hopeful that together we can break this deadlock. The clock is ticking, as they can't afford to renew the lease for the condo they are renting.

Our flights are landing at Miami International Airport at almost exactly the same time. Mine arrives first and I take up a position by the baggage claim, our designated meet-up spot. The seating area is located behind a freestanding billboard that blocks my view of arriving passengers. I can only see the travelers approaching from the knee down, and it's not like our family has such distinctively shaped lower appendages, but I am confident that I will recognize my sister's calves and footwear.

A pair of shoes comes into view, sophisticated black-and-white patent-leather pumps, but the legs stop tentatively. This can't be the locomotion of my executive-decision-making sister—she always gets what she wants, always wins, and she never stops. Never.

On a recent visit to her home in Georgetown, she suggested we take the scenic route into the city. That route turned out to be a steep nine-mile trail through a park. We missed a turnoff and found ourselves facing a tributary of the Potomac. We had to ford a stream in order to make our dinner reservations. She is my best friend and biggest supporter, but she also terrifies me.* While I can be tireless and overbearing, hence the nickname "Sergeant Gurwitch," my sister is known simply as "the General."

A pair of sensible but elegant shoes purposefully strides toward the bank of chairs. These are shoes that one might wear when helping to airlift refugees out of Ethiopia but would also be appropriate when conducting a board meeting. Though a hundred people have walked by and I've spotted her, before I can revel in this inconsequential victory, she appears and says, "I recognized your purse. Let's go." I carry a bag fashioned from recycled tarp, and the shoulder straps are made from seat belts, which is a bit distinctive, but still, she always wins. She's exiting the building before I even stand up.

OUR PARENTS' CONDO is only a few miles from the house they lived in for forty years, on the same stretch of sand where I spent weekends slathering on baby oil in my string bikini before I discovered punk rock and torn ballet tutus.

The real estate agents, a duo with big bright teeth and even bigger, brighter hair, known as the Debbies, found this temporary landing spot. The Debbies, anxious to get the prestigious Sunset Islands listing, were brought on with promises of selling the house and securing the next home for them. "We'll treat your parents like family." The house sold quickly, but they tired of clients whose

---

* My sister's underwear drawer is color coded and as organized as an Excel spreadsheet. My drawers serve as evidence of chaos theory and my closets are a case study in entropy.

finances shifted shape like images in a fun-house mirror, and a sublet was the best they could come up with.

I begged the Debbies to let me keep the Sunset Islands home's brass knocker, an absurdly and disturbingly realistic woman's hand. I became obsessed with the idea that this disembodied limb must remain in our family. *It's a family relic*, I explained in a series of impassioned e-mails. So much for *family*, or maybe it's because we're *family* that I never heard back from them. My cousin Ruth recently confessed to having several e-mail addresses, including one dedicated to annoying family members that she "forgets" to check regularly. "What a great idea," I shrieked before realizing that the address I'd been given is the one that's labeled *family*. I suspect that e-mails sent to clientrequests@thedebbies.com land in an account that gets checked neverly.

This luxury condo seemed like a soft landing. My parents were already familiar with the neighborhood, and making the transition from a 3,500-square-foot home on a gated island to the kind of downsizing they'd eventually need to do could have been a shock to the system. But it's time to move.

It's also been disappointing in ways we didn't anticipate. Each wing of the building has its own elevators, which means that they're basically private elevators, eliminating most opportunities for chance meetings. This has totally subverted my fantasy that my mother, who was becoming increasingly isolated on the island, could find a new social circle in the building. It's important to remember that even within tribes, there are subsets that don't overlap. One Friday night a couple about my parents' age got on the elevator with my father. The husband was wearing a *kippah*, and as they appeared to be coming from services, my dad said, "Shabbat shalom," only to be dressed down with, "How dare you address my wife!" Same religion, different tribe.

My parents are so anticipating our visit that they are standing outside of the lobby by the valet parking desk. How long they have been there is anyone's guess, as the ride from the airport takes at least an hour. My father looks stooped. His neck is thrusting forward, his face turned downward, and he's lost at least forty pounds. He's a shadow of his former self. My mother looks better than she has in years. This is despite the fact that she is dying. Not dying like we are all dying, but actually dying.

She has metastasized breast cancer that has spread to her bones and now is showing up in spots on her liver. We were told to expect maybe two years at best, but it's been over two years and even her doctors are puzzled by her continued presence aboveground. She's begun to take great pride in telling anyone who will listen that she doesn't take any medication on a regular basis. That is true; she's had her thyroid removed and takes a daily synthetic replacement; one breast has been recalled to the earth, and there are regular blood transfusions and rounds of chemo, but she is not on other medication on a regular basis. It's likely that the cancer will do her in before she will need to go on any other medication.

We don't know if she is aware of the diagnosis because my father has instructed us not to talk about a timeline or dwell on her impending mortality. The form that she's wearing in her mastectomy bra is peeking out ever so slightly from the neckline of her knitted top, because she's never quite gotten it fitted properly, but other than that she looks terrific.

This is not unlike how things ended for her mother. The week before her death, Nanny attended my wedding, where she danced and was in good spirits. Back in Delaware, she was feeling a bit under the weather and went to the emergency room, where it was discovered she had acute leukemia, and she died that night. She had never looked better.

Mom's health is one of the reasons it makes sense to move somewhere that offers varying degrees of care, but there's my dad's health to consider as well. Recently, he got stuck on the commode, nude. He has a slew of persistent health issues, including COPD, which causes bad circulation, and his legs went numb. Unable to lift him, my mother phoned downstairs and one of the valet staff was kind enough to come up and help him. I can't imagine assisting in the toilette of the elderly was part of the job description when they signed on to park and retrieve cars at a luxury condo building.

The miracle is that he's lived as long as he has. That my father still smokes isn't helping. Diabetes and heart disease have been guests at every family function for several generations. He's outlived his younger brother and is the oldest living Gurwitch but for one distant cousin.

My dad's voice sounds as strong as ever when we speak on the phone, so his appearance is a bit shocking. My mother hugs my sister first; birth-order privilege holds and she was always my mother's favorite.

"Did you know," she says, pulling me in close, "I'm married to a royal asshole?"

Do I know that?

My mother drove me to acting lessons, dance classes, debate tournaments, doctor appointments, and back-to-school shopping, but my dad was fun.

During the halcyon swinging seventies, I was more than willing to serve as his wingman. In the days when home movie screenings were exceptional occasions, I had cachet, inviting friends to his office screening room while my dad got free teenage market research. What could be done for *National Geographic* outtakes of natives engaging in cannibalism? My dad thoughtfully catered the screening with vats of barbecue ribs but the film never saw the light of day. For the record, the footage looked more like chickenalism.

I was not only my dad's wingman; I was his beard. The details of these exploits have thankfully faded from memory, but there was one incident that has stayed with me.

Not long after I started college, I received a call from my father. He'd dreamed that he was attending my wedding accompanied by his secretary and then-girlfriend, Loreli, a petite blonde whom I'd met on several occasions. In the dream, he was holding a baby in his arms. His and Loreli's.

"I felt like an asshole. Do you think I should break it off with her?"

"I guess so, Dad," I answered. Honestly, I don't even know why I said that. I'd completely bought into a "your mother's no fun" narrative. It would be a few months before my college funds would be depleted and he went into chapter 11 again, and thirty years before he'd reveal that he'd blown hundreds of thousands of dollars on this relationship. When I asked him why he'd thought it appropriate to include me in his dalliances, a few years back, he shrugged it off. He'd never thought twice about it; his dad had done the same with him.

I think it's safe to assume that the bankruptcy would have brought an end to the relationship with Loreli, but I'll never know how our lives would have been different if I'd answered the phone and said, "No, Dad, it's a grand idea to shack up with your lady friend and I look forward to babysitting my future siblings!"

These escapades are in our rearview mirror, but do I know that my mother is married to an asshole?

"Yes, I do, Mom," I tell her, knowing that I'll never be able to make up for the years of empathy deficiency.

Upstairs, our mother has laid out items she wants to divide between my sister and myself on the dining room table. There are piles of starched linens, a few sterling butter knives, silver iced tea straws, two silver-plated trays, and a collection of the kind of Waterford crystal bowls that people used to regularly give as wedding gifts. I rarely use the ones I have, so what will I possibly do with more? I imagine scores of us who married during what may one day be known as the Waterford Crystal Bubble Years, holding each serving dish close, as recommended by the guru of the anti-clutter cult, asking ourselves if this or that bowl elicits joy. I can't picture a single one of us mouthing the word "yes." Nostalgia? Sure. Sentimental memories? Maybe. Minor workout for abs? Possibly. But if joy is the measuring stick, I foresee many more entries to the almost four hundred thousand items that were for sale when I Googled "Waterford eBay."

The only thing I really want is her collection of Chinese porcelain, and she doesn't want to part with it. I pocket a piece each time I visit. They're even less useful than the Waterford; they're decorative Buddhist altar fruit. There's a longan, a lychee, a citron, and a buddha's hand, in cerulean blue, celadon, dusty rose, and goldenrod yellow. Maybe it's because they are so impractical that I love them.

Mom started calling me Sticky Fingers when she caught on that

I was stealing them. Now it's become something of a game. I have run out of room in my home but keep it up as a way to see how her memory is doing.

My sister would like us to split the assorted sterling pieces evenly, and while she is carefully counting the salad forks, I slide the citron into my pocket.

"Don't you already have a complete set?" I ask.

"Yes, that I paid for myself."

"Well, you also got your college paid for," I say, immediately regretting it. Any mention of how I got the short end of the stick, how she was already out of college when things fell apart, will only make us all miserable. I can't complain that she got a car on her sixteenth birthday and by the time it was passed down to me there were rust holes in the floor so big that you could see the road and people at school nicknamed it Gertrude. Wait a minute, I *liked* the name Gertrude, and it was punk and subversive that my car had holes. No. It's pointless and it's the past. It's immature and I promised myself I wouldn't go there.

"I'm sorry. You're right, we'll split it down the middle, but that won't include the pieces I manage to hide in an internal cavity."

We sit down in the living room, which is furnished and arranged in exactly the same way it was in the house on Sunset Islands. With the heavy drapes closed, they can keep the illusion they're still ensconced in their beloved home.

We need to plot out tomorrow's schedule, but I've eaten an orange and my mother is insisting that my father put the rind in a miniature plastic garbage can that has been placed on the kitchen floor by the sink. It's so tiny it looks like the one we had in my son's backyard play kitchen.

"Your father needs to bend," she says, "he's not getting any exercise. Bend over, Harry. He's got to bend over! He's got no muscle tone in his upper body."

My mother has always been obsessed with our father's weight. She's right to be worried, but her nagging can reach a feverish pitch. She claims that Dad tried to stab her in the hand once with a plastic fork because she complained about his salty-nut consumption on a cross-country flight. "That's horrible, Mom, inexcusable," I remember telling her, at the same time wondering how many times you would have to hear someone tell you that you can't eat that tiny allotment of peanuts before you'd want to stab them. Somewhere over Kansas. I think I might be moved to violence as we shadowed Topeka. This is one more reason why I am here to help.

"I don't think bending over builds upper-body strength," I tell her, knowing my father will not be able to lower himself enough to open the lid without toppling over. He would need to crawl on his hands and knees while clutching the orange rind in his teeth.

"Mom, it's a countertop can, and it's too small. You must have to keep emptying it. Can't you put it on the counter?"

"We're only two people and anyway, he should empty it down the hallway. He needs the upper-body exercise."

"Mom, you don't get upper . . . that's it! I am getting you a new garbage can while I'm in town." I put the receptacle next to the sink.

"Thank you," my dad sighs, as if I've negotiated a lasting peace in the Middle East. We've trash-talked our way through an entire hour. When we kiss our parents good-bye, it feels like we are practicing for some future finality.

Lisa and I roll our baggage to the Sun Harbour hotel. It's right across the street from their building, next to the Suncoast bank, and down the street from the Paradise Deli. Here, even medical offices contain the words "sunshine" and "beach." It seems wrong to be staying at a place whose name evokes frolicking in the ocean when we're on such a serious mission.

The Sun Harbour is more motel than hotel. The rooms open directly onto the busy street, the smell of bad decisions hangs in the air, and the upholstery is shiny in a way that recommends putting down towels before sitting. Our parents are safe in their heavily staffed residence, as if deposited in a bank vault, while we who have saved and budgeted, trying to be responsible, my sister more successfully than me, are stashed inside a Greyhound bus locker, but our parents are fragile and must be protected. We are running an egg-and-spoon relay race. We will have to be especially careful on the handoffs as we try to keep those eggs safe.

Lisa and I trudge through our nighttime rituals. She is ready for bed before I am.

"Are you prepared for tomorrow?"

Am I prepared? I am reminded of how I prepared to become a mother. There were months spent deciding to get pregnant and time spent trying to get pregnant. While I was pregnant, I had my head buried in books about healthy pregnancies, and when the baby actually came, I was already woefully behind. Our son is seventeen and I just made it to the chapter on introducing solids in *What Baby Needs*.

Even recently, it seemed like my dad might wrangle the extra income that would open up more choices. There was an engineering firm that had patented an innovative sewer monitoring system, but the company imploded in lawsuits and someone went to jail; a scheme to extract minerals out of an old gold mine that was just that—a scheme; a promising pharmaceutical company that even Lisa seemed hopeful about, but it too got mired in legal irregularities. Dad used to associate with disbarred attorneys and CPAs who'd lost their licenses, but his current circle includes poker players and a guy who lost his hairdressing license.

Only I didn't know that my father has been playing poker several times a week during the last decade.

"When you'd call him and you'd hear announcements in the background, where did you think he was?" my sister asks me.

"Airports? Traveling . . . for business?"

Even Dad says he was taken by surprise by a potential investor at the Texas Hold'em table at the Gulfstream Park Casino, where he has earned a nickname, "the Hammer,"* because "he comes down hard when he has a great hand." He inquired how much money the gentleman wanted to invest and where he was keeping his capital. "In a duffel bag," the dude whispered, "and I don't count my money in numbers, I measure it by the pound."†

"I am prepared," I lie. Despite my training as an actress, unlike our father, I've never mastered a poker face.

Lisa turns over and tells me to get some sleep, and in no time she's out. I tiptoe to the bathroom and turn on just enough light to peek into her suitcase. Her clothes are folded into neat piles, bras stacked like Dixie cups.

She should be handling this. She's decisive and never looks backward. I'm still stewing over a pair of metallic go-go boots I should

---

* It sounds a bit overly dramatic, but it's better than being the Nail.

† Dad informed me that twenty-two pounds of hundred-dollar bills adds up to a million dollars. Casinos can be educational.

have purchased in 1981. "You won't see that kind of thing coming and going," is something our grandmother Rebecca said when recommending styles that would make you stand out in a crowd.

THE NEXT DAY, my sister and mother set off early enough to make it to our first destination, the Tel Aviv Gardens, for the weekly Saturday morning Shabbat services. I arrive at the condo and Dad answers the door wearing only a towel. He is "finishing" his shower. It takes him over an hour in the bathroom. "Do you need any help?" I call out, hoping the answer will not be yes.

Waiting for our car, I try to make meaningful eye contact with each of the three parking attendants. I don't want to embarrass my father, so I tell each one in as cheerful a tone as I can muster, "Thank you so much for looking after my parents," wondering which of them is the one who performed the bathroom rescue.

"Let's hit the town, Dad!" I say as he lowers himself carefully into the passenger seat with the help of a "car cane," a $19.99 geriatric lifestyle aid he saw advertised on daytime TV. I hold my breath, wishing, for his sake, that we were on the kind of adventure we used to take back in the day.

The summer of my sophomore year of high school, my dad invited me to accompany him on a business trip.

We flew to Los Angeles and checked into a two-bedroom suite at the L'Ermitage Hotel in Beverly Hills. I have no idea what a suite cost back then, but you can't get a suite in the hotel for less than two thousand a night now. The room had mirrored walls, deep shag carpeting, and wicker furniture with chrome accents. If you ran your finger along any of the smooth glass surfaces, you'd probably have picked up trace amounts of cocaine. It was the opposite of my mother's home with its tasteful oriental rugs, altar fruit, and crystal sconces.

My dad wanted to show off the offices of his film distribution company, located on a high floor in a glass building in Century City. I remember opening a set of massive wooden doors that led to a vast space where only a few employees milled about.*

My dad also arranged for me to have my picture taken by a photographer he said was tops in the biz. The night before the shoot, I went clubbing on the Sunset Strip with a girl whose family had moved from Miami Beach to Beverly Hills. She knew where the doormen would let in underage girls. I found myself in the men's bathroom smoking angel dust and then making out with Danny Bonaduce.† I was so stoned that even though I was less than half a mile from the hotel, it was almost sunrise before I stumbled into our suite, only a few hours before what had to be a very expensive photo shoot.

The photographs have a distinct *Saturday Night Fever* disco vibe and tell the story of a girl who hasn't noticed she's gotten just a little zaftig. The face is a bit chipmunky—like she's storing nuts in her cheeks. I'd just given up my twice-weekly ballet class, but not the

---

* Ten years later, I got my first starring role, in a nighttime TV series on HBO, whose offices were in the very same building. This was the series that was "prophesied" by my psychic father, Van Zandt.

† Mr. Bonaduce lived until recently a few doors down from me. When he decided to sell his home, I went to the open house; the place was decorated in a style I call Celebrity Spanish Inquisition: velvet thrones, leather chairs, and full-size cutouts of the actor.

post-class chocolate milkshake. I am wearing more makeup than I have ever worn in my entire life, practically a kabuki mask.

In the pictures I am gazing at my own image in the mirror; I am plucking petals from a daisy; I am practicing ballet. Mostly, I am practicing looking intense. And hungover. It seems impossible that I was in the same city I now call home. The city where I had no history, no family connections—all a plus. I had completely blocked these memories out of my mind when I moved to Los Angeles.

I never used those photographs professionally. Would we be heading to these retirement homes if he hadn't frittered away so much money on that pricey photo shoot? It probably wouldn't have made a dent, but I feel sure that neither the Tel Aviv Gardens nor the Captain's Clubhouse, or wherever it is that we're headed, will be anything like L'Ermitage.

Unlike Princess Meritaten, eldest daughter of Pharaoh Akhenaten of the eighteenth dynasty in Egypt, I made my sheath out of the lining of old drapery I found on a street corner in the East Village of New York in the 1980s.

into the mystic

Everything was going to be perfect, just as soon as I became a Butterfly.

Or a Hollyhock.

What kind of hallucinogen do you have to be on to want to be shrubbery or an insect? None. Unless you consider reading an altered state. I was fifteen in 1977, when I cracked the spine of *Slapstick*, a novel by Kurt Vonnegut, and I experienced that kind of "everything makes sense now" ding that went off in Don Draper's head when he cooked up the Coke commercial in the final episode of *Mad Men*. Vonnegut spins your typical dystopian future, except that something wonderful has come from the slew of calamities that has befallen society. The world's citizenry has reorganized into clans: Butterflies, Orioles, Chickadees, and assorted botanically inspired fraternities.

Imagine each of us being instantly linked to hundreds of thousands of cousins spanning the globe, hence the subtitle of the book, *Lonesome No More.* We'd all be one big happy family. Well, more like lots of big happy families. Or lots of unhappy ones: the Hollyhocks, Chickadees, Orioles, and Butterflies, each unhappy in their own way. This sounded even better than caffeine and wedge heels, both of which I'd also just discovered and still pledge unwavering allegiance to.

Before I picked up *Slapstick*, it was through the adventures of the crew of the *Starship Enterprise* that I contracted my first case of family envy. Lots of girls were Marcias or Jans (no one ever admitted to being a Cindy), but I was a Trekkie. In the face of danger, the crew banded together, proffering unconditional support, as did the flattering rompers, precursors to full-body Spanx, worn by the entire Starfleet family. Captain Kirk and the gang were perennially plunked down on hostile planets, where they battled reptilian creatures in rocky amphitheaters.* Every day after school, I'd pack my paisley canvas overnight bag, intending to run away from home, but never ventured more than a few feet beyond the parking lot of our apartment building in Wilmington, Delaware, where I'd re-create scenes from *Star Trek* among the boulders lining an adjacent creek.†

My pencil case standing in for a transponder, I called out, "Beam me up, Scotty!" as I dodged imaginary foes. Sadly, the circuitry in

---

* Vonnegut borrowed characters from *Star Trek* and elements of his novels appear in the series and movies.

† I also used to swim in that creek, which was probably part of a sewage drainage system, but that has nothing to do with this story, except it may be why I am several inches shorter than my relatives.

my pencil case was just as unreliable as my current cell phone carrier, so at six p.m., when my mother called me in for tuna casserole and Tater Tots, I'd reluctantly head back inside.

Even at age ten, I suspected it was going to take a few years before we caught up to Gene Roddenberry's utopian vision, so I located the next best thing.

Mrs. Brownstein, my fifth-grade teacher, was a fresh-out-of-college hire at River Road Elementary School in Wilmington. One of those newbies who shows up each day beaming enthusiastically at students, before the light goes out in their eyes, as it did for my son's seventh-grade science teacher, a thirty-five-year veteran of the overcrowded Los Angeles public school system. Clutching her desk for support, Mrs. Lee looked like she'd been airlifted out of a tsunami. Her clothing was disheveled, her hair unkempt; one shoe was missing. "I have no idea what day it is," she told us. It was Back to School Night. School had been in session for exactly one week.

If you were an outstanding student in Mrs. Brownstein's class, you'd get the privilege of receiving an invitation to have dinner at her home. My mother, who has diligently saved the writing assignments and playbills from my childhood, sent me a report I wrote in Mrs. Brownstein's class. It was on how I wanted to be a teacher and be pretty, kind, and have good penmanship just like her. I got an A, but Mrs. Brownstein added in her excellent script, *Okay, Anne, you don't have to try so hard!* Lady, you have no idea.

I was included in the first group of students chosen. She and her husband, also an elementary school teacher, served meatloaf and an iceberg lettuce salad. The Brownsteins were sweet but a bit on the boring side. They were *exactly* the kind of people I wanted to bunk in with. If I were their daughter I wouldn't have a grandmother who'd call "on the long distance" to remind me of the importance of having a good bosom—I was ten years old. The only thing is, in my memory, Mrs. Brownstein looks a bit too much like the actress and musician Carrie Brownstein, and her husband too closely resembles the comedic actor David Krumholtz. I remember us as seated around a circular white plastic table on white plastic modular chairs, but that's also a description of the dining room set in my Barbie's Malibu Dreamhouse. Memory can be a trickster. One thing I am certain of is that I wanted them to adopt me.

This plan was thwarted because halfway through fifth grade, my dad announced we were moving to Florida, where I found plenty of enviable families that included parents with recognizable jobs, steady incomes, and homes that felt like secure harbors. Many of my new classmates had generations of wealth behind them and traveled through the world with an ease that I would later come to see as entitlement but at the time was something I desperately desired. My initial instinct, probably due to a genetic predisposition to criminal activity, was to kidnap my friends for large ransoms—you know, something on the order of *one thousand dollars*!

I enlisted one of my new pals, Noelle, in my plot. Unlike our tanned, sporty classmates, Noelle and I were preternaturally pale-skinned and bookish, took ballet lessons, and had outsider musical tastes. The other kids were boogying to Three Dog Night's "Joy to the World," while Noelle and I performed overwrought interpretations of Jethro Tull's "Thick as a Brick" for each other.

We drew up our kidnapping plots at the local soda shop while mainlining Cherry Cokes and popping candy dots, pure sugar baked onto what looked like cash-register-paper rolls.* No one would get hurt, because the kids would all be in on it; we'd get that *one thousand dollars*, spend it all on candy, and start our own secret society, a sort of mash-up of *Willy Wonka* and *Lord of the Flies*. I don't really need to note that nothing ever came of these plans, because I'm not writing this book from a prison cell, but my friendship with Noelle faded after we auditioned for the modern dance club with a routine choreographed to "Aquarius" from the musical *Hair*. Noelle got in, I didn't, and without a partner in crime, I turned my attention to spending as much time as possible at friends' homes, hoping that one of their parents would say, "You know that friend of yours? She really seems like one of us." I'd pack that paisley bag and slam the door shut behind me. *See you never, Gurwitches!*

No one ever did offer to adopt me, though I did form lasting bonds with classmates, some of whose parents have served as surrogate mothers and fathers throughout my life.† My mom told me recently that one of these mothers, someone whose favor I curried and cherished, knocked on our front door and offered unsolicited advice not long after we moved to Miami Beach:

"You need to buy your daughter new clothes. She's never going

---

* It's possible the daily consumption of bleached wood pulp is yet another reason why I am shorter than my family. Noelle ended up being the smallest one of her siblings as well.

† I've wanted to fold my son's friends who regularly hang out at our home into our family, though they may not see me as a surrogate mother—we have a converted garage/rec room that makes for easy late-night entrances, exits, and stashing of bottles of cheap wine.

to fit in here with those drab wool dresses, long knee socks, and Buster Brown shoes."

In my fifth-grade class photo, it looks like an Amish has been Photoshopped into the picture. I'm in a dull maroon smock with a high lacy collar. But in the sixth-grade shot, I'm wearing a bright blue short-sleeved blouse with puffy sleeves and hip-hugger bell-bottoms that laced up the front and back. By virtue of growing up with the children of these families and aided by my new wardrobe, I had much greater entrée into the world of privilege than my mother and father ever would. These bonds also led me into another, more unexpected realm.

I was at a Chuck Mangione concert with my high school boyfriend when I saw colors streaming through the air. It was easy to see the pattern: the rainbow of electric reds, yellows, and oranges was triggered by the sound of the horn instruments. When the music stopped, the colors disappeared, but for three weeks following the concert, if I heard something on the radio by Chicago, Steely Dan, or Earth, Wind and Fire (you couldn't get away from horn sections in those days), those hues would appear like a Peter Max flag waving in the air around me.

This neurological phenomenon of seeing musical notes as colors is a form of synesthesia, a misfiring of synapses in the brain, but I didn't know that at the time. I was afraid to tell my parents, as that might have involved mentioning exactly how much pot I'd been smoking during this foray into the mystic (which happens to be a song I experienced as waves of undulating amber and crimson). These hallucinogenic colors disappeared just as suddenly as they'd appeared, but I'd glimpsed the invisible magic in the ether. Both the high school boyfriend—let's call him Daniel, because that was one of the most popular name for males born in the 1960s—and I were sure it was a message from the divine portending a special destiny.

I'm sure that Daniel's family breathed a collective sigh of relief when, a year my senior, he went off to college and left me behind, because I'd spent an inordinate amount of time at their home. "Now what?" they must have said when I turned up in New York City the next year. Not only had I followed him into the same drama department at NYU, I'd moved into a dorm a block from the condo they'd purchased for him. I was a constant presence at their place, even after his sister took up residence in the condo's second bedroom. The summer after my freshman year, we traveled around Europe together, and when my parents' finances imploded and I dropped out of school, naturally, I moved in with them. The thing is, we'd broken up by that time, so Danny partitioned off part of the living room for me. When I finally moved out, it was to a studio apartment in the building next door. Was their kindness offered solely out of love and compassion? Maybe, but I think I just wore them down. Like an infestation of mold, it was really hard to get rid of me. There was something else at work here as well. Danny and I believed that we'd been reincarnated as siblings over many, many lifetimes.

When you read these next few pages, it helps to put in perspective what was happening in New York at the time. Many "seekers" were signing up for pop psychology seminars like EST or sampling sects of Buddhism like they were tapas platters; Shirley MacLaine was running around touting her psychic abilities and belief in past lives; and we became avid readers of books on "expanding consciousness."

It was Danny who introduced me to a new age psychic and medium.

Van Zandt was a classical pianist, a Fulbright scholar, and had won several competitions. Charismatic and strikingly handsome, he was in his mid-thirties when we met. He hailed from west Texas and his slight Southern twang went a long way toward fostering an instant kinship. He'd been a student of Jane Roberts, the author whose series of books is composed of the teachings of Seth, an entity who communicated from a non-physical plane. Under her tutelage, Van Zandt discovered that he too had a gift for channeling disembodied spirits. If you met him on the street, you would never have suspected this interest in mysticism. Outside of his fascination with new age philosophy, he was the organist at a church in Brooklyn, and gave piano recitals. The S & M scene was at the height of its popularity in the West Village but Van Zandt, a khaki-pants-and-penny-loafers guy, was pretty straitlaced for a gay man. Alas, he would never make it as a spiritual leader today: he loved his cheeseburgers.

A group met regularly in his tiny West Village apartment. We crowded around his waterbed, sitting crisscross applesauce, knees touching, surrounded by the artifacts he'd gathered on his frequent travels to the Far East. There was a perfumer, a clothing designer, a graphic artist, and a photographer, among other creative types. For many of the years of our association, I was the youngest, and the group was supportive of me outside our sessions, coming to see me perform and treating me to meals, as you would if your younger cousin had just moved to town. Thank goodness. I was so ill prepared to be on my own, I reverted back to the picky eating habits of my childhood. I lived on a "Southern comfort food with a New York deli twist" diet, eating a bagel for breakfast, a piece of fried chicken for lunch, and a mini cheesecake for dinner, for almost a year, until I developed symptoms of scurvy.

We were engaged in a dialogue about raising the consciousness of the planet so we could usher in what is often referred to in such circles as the dawning of the Age of Aquarius. I was being offered a second chance to dance my way in.

At the center of the teachings was a communal belief in God as the shared universal soul. I was on my own in the big city, without a school program to anchor me, and I was desperate for this divinely consecrated connection. I never spoke to anyone I knew professionally about the group, but it was the secret sauce that boosted my confidence.

One of the great things about new-agey stuff is that it doesn't require a lot of study; you don't have to do much except have a mind so open it might be a blank slate, or in the case of the EST training seminars, be able to sit through long lectures without taking bathroom breaks. But magical thinking takes a lot of work. We subscribed to the ideas in Louise Hay's *You Can Heal Your Life*, in which the author wrote that illnesses are created by errant thoughts. For example, diabetes, Hay posited, is created by "longing for what might have been."* Since everything happens based on your ability to create your own reality through positive thoughts—much like the premise of *The Secret*, which claims that you can manifest wealth

---

* I think Louise got that backward: diabetes isn't caused by but does give you longing for desserts that might have been.

through the "universal law of attraction"—it requires constant up-keep. If our thoughts create our prosperity, then if you don't envision it, vision-board it, or affirm it strongly enough, it's your fault if you aren't successful, develop multiple sclerosis, or get offed in a genocide.

Our talks with "David," the enlightened being that was chan-neled by Van Zandt, were peppered with concepts like the mul-tidimensional vibrational levels of the earth plane, energetic manifestations, and illumination of the most sacred. It was fairly typical new age vocabulary. We adopted seven Principles of One-ness. We parsed their meaning as if they were liturgical texts, just like Bible study. Principle number 7 gives you a good idea of the other principles:

> The dance of life becomes the ecstasy of oneness as the
> light of God floods the entire being of all consciousness
> and the new age begins.

Having contemplated the writings and messages of many teach-ers, I believe I can distill the sentiment of most new age philoso-phies into four words:

> Don't worry. Be happy.

David gave us a series of magical symbols with corresponding hand movements, mimicking the opening of lotus flower petals. I believe these may have manifested on this earthly plane when Van Zandt and Danny ascended the Great Pyramid of Giza and an illu-mination was vibrationally experienced on a multidimensional level, connecting to the most sacred transcendent energy. They were named Yorukai, Samtor, Nnehd, Rhenefe, Lahktum, Kirak, Obrhahahn, Libaan, and Nasareh.

As I write the symbols and puzzle over why we spelled Nnehd with two N's, I marvel at how I never questioned this entire enterprise and how I can still feel the loss of being swaddled in a spiritual security blanket like a stone in my heart.* Ours was a God whose grace was dispensed like a cosmic Klonopin drip.

Much of David's message to me was a reminder of the fourth principle, which stated that everything had to have a beginning—kinda like Genesis—so I needed to study and have patience. It's the same advice the acting teacher whose class I'd joined gave to me on a weekly basis. David also prophesized that I would win an Academy Award one day; that admittedly kept my spirits up as well. It was reassuring to know that I was guaranteed success, or in the parlance of my dad's poker wisdom, the deck was stacked in my favor. But most important, to borrow from Sister Sledge: we are family. Or rather, we were family.

We were told our group was the reincarnation of a family. Reincarnation is widely accepted by practitioners of a number of faiths, but we were lucky enough to get the inside scoop on it. The soul, David explained, is like a tree with many branches. Some souls are so powerful that their essence is shared by many people, so if you believe that you were Charlemagne in another life, like Napoléon, or Napoléon in another life, like John Lennon, it's possible.

---

* Some things can feel true, the way it can seem like eating ice cream shouldn't make you gain weight because it's just frozen liquid.

At the time, I was dating someone in medical school who was doing his internship in the psych ward at Bellevue.

"Sometimes," he told me, "we have a run on messiah complexes. We have to separate the patients because it's too upsetting for one Jesus to encounter another Jesus. They fight over what channel the TV should be tuned to."

Christ, it's a good thing I never mentioned our interpretation of why this was happening, or I might have ended up on his ward.

We were advised that we could draw energy from these other lives and they from us, and this idea helped me to feel empathy for people from different backgrounds.* It's a shame that I couldn't feel connected to the family of man simply because I was a part of the family of man, not to mention all species on the planet. We are all distant cousins, but cousins nonetheless, of the "last universal common ancestor," also known as LUCA, the very first, single-celled organism off the biological assembly line some four billion years ago that gave rise to everything that ever followed. LUCA thrived in hot vents at the bottom of the ocean. Reincarnation or not, it's obviously a straight line from LUCA to my love of steam saunas.†

---

* Physicist Lisa Randall explains, in *Knocking on Heaven's Door*, how Rhonda Byrne, author of *The Secret*, says she read about quantum mechanics and immediately understood it. Randall says, "No, you didn't." Quantum mechanics works on a scale too small for our thoughts or "souls" to create energy with physical properties.

† I blame the public school system of Florida of the 1970s, where science education wasn't as important as a class required to graduate high school titled "Americanism Versus Communism."

Our group shared one particularly spectacular lifetime. Much more exciting than being the great-granddaughter of a peddler and a bootlegger, we were the family of the pharaoh who introduced monotheism to Egypt during the eighteenth dynasty. Van Zandt had been the pharaoh, Akhenaten; Danny was one of his daughters; and I was his eldest, his favorite daughter, I might add, while others were extended family members or high priests. As such, we were an elite soul cluster: members of the Council. Our reunion was thousands of years in the making. Our eternal bond could not be broken, which conveniently absolved me from feeling guilty that I'd mooched off Danny's family. There were also other lives. I'd been a cobbler, a beggar, and a farmer—nothing glamorous—and that added to the verisimilitude, because you couldn't be royalty in every life, right?

I wouldn't know what kind of father the pharaoh Akhenaten was, but VZ was the best gay dad a girl could ever have. He couldn't have been more different from my own father. He didn't give a hoot about money, a fact that was helped by the smallest of inheritances, which allowed him to live extremely modestly, and happily so. He was one of the least neurotic people I've ever met. He was a disciplined musician, knew all the best thrift shops in Greenwich Village, was effusive with praise and generous with his time, and had complete and total confidence in me, both in and out of his trances. He was an inveterate world traveler who had fabulous taste in textiles, and like any good dad, he brought souvenirs home from around the globe, many of which still hang in my home.

My relationship with my parents and even my sister was strained. The illusion of my father's infallibility finally shattered. I was crushed to see him revealed as someone who'd put his needs before our family's well-being, and though I had boundless compassion for my past-life personas, I couldn't see beyond my own self-interest to have compassion for my mother's inability to fix things. I didn't come home for holidays and we spoke infrequently. On the two occasions I went to Miami for work, I stayed in hotels.

Everyone in our group seemed to believe in our glorious lineage. Recently, I was visited by one of the members of the Council. I hadn't seen her in over thirty years. Thanks, Facebook! We went out for lunch and I ordered a cheeseburger in Van Zandt's honor.

"I was always a bit dubious about having been Queen Elizabeth," she confided.

"Not me," I chirped, stuffing a fry into my mouth. "I had no trouble believing I was a princess."

Akhenaten is depicted on reliefs preserved from the eighteenth dynasty as receiving rays from the sun god, the Aten. *Or was he in communication with aliens?* This idea wasn't exactly original to our group. Extraterrestrial enthusiasts have long associated the pharaoh with an alien intervention, speculating that his elongated skull and curved spine were indications of his alien DNA. More likely is that he suffered from Marfan syndrome, which also explains his brief reign and early death.*

All of our spiritual development was leading up to an intergalactic date with destiny. At four p.m., on October 25, 1995, our family

---

* Many artists have been fascinated by Akhenaten, including Philip Glass, whose opera based on the pharaoh's life received its New York premiere on my birthday, November 4, in 1984. It had to be a sign! We found it so migraine-inducing that we skipped out and went for cheeseburgers.

was going to take part in the first recorded contact with aliens. The landing would take place on the coast of Italy, in Sardinia. We, the Council, were being called home as representatives of our planet.

Anthropologists have long puzzled over what caused the cognitive revolution that changed our brains and led to our becoming the dominant species. We had the answer. These alien life forms had sprinkled us with their fairy dust and now they were coming back for us! Van Zandt was receiving transmissions from the aliens, who had been monitoring our progress through computers buried underneath the poles. Delta Phi Epsilon is the name of a sorority founded at NYU, and an epsilon delta is a type of mathematical equation that deals with limits and is beyond my limited brainpower, but Delta Epsilon is also the name of the galaxy that was pinging us. We'd all seen *Close Encounters of the Third Kind* at least a dozen times, and that's how we pictured it. It was going to be a family reunion with all the production value of a Spielberg film. Our true celestial home awaited, and this one, unlike my parents' house, didn't have three mortgages and a lien from Phil Rizzuto and the Money Store.

Growing up, I was a sprinter, never a marathoner. I ran the sixty-yard dash on our middle school track team. I excel at beginnings and relish the last push toward a finish line, but middles have always been challenging. I run every day for exercise now and I'm not sure I've ever broken a twenty-minute mile. The prophecy offered a hop, skip, and a jump to a spectacular finale.

There was never any money exchanged, there was no recruitment, and there was no dress requirement. A few years ago, when that tragic Hale-Bopp cult committed suicide, it was revealed they slept in bunk beds (uncomfortable), ate fast food (bloating), and wore matching ill-fitting jumpsuits (unattractive). I would never have joined a cult that had a restrictive and unflattering dress code.*

We held a party where we all came as ourselves from other lives. I wore a sheath fashioned to resemble garments worn by Meritaten, based on the reliefs in the Metropolitan Museum of Art. No one blinked an eye as I strolled down the street; it was the 1980s in the West Village, and everybody was dressed as a princess.

There was also an event where I accepted my prophesized Academy Award molded with tinfoil and one of my high school debate trophies. I am eternally grateful that the ceremony predated the Internet and that there is no video footage of my acceptance speech, as that would be more embarrassing than acknowledging that I was FaceTiming with aliens.

When Van Zandt was diagnosed with HIV/AIDS in 1988, we Council members took turns taking care of him, sleeping at his place, mixing up batches of AZT, and accompanying him to doctor appointments. The decline was swift; at that time the HIV virus was sweeping through downtown New York. Before Van Zandt's health deteriorated so much that he no longer channeled, David told me in no uncertain terms to move to California. He insisted. I was going to land a television series within six months of moving west, and being the kind of father who wants to see his daughter

---

* The only person that I told about my interest in the eighteenth dynasty was Martin Scorsese. After I auditioned for *The Last Temptation of Christ*, we struck up a short-lived friendship based on a mutual interest in that time period and he sent me a book on the subject. I left the reincarnation part out of our conversations.

taken care of after he's gone, he predicted I would meet a tall, slender blond guy and marry him. It's really a chicken-and-egg question, but I managed to find someone who fit the bill and who, for his own reasons, agreed to marry me the same night we met. Nicholas had made his own *Star Trek* uniform when growing up in England, so it seemed an awful lot like fate. I didn't invite my parents or sister to the wedding—we eloped—but I did introduce him to Van Zandt.

Van Zandt died within a few months of my westward move. I was devastated. I'd become totally dependent on his guidance. The group disbanded and we lost touch, but I had a husband to lean on and had scored a TV series, so felt I was still living out the prophecy.

That marriage didn't last, and when the date for the alien arrival came and went, I barely noticed it. By that time I was so busy with work, and it's not an exaggeration to say that Los Angeles's legendary traffic jams render the idea of intergalactic travel moot. Still, I held out the very faintest of hopes that it might still happen one day. Did the date translate differently in their time zone? Delta Epsilon sounded like an awfully far-flung corner of the universe.

When I married my husband of twenty years now, Jeff, he was trying to distance himself from his own quirky family and was a card-carrying member of the clannish comedy world, which I slipped easily into.* A year after we married, our son, Ezra, was born. Prior to the 1960s, children born with his constellation of birth defects died upon birth, and it just didn't make a lick of sense

---

* I "neglected" to tell Jeff about being in communication with UFOs until fifteen years into our marriage.

to me that my son or I, or any other children, had caused this condition through negative thinking or through some karmic debt. Ezra's health was righted, but his birth swept away my attachment to God and mysticism, and also, as a practical matter, my desire to leave the planet.*

I use the word "cult" to describe this group, because of our deific bonding and the global belief system we adopted, although we don't fit the accepted definition of a cult. No one was harassed if they wanted to cancel their trip to Delta Epsilon. Van Zandt never trafficked in reverence or encouraged worship of any kind. No fortunes were made or lost based on his predictions, except mine, and by any measure, I came out ahead. No lives were lost, though I do feel a bit wistful about not getting to traverse the Milky Way. I was never going to have to concern myself with long-term care insurance or retirement plans, and it sounded like a glorious adventure. I'm convinced Van Zandt had no ulterior motives; he was a true believer.

My father was also a true believer. More people were harmed by my father's fantastical dreams of getting rich quick than our close encounter of the imagined kind. I'd never met anyone outside of our family who'd been caught in the undertow of my father's wake, until a dinner I attended in the early 1990s.

It started as a showmance. An actor and I worked together on an episode of a TV series and fell madly in something or other, and this particular dinner at a fashionable Hollywood eatery was to be my first introduction to one of his intimate friends.

---

* It never occurred to me at the time, but in hindsight, it does seem significant that none of the Council members had children.

We were spooning our panna cotta when his friend Bobby, a director of independent films and just the kind of dramas I aspired to act in, turned to me and said, "Is your father Harry Gurwitch?" A piercing tone (the kind of thing you hear in movies when a bomb goes off) whooshed through my head and all the sound dropped out in the room. My head was throbbing. I knew by the way he asked that I should say no, but what came out of my mouth was, "Yes." He told us that when he was just out of film school, he'd directed his first feature and had met with my father at the cavernous Century City office. My father said to purchase a plane ticket and he'd meet him in Cannes, where they'd set up meetings, promote the film, and launch his directing career. Bobby flew to France, but my father never showed.

"That was my first introduction to the shittiness of the film industry," he said.

"That's my dad."

That the actor and I ended up breaking up had nothing to do with this incident, but it might not be a coincidence that I've never appeared in one of Bobby's shows. I asked my dad about this once, but he has no memory of Bobby or his film or the promise he neglected to keep. My father has an uncanny ability to excise the inconvenient.

Really, the biggest tragedy associated with the Council is how appalling it would have been for Princess Meritaten to learn of her incarnation as me. I often dreamed about her life in the palace at Tel el-Amarna, but I hope she was spared the memory of that dinky film festival where I had to sleep on a futon on the floor of my distributor's damp basement apartment.

"What? A commoner? A mid-list scribe, a bit priestess on the stage, and what is this *screen* thing? She has no serving staff to help her dress or bathe her? OMSunG, what kind of karmic good deeds must I perform to avoid a lifetime as this Annabelle Gurwitch? What kind of ridiculous name is that, anyway? Well, at least she has cats."

My father wants to go where there are thin women and thick steaks.

the best of all

possible homes

The Tel Aviv Gardens Retirement Home is located in a neighborhood of Miami known as Little Haiti. Many of the residents landed on our shores in small boats during what's broadly termed the Haitian diaspora. Soon after strongman François Duvalier, known as Papa Doc, took power in Haiti, waves of Haitians fled the country and arrived in circumstances not dissimilar to those of my own family. The streets are lined with bodegas where you can purchase candles, herbs, and spiritual baths; *carnicerias*; and restaurants that serve Creole-style cooking.

My parents are trying to make the most of their waning mobility, but it's a stretch to imagine them strolling leisurely through this neighborhood, because they've never sought out friendships with people of any color other than their own, much less felt comfortable in their company.

My father's earliest memories of growing up in Prichard in the

1930s include stepping over the bodies of African-Americans who'd been caught out after the curfew, a loathsome prong of the Jim Crow laws, shot, and left for dead on the unpaved streets in front of the family home.

An incident that took place in the early 1970s perfectly encapsulates how ingrained attitudes about race were in our family. My grandmother Rebecca stopped a well-dressed black woman while crossing the street in Atlanta and asked if she could put in a day of work cleaning her home.

"Madam, I am a superintendent in the Atlanta school system."

"Do you have a sister?" Rebecca inquired.

In Mobile, my mother worked as a social worker with the county government. As the "government lady," it was her job to deliver assistance checks to the descendants of the Africans who came to the U.S. on the *Clotilde*, the last slave ship to arrive on American shores, who were living in Plateau, or as it's also known, Africatown.

In 1860, the *Clotilde*, a two-masted schooner, set sail from Ghana and headed for the U.S. with approximately one hundred Africans on board, despite the fact that importation of slaves had already been declared illegal fifty years earlier. Mobile holds the dubious distinction of being the port of entry for the *Clotilde*. Many of my mom's clients, deeply rooted in West African culture, cooked over open fires and generously shared meals with her. But these weren't people she'd play bridge with or meet up with for a coffee klatch. When she turned sixty, she got a job at the housing department in Miami, where she worked with people of every background imaginable. Still, she rarely thought to invite them to her home or socialize with them.

Odds are that the majority of the residents at Tel Aviv Gardens are not familiar with the community, so it's not a surprise to see that the facility is surrounded by high walls.

Driving onto the gated campus, we find ourselves in a pink ghetto. All of the buildings, including a rehab center, a hospital, two residences, a nursing home, and the Alzheimer's Care Center, are painted shades of pink. Pink is the color that aura readers tell you represents nurturing; a pink skin tone is an indication of healthy circulation or that you were recently on the receiving end of a facial peel; pink is the color Molly Ringwald was the prettiest in when she was a Brat Packer; but since the turn of the last century, pink has also been a color associated with babies. This seems appropriate because of the way age returns you to your youth, but not the youth you might wish for; no, it propels you much further back, to infancy. Pink is most often associated with baby girls, to be precise, which seems fitting as, in keeping with expected life spans, there are more women than men at the Gardens.

My father and I park and walk, slowly and deliberately, as he must do now, toward the residential towers. We pass several geometric statues artfully placed on the grounds, pausing to admire a ten-foot-high ceramic flamingo inlaid with glittering mosaic tiles. The flamingo isn't the official bird of South Florida, but it is the kitschy mascot.

A plaque lets us know that the bird's name is Mayim E. Flamingo. "*Mayim*" is the Hebrew word for "water," but what does the "E" stand for? "Elder"? We are both stumped.

"Mom will love this," I say, and my dad nods his head. "Or she won't," I say, and my dad nods his head at this as well. In the mid-1980s, Mom happened into a John Waters film festival and for a time, she told everyone who would listen that John Waters was a genius and *Pink Flamingos* was her favorite movie. She was so obsessed with the actor Harris Milstead, better known by his drag name, Divine, that for years, I'd receive greeting cards featuring an outrageously outfitted Divine with messages like *Happy Birthday, Hope it's Divine!*, even when it wasn't my birthday, and pink flamingo tchotchkes (that's Yiddish for "junk") of all sizes and shapes: mugs, pencil holders, figurines, and even a pair of pink plastic lawn flamingos. More recently, her brain has been hijacked by Fox News and she's taken to repeating things she hears on the network, like, "Gay people shouldn't have children." So it's either good luck or bad luck—one of the lucks—that Water Elder Flamingo is standing watch outside the home.

Palm trees line the driveway, a fountain cools down a plaza in front of the rehab center, and an ancient cypress shades the entryway to the residences. The grounds appear well maintained, with large expanses of grass, but unlike what was pictured on the website, there isn't an aging marathoner or geriatric lovebirds engaged in a tête-à-tête on a bench. There's no spry octogenarian and her aide perusing a rose garden—was the older woman winking at the aide? How insouciant of her! There's no one outside except several nappers nodding off on patio chairs in front of the entrance to the residence.

A couple of snoozers list slightly in their seats. Can't they put them somewhere we can't see them? It looks like a tenement. This shouldn't be the first thing you see. I flash back to the day after we moved into the house that my husband and I have shared for twenty years. The cable guy came while I was out. As I pulled into our driveway, I saw bright blue cables threaded through holes that had been drilled into the white stucco facade. "Can't they put them somewhere we can't see them? This shouldn't be the first thing you see!"

I shouldn't have yelled this at my husband, and the same words are forming in my head now. What's wrong with me? Why am I so concerned with appearances?

We enter the building and I'm relieved to see that it's immaculately clean, brightly lit, and decorated with modern furnishings. It looks like any number of moderately priced chain hotels that I've stayed in, except that the hallways are wide enough for a tractor to pass through. The lobby has a list of activities for the week. There is an ice-cream social, bingo, an exercise class, crafts, and a book club. There's even a cocktail party every Wednesday. It's the first happy hour I've seen that has a start time of three p.m., but most of the residents are in their nineties—some may not live to see five p.m. There are excursions to the local symphony and a performing arts center. This week there are a variety of films: oldies like *Paint Your Wagon*, Jewish fare like *Woman in Gold*, and *Still Alice*, in which Julianne Moore stars as a professor with early-onset dementia, which makes me wonder if any of the staff have actually seen the film and if we should inquire about suicide rates.

My sister appears and swoops in with the kind of manic energy she and I both veer toward when we feel the world sliding out of our control.

"Annabelle, Shula is here."

"Who?"

"She taught you your haftorah."*

"I don't think I remember her."

"Oh, you will," she says with a tone that sounds a lot like a threat.

Lisa whisks me into the home's synagogue, where a woman in a wheelchair waits for us.

"Anne, it's so good to see you!" Shula says. There was a time when people calling me by my given name bothered me. It also bothered me that for years after I legally changed it to Annabelle, every member of my family added the suffix "-belle" to their name in conversation. I'd pick up the phone and hear, "Sisterbelle, it's Lisabelle," or "Hello, it's your motherbelle." Now I find it endearing.

"I see all the kids I taught," she says, bursting with pride. "Everyone comes to see me."

Everyone is a better person than me. Shula wants to reminisce about Temple Beth Shalom.

"Do you remember when the rabbi said that Jonathan Spivak and I caused Nettie Goldstein's heart attack because of our disruptive behavior in Hebrew school?"

"I remember him, but I don't remember that. Weren't you the president of your confirmation class?"

"Uh-huh . . ."

I don't mention that I'm an atheist now, even though I rarely miss a chance to work that into a conversation; it doesn't seem important.

---

* That's the passage you learn to read from the Torah for your Bar or Bat Mitzvah.

It seems important to politely laugh and look surprised when she begins loading up slices of lemon cake from the Oneg Shabbat (post-services snack tray).

Snacks were served after services at Beth Shalom. As the congregants filed out, you'd hear the sound of purses snapping open. The Hadassah ladies carefully wrapped bread, cookies, and anything else that wasn't nailed down into paper napkins and secreted them into their handbags. We kids always made fun of this, never stopping to consider how many of them lived through the Depression or that these matrons were the forerunners of the campaign to reduce landfill waste.

Shula doesn't want to talk about my spiritual failings, she wants to talk about how she's heard I'm doing so well. I know I am practicing for my future when I look her in the eye, grasp her hands, and affirm that her life had meaning by telling her that any success I've had can be traced back to the time I spent with her, and who's to say that's not true? With any luck, someone will do this for me one day.

I'm disappointed to learn that she's only staying at the Gardens until her broken leg heals. It would be so good for my mother to have someone who knows her, even if it's just tangentially through me, and I'm contemplating breaking her other leg when Lisa spirits me into the dining room.

A row of walkers rest against the wall and several residents are being fed by attendants, but I try not to stare as we make our way toward our table. My sister has already introduced herself to everyone who is able to chew with a closed mouth. My parents are perusing their menus, so I head over to a lively group of female diners, where Lisa has ingratiated herself.

"Your mother will fit right in. She'll love it here," a bubbly bubbie type says.

I'm pimping my mother to Bubbly Bubbie for a full ten minutes before I notice that she's got on a bib. It's a pattern that blends in well with her blouse. *Don't look at the bib*, I tell myself, *avert your eyes, don't embarrass her.* As I move down the row, I catch the interest of Twinkle Toes. Twink jumps up and does a little jig. "I'm ninety and I'm one of the only ones here without a walker! We came here with our husbands, but when they passed, we formed this group. We go to the ballet, concerts, and play cards together."

I'm not sure which part of what she's said is the source of her joy, that their husbands have passed or that they go to the ballet. She gestures to a lithe woman seated next to her. "Her husband is still alive." She points to a man with a grumpy expression seated across the room. "He says she nudges him when they eat, so he eats by himself." Now I am certain that this is the right place for my parents. The idea that my father can eat a meal far from my mother's haranguing sounds ideal, although I can't imagine what my mother will do, as her raison d'être seems to be giving him a hard time. I look over the crowd. With its collegial air, it has a senior hostel vibe, and as impossible as it is to picture her here, it makes sense. Mom's early life was populated by women who looked like these ladies, and the food is just bland enough to be reminiscent of Nanny's cooking.

I order a chicken salad, and it's not Le Cirque but it seems like a small mercy that they have gumbo on the menu. It's nowhere near as flavorful as my dad would prefer, but given the state of my parents' finances, that even this comfort is within reach seems like a miracle.*

Because Twink appears to be the leader of the pack, I ask, "Who are they?" nodding toward a man who is neatly dressed in a polo shirt and pressed trousers. He appears younger than my parents but he's in a wheelchair and is being spoon-fed by a middle-aged woman with the kind of angular haircut that requires regular mainteance. I've lasered in on her as another potential BFF for my mom.

"That's Bruce; he's sixty-five years old and he lives here. He was an architect. He designed this building and now he has Parkinson's. His wife comes every day to visit and have meals with him."

I start to tear up, so I put my glasses on. I can't let them see me cry.

"You're going to like my mother," I tell her, leaning in to kiss her cheeks. "She's smart and funny and always full of surprises."

"We already love her." And with that, Bubbly Bubbie kisses my hand and I take a seat at my family's table.

"This is going well," I'm whispering to my sister when we hear something in the distance that sounds like an alarm going off but, as it gets closer, is unmistakably a human scream. A sturdy woman, with a build like a tree trunk, bursts into the dining room. I noticed her in the hallway walking (unassisted!) and pegged her as a possible buddy.

"Help! Help!" she screams. "They're trying to kill me. They're trying to kill me!"

---

* Seventeen percent of seniors in America suffer food insecurity, which makes me really happy that at least bubbies get dessert after services—reason enough to join a temple.

She's jabbing her index finger in the direction of a soft-faced attendant who is standing in the doorway, arms hanging slackly by her sides. The aide doesn't appear to be in a murderous mood.

"Help me, help me," the sturdy woman pleads. Her eyes search the room and meet mine.

A shrunken man, skin hanging loosely off his slender frame but dressed in a sartorial tweed nonetheless, shakes his fist at her and whines, "You've got to stop saying that. Why are you saying that?"

A sudden calm comes over her. "I wouldn't be saying that if it weren't true."

No one is moving toward her. I stand up. "Someone has to help her," I whisper under my breath. What if they are trying to kill her?

"They're all over me. They're crawling all over me!" She rushes out of the dining room screaming and waving her hands in the air. The diners return their attention to dessert.

Are we in a senior-living version of *Rosemary's Baby*? *They're all in on it*, I think, *no wonder they're so welcoming*. My parents are Mia Farrow's baby and these people are members of Ruth Gordon's coven.

In the distance I hear some island-accented voices— the aides at the Gardens are uniformly Jamaican or Haitian—trying to calm the screamer down, and I realize what everyone else knows. This is not their first time at this rodeo. I also realize I'm an idiot. There's a compelling reason that has nothing to do with the ethnic makeup of the neighborhood for why the campus is ringed by high walls. "Well, that's not good timing," I say to no one in particular as I push my food around my plate.

I excuse myself to go to the bathroom. Now that my eyes have adjusted to the surroundings, I notice the emergency pull cords that are stationed along the walls, little scuff marks near the floor moldings—the turning radius of wheelchairs must not be terrific, or maybe it's marks from the walkers and carts most of the people are pushing—and an extremely faint smell of some sort of human excretion. I lock myself into a double-wide bathroom stall, sit, and weep.

When I've collected myself enough to wash up, I see that my mother is drying her hands at the sink. I have no idea how long she's been standing there.

"I can really see you here, Mom. You'll be the one screaming, 'They're trying to kill me,' in no time at all." We laugh and dab at our eyes.

There isn't an apartment available for us to visit, but my parents and sister have already seen one on a previous trip. We take a cursory look at the pool, gym, and hair salon, and it's time to go. It won't be until months later that I will wonder why didn't I check out the rehab facility. But I'm not thinking clearly. My sister was right to question if I was prepared. It was like being on a moving walkway: I went in the direction we were going and I didn't think to get off, or maybe I couldn't bear to see the advanced care units, which my parents will likely graduate into, because if I did, I'd never be able to make a decision.

None of us have visited the next destination but it's the only other place my dad found online that's within their price range and that has the word "club" in its name.

The Admiral Club is in what might be considered a nicer part of town. The palm-lined entrance reminds me of the driveway leading to the Jockey Club and seems promising, but as we get closer, we see a nondescript midrise apartment building, one of the few stucco structures that haven't been replaced by the glass monoliths that crowd the Miami skyline. The windows in the building look small, there are no grounds, and there's no security.

My spirits rise when I see that we've made the lobby LED screen. *Welcome Gerwartz Family!* But it's the thought that counts.

Then I see the parlor. Mixed-and-matched dining room chairs are crowded into an area that is poorly lit. Rows of seats are facing in the same direction, a television is on, and it looks more like an emergency room than a community room. The upholstery is visibly worn, the carpet well trafficked; even the wrinkled wallpaper looks tuckered out. Along the back wall, residents are lined up in their wheelchairs, gazing inertly at the screen.

The director of the Club, Faith, greets us with flight attendant efficiency and invites us to tour an apartment.

The apartment has low ceilings and that same sad carpet. When my father learns that cooking is not allowed in the apartment, his mouth falls open, but the bathroom is by far the saddest part of the place. A plastic tub has been hastily modified for seniors unable to lift their feet by sawing out the middle section and sealing the edges with caulk. My parents take it in silently. It's only when my mother looks over at a window, with its crooked aluminum blinds, slats bending in the wrong direction, and a window air conditioner unit, that she sighs defeatedly, "I thought we left that behind in Delaware."

My mother says she never shared my father's first-class fantasies, but life on Sunset Island II was awfully seductive.

I've lived in far less glamorous places. But she doesn't know that. My mother couldn't bring herself to visit my apartment when I lived in New York. "I know my limitations," she'd said. Fearing the place would be so ratty that it would upset her, she asked a friend who lived in New York to check it out. Ruth stepped over the vagrant who lived in the garbage-strewn vestibule of my building, trudged up the five stories in her full-length mink coat to my cramped sublet, and reported back, "Yep, it's just as ratty as you expected!"

But it's different when you're young and hopped up on dreams of your glorious future and cheap deli coffee. There was also something special about each of my chosen hovels: a view of treetops, an antique lighting fixture, purple tiles in the bathroom. Here, there is no place to rest your eyes that isn't industrial, uninspired, and it's likely that many hours will be spent inside these walls.

In that moment, my heart breaks for my mom. I spent so many years angry at her passivity, how she looked the other way even when Dad's irresponsibility harmed her children, but depression makes you selfish, and that is the tragedy of her life.

My sister has gone quiet, which is not a good sign. She has a constipated smile plastered on her face.

"So what brings you here?" Faith asks my sister and me, not making eye contact with my parents.

"We were thinking this might be a weekend getaway spot for my teenage son," I'm tempted to say.

"Your parents present very well," she says, as though sizing them up like they're farm animals at a state fair. In all of the arguing about the garbage can, we neglected to discuss whether to mention that Mom is sick, but it seems better not to bring it up because we need them to get a place in independent living. We don't want to have them put in a higher level of care, because they won't accept that. Not yet.

"It's time for our parents to think about the next place," I say.

Faith nods and generously proffers an impromptu dinner invitation. We peek into a cafeteria that is markedly shabbier than the one at the Gardens. It's four p.m., so the dinner service is about to commence, and the featured dish is displayed under plastic wrap. My dad looks heartened to see that it's sliced ham, but the vegetables are overcooked. Before I can answer, Lisa says, "Thank you, but we have other plans." She all but breaks into a sprint and my parents move quicker than I've seen in years to exit the building.

We do actually have plans, because my one-step-ahead sister wisely made dinner reservations at my parents' favorite haunt.

We consolidate into one car and to break the silence, I ask my parents to hand over their new iPhones. In an attempt to retire their outdated flip phones, my sister has generously treated them to new ones. They've already expressed concern about using the touch screens, but I am going to make it easy for them by transferring their contacts, starting with my father's phone.

"Who is Artz?"

"That's Gary Artz."

"Is he dead or alive?"

"Dead."

"Who is Ellis?"

"I'm not sure."

"Alan?"

"Not sure."

"Myer?"

"Dead."

"Oh, is that Cousin Mike?"

"Yes, dead."

"Brother?"

"That's Cousin Brother. Dead."

"Dad, why do you have Christie Hefner's phone number?"

"I put some investors together to buy a Playboy Club, but it didn't pan out."

"When was that?"

"In the late eighties."

"Who is ann345mwx?"

"That's you."

"Not dead, just resting," I say, borrowing a line from the terrible *Ishtar.*

Now I'm facing that singularly twenty-first-century dilemma: to delete or not to delete. That is the question. In the past, one might have drawn a line through the deceased's name in a bound address book or Rolodex, allowing the presence of absence. Electronic deletion is so swift and complete that I can't bring myself to remove the departed from my own lists, but given that 99 percent of Dad's entries are no longer living, scrolling for a phone number has got to be an emotionally draining exercise.*

The irony is that everyone who knows me has either called or texted and gotten my standard reply, "What wonderful person is this?" because I've never managed to enter contacts in my phone, but I want to exercise some small control over my parents' future. I'm determined that they are going to know who is calling them, damn it! Texting? We probably don't have to worry about it, people

---

* This subject has been tackled by numerous writers, most memorably Edward Zuckerman in *The New York Times*, who at last count had seventeen deceased entries, but no one has come up with an acceptable ratio of dead-to-living contacts.

over eighty don't tend to text, but you never know with my dad; he's always been an early adopter.

A month ago, Lisa was on one of our rotating tours of parental duty and invited a high school friend, Stephanie, over to our parents' condo. Stephanie suggested setting up a Skype account on their home computer. They might want to see their grandchildren when conversing, not to mention that my sister and I could keep an eye out for signs of decline. Our parents agreed. Lisa, Stephanie, and Dad gathered around his computer, but when they tried to sign up, they learned that he'd already opened an account and had been Skyping with Hot Babes, Really Hot Babes, and the Hottest Babes on the Web for quite some time. Mercifully for all involved, Mom was busy emptying the trash bin. Someone had thrown out a paper towel, so with the celery stick already there, it was overflowing.

I decide to delete only the longtime dead, ten years or longer; to leave Christie Hefner for old times' sake; and to leave ann345mwx as is because it has a certain ring to it and there's also a chance that it's not me. I can't bring myself to open the contact and see what number is listed. I hope that I am ann345mwx.

"Can I interest you in a cheap Merlot?" my mother asks when we arrive at the restaurant. Tonight will not be a good night to give up alcohol. We're so relieved to be in a place where everyone is ambulatory that we don't discuss anything other than our food, and polish off two bottles between us.

Back at the condo, Lisa and I parcel out the silver, politely declining the iced tea straws. We are cordial, verging on solicitous, in our distribution of the linens—four napkins is the equivalent of one tablecloth—but we hit a snag on two silver-plated serving trays that once belonged to Becca. We both prefer the rectangular to the round. My sister suggests we play rock, paper, scissors.

"I can't. I just went to adult summer camp and am still traumatized by the memory of two hundred people in onesies pointing their scissors at me."

"What about a coin toss?"

"Sure, no problem, whatever you want," I say, but something in my brain breaks. I have to win this coin toss. My sister throws a quarter up, catches it in her palm, and invites me to call it. But I can't do it.

"Call it . . . Call it, Sisterbelle!"

"Hea . . . ails."

"What did you say?"

"Hea . . . ails," I repeat in an effort to form a word that sounds exactly like both "heads" and "tails." "Hea . . . ails," I stutter. "Hails. Hails."

"Hails? Are you calling hails?"

"Uh-huh. Hails." Something must have broken in her brain as well, because she punches me in the arm. Playfully, but her fist *is* closed. I punch her back. She punches me. I punch her. She punches me. We pummel each other like five-year-olds. Our mother sashays in and wants to know what's happening.

"Mom, what are you wearing?" I gasp. She's got on a high-collared full-length flannel granny nightgown.

"It was Rebecca's, it's so comfortable," she says, executing a wobbly but passable fashion show twirl. "What's going on in here?"

"Hails! Hails!" we say, but it doesn't make any sense. Our mother, who had a bit too much of the cheap Merlot, starts laughing, and all three of us are giggling now. My father, hearing the noise, shuffles in. He is wearing a bathrobe that barely reaches his thighs.

"What's so funny?"

A spinning spectral figure, like something from a children's ghost story; a stooped colossus in a Lilliputian bathrobe; and two middle-aged women duking it out over serving trays. This will be the last memory we make as the Gurwitch family relaxing at home on a Saturday night.

When none of us can offer an explanation, Dad shrugs and shuffles back to the bedroom. He's probably got a Hot Babe waiting. How much dough he is spending, we don't know, but it's better than risking getting hit over the head or worse at a "golf tournament."* Thank goodness for porn on the Internet!

I sober up quickly with the realization that I'm going to have to call heads or tails after having thought about porn.

"Heads?" I say because it conjures an only slightly less vivid image.

Lisa turns the coin over and it's tails. She slips the long, thin tray into her tote. You can never beat the General.

Back at the Sun Harbour, I ask Lisa if she'll miss our parents when they're gone. She says that she will, adding in a measured voice that she knows they always believed in her. "Always." She repeats the word "always," and I know she means they always believed in her, but I hear it as a reminder that they were always so predictable.

---

* Dad told Mom he was going to a golf tournament, but a credit card bill told the story of a hotel room and an escort service. She donated his golf clubs to a local thrift shop while he was at a casino. Unfortunately, she can't remember if this happened last month or last year.

That summer I went to Los Angeles with my dad, my next stop was Northwestern University's summer theater institute, known as the Cherubs program. If I wasn't sure already that I wanted to head to a life in the arts, that summer convinced me. I also met Tonya Pinkins, who would go on to win a Tony Award and every other honor you can win as an actress on the New York stage. Tonya and I have seen each other through failures and felicities since we were fifteen years old, and it's hard to imagine my life without her and that program.

A few years ago, an administrator tracked me down to inquire if I wanted to make good on a pledge my father had made. Unbeknownst to me, I hadn't been accepted into the program. I was a sophomore at the time, and students were supposed to be juniors. Knowing how much I wanted to go, my father intervened, promising a generous donation. Who knows what would have happened if I hadn't attended that summer? Surely a domino effect of differences, maybe for the better or maybe for the worse. I'll never know. Was my mother aware of this bribe? Probably, but in this instance her passivity worked in my favor. For so many years, I told myself that anything good in my life had happened in spite of them, but who's to say that any success I've had can't be traced back to their being my parents? And they will always be my parents. And they did always believe in me.

"Always," I repeat several times, mimicking my sister.

We're in our pajamas when we start surfing the Web for senior-living communities. We check out the website of the luxury residence Dad has e-mailed as a better alternative to today's offerings: Villa Grande. It's close to my parents' doctors' offices and it has a lecture series, high-end wine tastings, and shellfish! But it's out of reach of their budget. There's another enclave, Villa Even More

Grande, that has cottages, town houses, and ranch-style haciendas to choose from. The layouts are named for artists ranging from Renoir to Chagall. The Michelangelo is the size of New Hampshire. Not only are the ceilings higher and kitchens stainless, the photographs hint at perhaps the greatest luxury of all. In the staged shots, a stylish woman contemplates a biscotti by a bay window, and on a couch in the background, in what looks like a galaxy far, far away, maybe even Delta Epsilon, a man reads the newspaper. They'll need walkie-talkies or smoke signals in order to communicate. It's an unmistakable message that the greatest luxury is to be able to put space between you and your spouse. It's the perfect place for my parents.

The seniors are dressed in someone's notion of classy: ladies wear pearls and the men are uniformly outfitted in pin-striped shirts, expensive watches on wrists. What will the marketing be like when we, the punk rock generation, are looking for the "next place"? My new goal in life is to live long enough to see senior-living ads featuring aging hipsters sporting vintage Ramones T-shirts and to afford a Banksy.

"Should we try to get them in there?" I ask my sister, knowing full well that we'd have to borrow against our own futures to get them into even a Pissarro.

Our dilemma is just one more way in which the disappearance of the middle class is playing out in our country. There are plenty of choices if money is no option, Medicare subsidies for those without any assets, but the in-between barely exists.

Companies are putting resources into the super-high-end retirement market, just like in the cruise industry. In fact, Villa Grande advertises with the tagline "When your ship comes in, why not make it a cruise liner?" and touts their services as unmatched by the top cruise lines. Forget a sponge bath; at these sanctuaries you could probably get a tongue bath if that's what floats your boat. Places like Tel Aviv Gardens used to be the primary destination for Jews of a variety of income levels, but if families are monied, they go elsewhere. The Gardens doesn't have access now to the donors who used to fund improvements, so it seems like steerage in comparison.

When you add in the lessened mobility that age brings, a geriatric caste system is inevitable. Of the few lasting friendships Mom and Dad have made, the well-heeled folks have moved to areas of the country like North Carolina, considered a desirable retirement spot, where they'll either hire expensive in-home care or be ushered into one of those gilded golden-year havens.*

I get excited when I find a mid-priced community in the middle of Florida called the Villages, but our hearts sink when we read that the development is owned by a conservative billionaire and there've been reports of incidents of harassment of residents who aren't in lockstep with the politics promoted by the Villages' newspaper and radio station—dog poop on doorsteps and public shaming of Democrats. My parents would be in their element, but what will happen when Lisa's and my families visit? There's also a 0 percent Jewish population there, which would be unacceptable to my mother, and the hundred thousand or so residents of the Villages rarely leave the property, which sounds a lot like a senior internment camp.

---

* I wonder if there's ever a time when friends say, "You know, I'm going to forgo that place that serves sushi and settle for tacos and better company." I hope so, because I have a few friends I'd like to grow old with.

We search for a place like I read about in Atul Gawande's book *Being Mortal*.

"I read about a retirement community that has one hundred parakeets, four dogs, two cats, a colony of rabbits, a flock of laying hens, and after-school care for the children of the aides, and it shares a campus with a school. Some of the residents write up daily reports on the birds."

"Can't you see Mom writing reports like, 'Parakeet number 32 isn't cleaning up after itself. Messy! Fat; halved birdseed rations today. Too much singing; annoying. Put a thimble of cheap Merlot in the aviary and it settled down fine.'"

We can't find anything like that in Florida. Just for kicks, I search for the place that Gawande wrote about and find that the minimum buy-in is six hundred thousand dollars, not including the monthly fees.

Lisa and I talk about the money, how we can swing it. As I fall asleep I add up my savings, our son's college fund, our retirement plans, and try to guesstimate how much I could get for the hand-painted Dolce & Gabbana skirt a TV network bought me once, but I can't make the numbers work and my sister has two sons who are graduating college in an economy where entry-level jobs are hard to come by. My dad has squandered his and Mom's money, for sure, but if their savings had been wiped out by a tornado, would that make them any more sympathetic? The Torah says the greatest charity is to give without judgment, and then there's that old "Honor thy father and mother" commandment. It's the fifth one. Oh my God, I don't even believe in God, so why am I so Jewish? I would just like them to have something beautiful to look at.

I'm mad at my grandfather Ike for not making more money, I'm mad at our dad for not making more money, but mostly I'm mad at myself for not making more money and at Atul Gawande because I wish I didn't know about parakeet paradise.

Our flights are scheduled to leave early in the morning and we try to reach our parents' cell phones but they don't pick up; we can only reach them on the landline. It's been less than twenty-four hours and they've already given up on the new phones. My sister and I say our good-byes at the airport but we still haven't made a decision. We just don't want to pull the trigger.

"Tonight," we agree. "We'll talk tonight."

I'm snaking my way through the long security line at Miami International Airport when the TSA screener pulls the citron altar fruit jar out of my purse and asks what's inside. "Memories," I tell him, which reminds me that I've neglected to buy my parents a new trash can.

That night, I call my sister, but before I can say anything, she beats me to it.

"Tel Aviv Gardens."

"Right. At least there are grand pianos. Lots of them," I add hopefully. "There was one in the lobby of the rehab center, the hospital, both residences. I wouldn't be surprised if there's a piano in one of the bathrooms on the campus; those stalls are big enough."

It's a point of pride for Jewish people to be cultured, or at least appear to be cultured. My parents had a piano in their home. I have a piano in my house even though none of us play it.

I tell her I'll break the news to our father.

"Hi, Dad, this is your daughter, ann345mwx. I'm calling to tell you that Lisa and I feel that the Gardens is the best of all possible homes for you and Mom."

My father says he might be able to hit up a cousin for some money so they can go to Villa Grande.

"Dad, I'm sorry, but I really don't think you should do that," I say, knowing full well that there's no way he's getting any more money out of our cousins.

"Well, it's best for your mother."

"Yes, it's best for Mom," I repeat. "And, Dad, I promise, I'll get you a new garbage can."

There is a whole world
that exists between knowledge
and belief. You and I exist
(necessarily) within that
continuum, however, as a
former "atheist in a foxhole"
(Viet Nam) I understand the
fine line you walk every
day you wear your uniform.
Those in authority are almost
always in the "believers" camp,
and they are also in a position
to make your life miserable.
For someone who was highly
trained to fix very complicate
ejection seats, I can't coun
how many days of K.P. duty I

We have no martyrs—we have no saints
No cross to bear, but we still have some complaints
—Penn Jillette

and they shall enter singing the songs of mumford and sons

When you let it slip that you're not a believer, well-meaning friends will say things like, "I can prove there is a God." Recently, the husband of a friend took up this challenge. Not only hasn't he devoted his life to studying man's search for meaning, but he's untroubled by his lack of cultivated knowledge. "Go for it," I said, harboring just the tiniest hope that he might be onto something. I'm not a "Hooray, there's no God" person. I'm an "It sucks that there's no God" person, but I am resigned. I'll have a double shot of espresso and the latest by Sam Harris.

"Okay, if there's no God, why is the ratio of males to females in the world always in stasis? Even after wars where large numbers of men die, the numbers always return to the same level. It doesn't make sense unless the hand of God has intervened."

"I'll get back to you on that," I told him, wanting to do my due diligence before commenting. I asked the brilliant physicist Lisa Randall, author of *Knocking on Heaven's Door*, if she might weigh in.

"What's the statistical probability that Jeremy Wright, patent attorney in Los Angeles, has solved the riddle of the ages?"

"That would depend: Are we talking about the probability using the amount of people who've tackled this issue since the beginning of recorded history or just in our generation? But for the real question, this doesn't prove anything. 'Intelligent design' arguments invoke God to account for something someone doesn't understand before exhausting possible scientific contributing factors such as birth rates for men versus women or a more detailed statistical analysis. The arguments also seem to often refer to robustness of men for some reason."

As a C-minus science student, I find the intelligent design argument faulty for a more practical reason. In a truly intelligently designed world, there wouldn't be pedophiles, dictators, or the need to eat lentils. There wouldn't be AIDS, Alzheimer's, or athleisure. There would be equal pay for the sexes and a livable minimum wage, and people would stop saying, "It's all good." There would be eye creams that really lift, iPhone screens that don't crack; politicians peddling falsehoods would be struck down by lightning, and booty shorts would be outlawed. If someone posited a theory that reflected a more realistic assessment of our world, I might be more inclined to accept it, but I'm skeptical that "God's doing his best" design would be met with much enthusiasm.*

---

* Saint Augustine argued that the flaws in our world are God's challenge to us. Also, that pesky free will thwarts the perfection of life on earth. Still not buying the intelligent design argument.

Still, I never felt compelled to seek out non-theist fellowships until the day I got sucked into a video about citizen volunteers helping Syrian refugees ashore in Lesbos, Greece. I was jotting down the name of the sponsoring organization, intending to contact them about joining the rescue effort, when one of the volunteers turned to the camera.

"I just want these folks to have a good experience with Christians."

Can we humanists ever hope to hit the ground running in the way that faith-based groups respond to disasters and crises? I wondered. Folks who identify themselves as unaffiliated, "nones," according to Pew Research, are the least trusted people in America. "I just want these folks to have a good experience with secular humanists," I picture myself saying as I grasp the hand of a refugee. Could I be a part of changing that perception?

If I'd spent a little less time contemplating my past lives, I'd have known that greater minds than mine have been working toward organizing secular communities across the globe.

A quick search on the Web lets me know the humanists in my part of town are outdoorsy types who like to hit the local hiking trails together. There is a healthy streak of humor running through many of their online meet-up profiles:

I am an atheist because I like to sleep in on Sundays.

I couldn't go home for Passover because I had a yeast infection. If that's not a reason to give up God, I don't know what is.

I'm an agnostic, satirist, writer and Rasputin impersonator. Check out my blog for shits and giggles, mostly giggles.

Then I heard about Sunday Assembly Los Angeles. The Assembly movement was started in England by two British comedians,

Sanderson Jones and Pippa Evans, who were looking for something that was "like church but totally secular." "*Live Better, Help Often, Wonder More*" is their trademarked slogan, which has been adopted by the seventy Assemblies in eight countries that have cropped up since 2013. The Assembly website announces their intention to be "radically inclusive," noting, "We don't do supernatural but we also won't tell you you're wrong if you do."

They sounded like my kind of people, but it was their call for volunteers to make holiday care packages for the Military Association of Atheists and Freethinkers, MAAF, that got me out of the house that Sunday morning. The lecture that week was also impossible for a sci-fi fanatic like me to resist. It was titled "Where Science Meets Science Fiction." I invited my husband, who prefers to remain undecided if skeptical about the existence of a deity, noting that the service included live music, but he disdains anything that even remotely resembles a religious service.

"Mark my words, they'll play something by Mumford and Sons." He despises their peppy, folky sound. Bands like Modest Mouse make his skin crawl.

"For an agnostic, you think you know everything, don't you?"

I was welcomed into the Assembly by two super-friendly male greeters. The guys were in good enough shape to be confused with personal trainers—we were in Hollywood, after all. If I wrote a scene in a movie in which one greeter revealed that he was an emergency room EMT and the other that he was an alcohol sales rep, and both said that after seeing drunken carnage all week, they were looking forward to something uplifting, any skeptic worth her salt would say that was too great a coincidence, but that's exactly what brought both of them into Sunday Assembly. The alcohol rep also said that after growing up in a churchy community, he felt "orphaned" as an unaffiliated person, a word I will hear numerous times during the day. I have an innate distrust of too much cheerfulness, so I almost turned around and left, but when I saw that the refreshment station was serving espresso drinks, not your typical tepid institutional brew, it seemed like a sign that I should stay.

I suppose it shouldn't be surprising upon entering an auditorium of self-professed freethinkers to hear, "NPR is not leftist enough for my taste." There were about two hundred people milling about, families with young children and a smattering of vintage Woodstocky types. It was refreshing to see that there wasn't a recognizably famous face in the crowd, which is unusual for Los Angeles, though if the celebrity Twittersphere is any indication, Hollywood is almost as churchy as my hometown of Mobile, Alabama. Tweets regularly teem with invocations of blessedness and gratitude and shout-outs of thanks to God.*

So many of the male Assemblers were on the younger side that we might have been confused with a ManBunCon. The varietals of hair bordered on the miraculous, some designs as improbable as an immaculate conception: man knots, man buns, the "hot crossed buns" (a double bun), the "bun run" (a vertical row of buns), "the debunoir" (a slicked-back bun), and the "I can't believe it's not butter bun" (this style aims to fool you: it's got shaved sides like a Mohawk, but wait, there's more—there's a bun back there). And most of the men had beards. I found it strangely comforting that though unwilling to embrace religion, these men were not agnostic about

---

* If you're looking to kick organized religion to the curb, consider that Justin Bieber just had a cross tattooed on his face.

all things. They were deeply committed to the grooming and maintenance of body hair.

We non-believers are funny! Someone in my row sneezed; I said, "God bless you—oops, gesundheit," and shared a titter with those seated on either side of me. An announcement over the PA system let us know that the event would be live-streamed and that the (all-volunteer) staff was checking the audiovisual hookup because, as we know, you can't leave anything to chance. Thinking I'd gotten the hang of this secular gathering, I made a kind of inside joke about how that's because we live in a random universe. My entire row chuckled. We're hilarious!*

The first order of the day was the "ice breaker" moment, meant to spark conversation among strangers. Instead of wishing the person next to you a blessed day or Shabbat shalom, we were instructed to turn to the person next to us and observe a moment of silence. I embarrassingly interpreted this to mean a theater exercise where you stare at your partner in an attempt to learn as much as you can through silent, probing observation. After two minutes of enduring my unflinching gaze, my neighbor cleared her throat, shifted uncomfortably, and turned away. The people around us were conversing casually, probably conspiring to politely freeze me out of the Assembly.

A song whose lyrics appeared on the screen in front of us blasted out from the speakers and we were encouraged to stand up and sing along with "I Will Wait" by Mumford and Sons, followed by "Float

---

* One of the hallmarks of urban tribes, subcultures, and families is shared common language. We secular folks have in-jokes and if someone mentions Sam or Richard, we know they mean our guys Harris and Dawkins.

On" by Modest Mouse. It wasn't the second coming, but I was in heaven; these are two of my favorite peppy, folky tunes.

After the musical interlude, Assemblers were invited to stand up or call out milestones they were marking this week. Someone was celebrating thirty-five years of marriage, another got an A on a college exam, a kid won a national prize with the Boys and Girls Clubs, and one little girl announced that she felt awesome. I was so charmed, I almost yelled out, "I'm experiencing a genuinely heart-warming moment without judgment, although I will write about it in a manner that is laced with sarcasm," but reason won out and I resisted the temptation.

The featured speaker was Dr. Foad Dizadji-Bahmani, a fellow at the London School of Economics and professor at one of the UCs in the philosophy of probability. He was impossibly good-looking; it seemed unlikely he didn't have a degree in handsomeness. He told us he'd be speaking on a concept that was a lot like the premise of the TV series *Fringe*. That show followed the chaotic disruption caused when parallel universes overlapped.* I was such a fan of the series that I stayed awake once for an entire cross-country red-eye because one of the show's stars was on my flight and I felt compelled to watch as her chest rose and fell with each breath while she slept, which qualifies as stalkery in any universe. I took notes:

Inflationary cosmology . . . there are other potential yous . . . bat shit crazy (is that a legitimate scientific term?) . . . truth important if true . . . Possible world semantics . . . quantum events . . . infinity universe . . . infinity pool (might not have heard that, but going for a cool dip is always welcome in Los Angeles) . . . quantum suggests there is an infinity

---

* Leonard Nimoy, Spock, played a pivotal role in the show.

of universes . . . quantum (again with the quantums?) of quantums (does he have a licensing deal with the word quantums?)

 jam jar water

 Birkenstocks

I don't recall what the note about jam jars and Birkenstocks had to do with the talk. Was he drinking from a jam jar? Maybe. Others in the crowd were. You see that a lot these days. Mason jars have supplanted reusable water bottles in the Hipster Ethos.* Was he wearing Birkenstocks? Possibly someone in my row was wearing them. I don't think his talk was intended to encourage this kind of speculation, but I would like to live in the alternate world where Birkenstocks were never invented.

I'm sure Dr. Dizadji-Bahmani's degrees were earned with unimpeachable scholarly research, but it all sounded a bit . . . just a bit . . . almost exactly like the channeled wisdom of free-ranging entities I was privy to as a member of that UFO cult in the 1980s. The talk probably landed him a development deal at the Syfy channel.

We observed a moment of quiet reflection, as you do, and then we were back into gear with the day's featured live musical act. A folk band from Hawaii leapt onto the stage. Accomplished young musicians, they struck me as so clean-cut and unencumbered by self-reflection, it was almost unseemly for non-believers. Aren't you supposed to wrestle with existentialism and be miserable in your twenties?

Their musical offering was perfectly charming, but I have to

---

* First there were plastic water bottles, followed by stainless and glass, and now you can't buy one, no, you have to have an artisanal water container. Can everyone be buying so much jam that they have jam jars to spare? I'm dubious.

confess, I was losing the thread. Were we at a God-free hoedown?
I was pondering this when a middle-aged woman sporting wire-
rimmed glasses and a grandmotherly warmth approached the mic
stand. She told us how her zest for life had waned after the death of
a family member and that feeding the homeless with Assemblers
had returned a sense of purpose to her life. This is a regular feature
of the Assembly, a three-to-four-minute testimonial on "doing our
best."

As she testified, I felt queasy. She reminded me of the women my
son and I had met working in the soup kitchen of his Episcopal
grade school. You can take the lady out of the church, but you can't
take the church out of the lady. I too find being of service a salve for
depression, but good lord, the service was getting awfully churchy.
All of the songs seemed to strike religious thematic notes: *Take my
flesh / And fix my eyes* . . . Is Mumford and Sons' song actually a
call to religion? And what if you don't like the musical selections?
That's really going to be a buzzkill. There's something comforting
and even pleasurable about showing up at your house of worship
knowing there will be the same old songs, even if you don't like
them. They carve a familiar if mortifying groove in your brain.
Just like if someone sings the Nair hair-removal commercial song
from the 1980s—"Who wears short shorts, we wear short shorts, if
you dare wear short shorts, Nair for short shorts"—it's impossible
for me to resist happily joining in.

As she spoke, I thought about my conversation with Ian Dodd, one
of the founders of the Sunday Assembly Los Angeles. I'd called to ask
about how he, a director of photography for TV shows, came to be
involved and he'd told me how he met the founders at a local watering
hole and got swept up into starting a chapter. He candidly addressed

the difficulty of coming up with a format. "Some people feel the Assembly is too churchy, for some it can't get churchy enough."

Music has been an issue, he allowed. Every secular community is trying to get away from endless covers of "Imagine." The Los Angeles Assembly often invites a local atheist choir, Voices of Reason, whose signature number that year was "The Rhythm of Life." It's from the musical *Sweet Charity*, in which Daddy, a role played by Sammy Davis Jr. in the movie version, an improbably jazzy, flower-power, hippie guru, sings about forming a church where his followers will "hit the floor and crawl to Daddy." Dramatists and audiences have puzzled over the song's inclusion in *Sweet Charity*, and it doesn't seem like an obvious choice for the Assembly either, although my questioning the selection affirms my status as a card-carrying skeptic.

Ian was a witness to what's been called the Second Atheist Schism, the first being the break from God. A faction of SA in New York, where he was living at the time, accused founders Jones and Evans of trying to form a centralized humanist religion. Guided by a more hard-core vision, they formed a splinter group called the Godless Revival. They proudly label themselves atheists and meet in dive bars.

I'm so glad I'm not in charge of figuring this stuff out, I thought as the Assembly drew to a close and we were treated to the full "tastes like chicken" religious institution experience. An announcement was made of this exciting news: "We're planning to hire staff, so we need money." In what must have been a nod to the newness of the group, the collection box that made its way to me was a diaper wipe container.

We service project volunteers were handed the boxes that were to be sent to the members of the Military Association of Atheists and Freethinkers who were serving on bases around the globe. Our secular stocking stuffers included books by Richard and Sam, mints, gum, and board games.

We were encouraged to include personal notes in our packages. I felt a bit silly, so I tried to strike a lighthearted tone and after several attempts settled on:

Dear third chimpanzee, merry everything, happy everybody!

I thought it was pretty clever until I peeked over the shoulder of the guy sitting next to me. Allen was composing a letter that was several pages long. I couldn't make out the text, but it was filled with underlined words, caps, and lots of exclamation points.

Allen, a surgical sonographer, served in the Air Force in Vietnam. Once his commanding officer found out he was an atheist, he'd pulled way more than his share of KP duties and cleaned more latrines than anyone else in his platoon, he told me with venom in his eyes as he spoke.

"Atheists aren't officially recognized by the military and are still required to pray at some ceremonial events. Even Wiccans have chapters on bases," he told me, his voice rising with anger. Had I composed my holiday greeting with enough sensitivity? It seemed doubtful, but my packages were sealed and whisked away. I'd also neglected to note that *The Third Chimpanzee* is the title of a book by Jared Diamond on how alike human behavior is to that of the chimpanzee, our closest relative. Without context, my letter could be misinterpreted in an antagonistic way. Unsuspecting women and men serving in conflict zones might open these boxes and take offense. Was it possible that Allen was exaggerating the importance of these care packages? He was wearing Birkenstocks.

I headed home and immediately put out the word through MAAF channels that I was interested in speaking with package recipients. I started receiving e-mails from people like Staff Sergeant Sawyer Braun, who told me about his "transition" from his Catholic upbringing. He was binge-watching George Carlin videos during a tour in Bagram, Afghanistan, in 2005, when he had an awakening. He started a branch of MAAF at Fort Campbell as a way of reaching out; being from a small town, he'd never met anyone who was a non-believer. "Humanism isn't recognized by the military, and we can't officially congregate as a group on base, so we hold our annual Darwin Day in my apartment." They are also looking for alternatives to "Imagine." He was hoping to convince his group to adopt "Let It Go," from the Disney animated film *Frozen*. A Marine sergeant, Cody Heaps, phoned to let me know how much he valued getting his package fifteen months into a deployment last year in Bahrain.

"Many well-meaning people send religious propaganda and I was so happy to receive something from 'my people.' You know what else is great about your gifts?" he added. "They're not too big. We get these huge hauls and it's just not practical in a war zone." Score one for the practicality of skeptics.

I had no idea how much attention was being paid to this small gesture, having never experienced this kind of marginalization for my faith or lack thereof. Their stories reminded me of the isolation I felt in my youth, for completely different reasons, but it was out of this feeling of solidarity with the soldiers that I found myself standing on the National Mall, facing the crowd of ten thousand freethinkers at Reason Rally 2016. I was so overcome with emotion, I blurted out, "I'm so glad to be here with my tribe," before I introduced retired lieutenant colonel Thom Grey, founder of the humanist group at Offutt Air Force Base, one of the members of MAAF I'd connected with. After he spoke, I didn't think twice about joining in the rousing rally-wide rendition of "Imagine."

I'd been expecting legions of Holy Roller protesters damning apostates to hell, but the mall gathering and subsequent parties had all the hallmarks of a large family reunion whose members had never met, everyone angling to figure out how they were connected and reveling in their commonality.

"I'm disappointed," Emery, host of the *Ardent Atheist* podcast, told me when I mentioned my dashed hopes of a bit more Sturm und Drang. "There's just one Flying Spaghetti Monster.* At the last rally, we had a Jesus riding a dinosaur."

You know a movement has gone mainstream when it goes meta. Scattered throughout the crowd I spotted fresh-faced acolytes of the Flying Spaghetti Monster with colanders on their heads, strands of yellow yarn just peeking out over the rims.

When I saw that the founder of Recovery from Religion, Gayle Jordan, was going to speak, I thought, *Well, that sounds a bit dramatic,* and grabbed a front-row seat. Gayle, who turned out to be as high on the dramatic scale as any CPA I've ever met, spent most of her life immersed in a Southern Baptist community. She was in her thirties when she informed her family she'd had an awakening and

---

* That's the unofficial mascot of some atheists who liken worshipping God to pledging allegiance to pasta. Legislation to make it an official religion to worship his divine Noodleship was introduced but ultimately failed in South Dakota.

was renouncing her faith. Her parents threatened to have her declared an unfit mother and tried to enlist the help of the local social services agency to have her three children removed from her home. Her group offers counseling hotlines specifically targeted for those in remote locations who live in households or within religious sects where they are afraid to "come out," in her words, to their families.*

One of the founding members of Black Nonbelievers, in his early thirties, said he'd had to join a church "'cause it's hard to meet women otherwise, you know? Church is part of the expected equation of family and community."

"You gotta keep your priorities straight," I told him, and I meant it.

But as with all clans, an in-family fight was in full swing. I inadvertently entered into this squabble by uploading to my Twitter account a shot of the golden uterus that Lizz Winstead and her Lady Parts feminist posse temporarily tattooed on my bicep at the rally. When my account blew up with angry tweets—"Nice one, Annabelle, what would you think if I got a golden penis tattooed on my forehead!" or "Annabelle Gurwitch has a golden uterus on her arm and you wonder why so many people are boycotting the rally?"—"What's going on?" I asked fellow presenter Yvette d'Entremont, whose nom de science is SciBabe.

An incident that took place in 2011, known as Elevatorgate, exposed what some feel is a culture of sexism in a community

---

* Freedom from Religion receives many calls from young people and often counsels teenagers not to identify if doing so might compromise their future—for instance, by costing them funding for their education.

admittedly dominated by white males. Rebecca Watson, a podcast host and blogger, known as Skepchick, mentioned an unwanted invitation from a random atheist in an elevator during the World Atheism Convention in a blog post. Her offhand remark escalated into a full-blown brouhaha when Richard Dawkins published an open letter contrasting her complaint with genital mutilation and other horrors that women suffer in the name of religion. Apologies have since been issued. The Dawkins Foundation has outposts in numerous countries and is an essential player in the secular world, and no one really wants to demonize them.*

Attempts at inclusion have been made, including a focus on LGBTQIA rights and the adoption of an anti-harassment policy. Still, there was a minor amount of boycotting of the rally and some online pushback, but it's easy to vent on a platform like Twitter from the comfort of your own uterus-less household. I had no idea about any of this, but then, what can you expect? The *Family Feud* game show first aired in 1976 and is still popular today. At least, as Penn Jillette likes to remind us, "We have no martyrs and no saints," so no one in either camp can claim God is on their side, and any controversy, at least publicly, died down in about the same amount of time as it took for my tattoo to fade.

If history is any example, it takes years, even centuries, for a movement to really take hold. If we want to have own secular hub, something like Vatican City, or even Salt Lake City, it will take a

---

* I also don't want to demonize them. I think of Dawkins as my beloved but dotty uncle when he says impolitic things. The Dawkins Foundation just merged with the Center for Inquiry, making them atheism central. In 2016, they raised fifty thousand dollars to extract activists and writers from Bangladesh who've been targeted for death by militant Islamists. Huzzah!

lot of diaper boxes full of cash, but then, the nones are young and in their most fertile years. Maybe we'll come up with new rituals and anthems yet to be written, or we'll keep singing peppy folk tunes and in a few hundred years, the songs of Mumford and Sons will become part of the atheist canon. Some congregants will roll their eyes as people around them sing out, and those who have forgotten the words will find themselves mindlessly humming along because they can't remember a time when they didn't know the melody of "I Will Wait."

Mayim E. Flamingo, who watches over Tel Aviv Gardens.

suddenly sequins

Encountering sequins where you least expect them can elicit a kind of startle response, especially if they are located along the seams of a T-shirt that already has coin fringe sewn onto the padded shoulders.

I'm wandering the aisles at the Ross Dress for Less in a daze. It's not like I'm unfamiliar with bargain shopping. I've schlepped through enough thrift stores to appreciate the patience and fortitude it takes to rifle through the many misses to find a few hits, but this store is like entering another landscape altogether.

If you want to visit the real America, shop the Ross Dress for Less in North Miami. Ross, like America, is a jumble of discordant singularities, all of which are competing loudly for attention. A single blouse has so many design elements it brings to mind a vase that has shattered and then been reassembled by raccoons. All logic has been dispensed with. Some items are so packed with studs and nail heads, I half expect the rack to be labeled *Fashion for People Who Never Travel*, as you'd never make it through TSA without ending up entirely in the nude, because even the bras and panties have metal accents. What appears to be a lumberjack plaid shirt, very Brooklyn 2016, is made of polyester, which, here in the tropics, forms an insulated casing around the torso and traps odor like a bathroom on a Greyhound bus.

I'm shopping because of the holocaust. Not the Jewish Holocaust, but my mother's personal holocaust, although for her, they have morphed into the same thing.

In the less than four months since my parents moved into the Tel Aviv Gardens her breast cancer has declared all-out war on her body. Pieces of our mother are disappearing like she's Swiss cheese. We have been told this progression will continue until there is nothing left but empty space. The latest outbreak of violence is an assault on her digestive system in the form of a tumor the size of a grapefruit.

By the time I arrive in Miami, she's made it through a seven-hour surgery and been sent to the Gardens' recovery center, just a few yards from the apartment building that my parents now call home. What's left of her midsection is saddled with not one but two colostomy bags. It seems like a cruel punishment for a woman who's looking at potentially months, not years, left to live, but death was imminent, so it was unavoidable.

I have been tasked with finding clothes that can accommodate the appliances and that will help, in some minuscule way, to ease her suffering. Ross is the closest store and I don't want to leave her side for long periods of time. As she is shrinking—every day she seems to lose a size—it seems imprudent to be purchasing "investment pieces." She would like stretchy pants, long shirts, and loose-fitting jackets. It appears likely that whatever I pick out will be accented with sequins, but if I'm lucky, I'll find something in a tribal print.

Teenagers tend to dress like their peers. It's a phenomenon called "twinning." According to psychologists, dressing alike bolsters adolescent girls' fragile self-esteem, and I've witnessed a similar dynamic at play with the women at the home. There is a pervasive style that they all seem to have adopted—colorful Aztec geometrics and Native American Hopi bat-wing patterns. My mother is mirroring her peers with a newly acquired collection of bold-patterned jackets and leopard-print scarves. The sight takes some getting used to: elderly white Jewish women in tribal prints being attended to by Haitian and Jamaican women in pastel uniforms. She'd like me to pick up something "fun"—a blouse in a tiger or giraffe print would be wonderful—and I want her to fit in.

It turns out, we had gotten them situated just in time. Two weeks after moving them in, we Airbnb'ed a place in Fort Lauderdale big enough to accommodate my parents for Thanksgiving weekend. It was to be a model for future weekend excursions.

The rental had slippery tile floors and we witnessed my dad fall—it was like watching an elephant get shot and go down in slow-mo. My mother had a persistent stomachache; we didn't know about the tumor yet. If you're looking for a guided tour of bathrooms in the greater Fort Lauderdale area, I can give you one. Despite her discomfort, she insisted on wine with every meal, which she dispensed from a three-liter box that she refused to be separated from. It was on that trip that I learned my dad was carrying a weapon to the casinos. We'd been driving around with a gun in the glove compartment.

On our last day together, I made my move. Feigning the need to find a UPS store for "urgent business," I charged my son with keeping my parents entertained while I excused myself, jumping into the car in search of a police station. I called my sister.

"I've got the gun! There's a holiday amnesty program, or when I get pulled over for speeding, I'll just hand it over to a cop," I said, flooring my father's Honda Accord.

"You're stealing his gun?"

"He's got a leg holster—he's going to bend over and shoot his foot off. Someone could take it from him at the casino and kill him. What if Mom tells him he needs to build his upper-body strength one too many times? He might shoot her."

"You're not allowed to do that," she said in the same authoritative tone The Little Man had used to get me to eat lima beans when I was five years old.

I reluctantly returned to the house, took my dad aside and opened my jacket. The gun was tucked into my pants. He told me in his best Big Daddy drawl that if I didn't give it back to him, he'd leave Ezra and me in Fort Lauderdale. I caved, but convinced him to let me put the .357 Magnum in the trunk. We drove back to the Gardens. Ezra didn't know, but he had their portable toilet seat on his lap (in a carrying case). My mother clutched her box of wine as my dad and I stewed in silence. That was the last road trip for the Gurwitches. Only later did I learn the gun was loaded.

I arrived at eight p.m. the night before my shopping safari. Dinner is served from four to six p.m. and I've gotten used to the hush that falls over the campus after sundown. Because there is a surfeit of empty apartments, I'm able to stay in the unit next door to my folks. One of the front-desk attendants said she thinks of my sister and me as part-time residents. I smiled when she said this, although the reality that independent-living unit #609 is the closest I have come to a vacation time-share is something I try not to think about.

One of those ubiquitous violin-playing-goat Chagall prints hangs on the wall of my place and it seems likely that the furnishings came from previous tenants, but I try not to think about that either. On my first visit, the bathroom, with its metal railings and emergency pull cord, depressed me so much that I didn't shower for my entire four-day stay, but now I find the "daily living aids" a delightful reminder that I am still young enough to use the loo without needing assistance, making each trip to the bathroom a cause for celebration.

Any adjustments I make are insignificant compared to my parents' acclimation. The Gardens renovated their apartment, updating the kitchen with a granite finish and replacing the carpet with bamboo flooring, but my mother still finds it wanting. My mom has started documenting a compendium of complaints in a notebook that I've named *Shirley's Little Book of Big Indignities*. They range from "At dinner, they gave me fruit but not a cookie and I'm supposed to get a cookie too" (which is true), to a suspicion that the cleaning service is siphoning off cups of her laundry detergent (which seems doubtful). This is not unexpected; entering a retirement home is difficult for everyone.

Lisa witnessed the initial move-in meltdown. She called to report on our parents' nonstop bickering and how Mom went into a rage, convinced the bargain-basement-priced movers were overcharging her.

"But Lisa, it sounds quiet right now."

"Uh-huh."

"Where *are* you?"

"I locked myself in the bathroom and I'm eating a salad in the bathtub."

Even the smallest details, like sounds and ambient light, take getting used to. Their place faces the exterior of the campus, a brightly lit boulevard. The amount of traffic whizzing by each week is greater than the number of cars that went past their Sunset Islands home during the entire forty years they lived there. As a constant reminder of their perch in the unfamiliar neighborhood of Little Haiti, their apartment looks out onto the Dark and Lovely Beauty Supply.

As expected, the Gardens' dining room and classes provide more interactions with other humans, but there have been unanticipated opportunities for community building as well. A few days after their arrival, my father was interrupted during his morning toilette by an insistent knock on the apartment door. When the knocking persisted, he answered the door and one of the oldest but admirably ambulatory neighbors burst into the apartment demanding to know why a nude man was in her dentist's office. She drops in once a month, and on the days when my father is clothed and able to convince her that the apartment is not the waiting room of Dr. Blaustein, DDS, she'll ask if he can stand with her until the elevator comes.

I can't say it seems like an unreasonable request, as each episode is much like *Waiting for Godot*. The elevators operate with an indifference to logic or reliability. Let's say an elevator arrives. The doors open, you enter, the doors close, and just when you think you're about to go somewhere, they'll open again. Repeat. I've been unsuccessful in finding a pattern, which means that the already slow pace of life at the Gardens requires even more patience and resignation to things being out of your control than you think you can muster. There is an old saying, "Florida is God's waiting room," and I now know that room is an elevator.

Out of all of Mom's well-documented observations, it is an unimpeachable fact that the Gardens is having trouble attracting younger folks like my parents, aside from the seriously broken, of body or brain. My mother's been tallying the diminishing number of residents. "We're down to seventy-eight in our building," she told me, which does seem to be worrisome, though I have no clue as to the accuracy or the method of her census keeping.*

There is a somewhat related culture clash, a palpable low-level hum of insurrection brewing at the home. Earlier generations were more religious than the newest crop of seniors, who aren't all on board with the strict kosher kitchen. As a part-time resident, I don't feel I should weigh in, but it does seem a bit much that even if you supply your own set of glasses, you can't bring a bottle of non-kosher wine into the dining room. My father has been caught smuggling bacon into the cafeteria in his trousers. We've tried to convince him to enjoy his pork in the privacy of his apartment, but he won't do it.

Still, there are thoughtful therapeutic touches. Each floor has its own motif of framed photographs that serve as visual mnemonics. Some floors have birds, while others have flowers. The only problem is they are a tad similar to my eye. My parents' floor has pelicans, while one floor up is whooping cranes. You'd have to be an ornithologist to tell the difference.

And there are highlights. My mother takes advantage of the "out

* The practical effect is that there are fewer stimulating services for the still mobile in the building.

trips"* to concerts and we are regulars at the chair exercise class. Her mother went to the gym several times a week up until the day she died, so my mother's new dedication may be another one of the habits she has adopted in Frances's honor.† Our instructor is tirelessly encouraging, although I found it troubling that her playlist for our group, which includes stroke victims in wheelchairs, opens with Mel Tormé singing "Don't Get Around Much Anymore." It seemed particularly a punishment to residents with more eclectic tastes, like my mother's new dining room buddy, Inez, a record producer whose music label included KC and the Sunshine Band. If I accomplish nothing else in my tenure at Tel Aviv, my legacy will be to have successfully lobbied for the residents to shake-shake-shake, shake-shake-shake, shake their booty from 11:23 to 11:27 a.m. every Tuesday and Thursday.

After his initial resistance, Dad has made an easier transition, or is at least making a good show of it. As there are fewer men at the Gardens, my father, who stands now at six feet, having lost a few inches, cuts a memorable swath and has gotten the nickname "Handsome Harry" around the campus. The front-desk staff seem to get a kick out of his feistiness and never tire of repeating that Dad told them in no uncertain terms, "Don't fuck with me in the morning." He announced that he was hanging up his pots and pans when they first moved in, but since he discovered the Seven Seas seafood

---

* "Out trips" is the lingo for excursions to concerts and the ballet. It sounds like prison lingo to me, but it's amazing how quickly phrases normalize into your vocabulary.

† I wound up with a ring given to my grandmother by Jack LaLanne's European Health Spas, in honor of her lifetime membership. It's twelve-karat gold. Can you imagine your gym giving you a gold ring?

store, located next to Dark and Lovely, he's come out of retirement.* When Lisa and I or his grandsons visit, he makes his gumbo, though his measurement skills have gone a bit wonky. On this trip, we will spend an hour spooning gumbo into a dozen containers to freeze and give as gifts to the downstairs staff. I presented him with a taller garbage can and he purchased a gadget called a Folding Helping Hand Long-Reach Pick-Up Gripper™. I have seen it in action. My mother spots a speck of dust on the floor and tells him to bend over and pick it up. Dad retrieves the FHHLR Pick-Up Gripper, extends the mechanical arm, probes the area for the particle, grasps it in the tongs, and deposits it in the foot-pedal-operated trash bin. The process only takes up most of an afternoon.

You will find no highlights, however, at the hair salon. Literally. They only do frosting, so don't even ask. In an attempt to go full-on Garden fashionista, I've had my hair done there. The stylist, who has not one but three signs that read *I'm a Beautician, Not a Magician*, gave me tight pin curls, though I requested a blowout, transforming my hair into an exact copy of my grandmother Frances's wig. To be fair, I was the only client who wasn't sleeping during their appointment, so I may have distracted her. The ladies of the Gardens complimented me, because I was twinning their preferred hairstyle, so it was worth it.

My mother is a poetry class regular, although she is not a fan of the modern poets featured in the *Sewanee Review*, which the thoughtful teacher, Kaye, a writer herself, tries to nudge the class toward.

"What does this mean? It's meaningless: 'Time is a graceless

---

* I have to give it up to my dad; he is the first resident of the Gardens to venture into the Haitian market.

enemy'?" Mom complained after one class, quoting from a Charles Wright poem. "I love the Russian tenement poets, their poems about life on the Lower East Side in New York and working in factories in the garment district, don't you?"

"Mom, you never lived in New York, nor in a tenement, or worked in the garment industry. You do know something about the march of time, but I'm so glad you are enjoying immersing yourself in turn-of-the-century squalor."

Regulars include Ilene, formerly a college professor, who still does some part-time tutoring, and Marvin, a libertarian Zionist who Xeroxes articles from Judicial Watch, which he leaves by the mailboxes with handwritten scribbled notes: *Israel, love it or LOSE IT, people!!!* At the class I attended, Ilene brought in something by Kipling, Marv recited Shakespeare from memory, and because I'm an asshole, I brought in obtuse musings by Gertrude Stein and got into an argument over interpretation with Marv.

"You're just like your mother," he said on our way out of class, a comment that sounded like a reference to both my appearance and my temperament.

"Thanks, I have to jump off the roof now, Marv."

My mother's sense of humor is still intact. "Me first," she added. "But let's make sure we do it from a high enough floor that we don't just break a leg."*

---

* Nothing is more frightening for the residents than losing their mobility and being in a "chair"—that's Gardens lingo for "wheelchair." In prison lingo "chair" is the electric chair, which for some Gardens folk would be preferable to their "chair," which portends a slow decline instead of a more desirable quick demise.

I started the day, as usual, by greeting the Yettas, the Shirleys, and the Lillians at breakfast. There are three distinct groups among the women at the Gardens. Some of the Yettas, the oldest of the residents, are Holocaust survivors. The most religious of the bunch, they wear head coverings while napping in the lawn chairs outside our building. In general, the Lillians are active in the Jewish community and are older and less mobile than the Shirleys, who still drive, leave the home on a regular basis, and are less religious. I kiss and greet them all.

"Lil, I love your blouse, it looks Navajo. What's your book club reading?" I say to the president of the building association and the oldest person in unassisted living, whose name is Lillian, though her mobility makes her more of a Shirley.

"Hello, darling, you look so glamorous today. You used to make your own jewelry, I know, that's clearly why you are stylish," I tell Esther, who, because she is losing her sight, is a Lillian. She moved in only a few weeks after my parents and often sits in the lobby and cries, so I always try to compliment her.

"How are your new students?" I ask Ilene from poetry class, a Shirley.

"Shirley," I say to one of the Shirleys, whose name is Shirley, "if you go to exercise class today, please do a Rockettes kick for me and my mother." Being the most mobile, there are usually three Shirleys, including my mom and this Shirley, in class. Rhoda invites me to stand in for my mother at Friday night services. Until recently, Rhoda was a Shirley, but an escalating short-term memory loss has sent her into Lillianville.

There's some competition among the residents about whose kids visit more often. It's not unlike how kids at summer camp know whose parents sent care packages and whose didn't. Some of them have the advantage of having kids who live nearby and I don't want my parents to fall too far behind, so I try to make sure everyone sees me.

We catch up on Gardens gossip. Bruce, the Gardens' architect with Parkinson's, has died.

"Oh, no, what happened?"

"It was sudden, in his sleep," Lillian tells me. We nod and make the little clucking noises customary upon learning of a sad inevitability. Still, the news is shocking. There is also a budding romance on campus, which is causing a big rift in the population. Two residents have fallen in love. The Yettas aren't pleased and don't approve. One stood up at bingo night and admonished the woman, "You should be taking care of your husband," because the woman's husband is a memory care patient.

"How do you feel about it?" I ask.

"Love wins," one says, and I'm not sure if she knows she's just summed up the gay movement in 2016 America, but it's a sentiment shared by the majority of the Shirleys and Lillians. One of the things you notice when you spend time here is that even an insignificant chat is charged with an unfamiliar intensity. No one is checking their phone, updating their Facebook, or posting to Instagram, making interactions that would once have been considered normal human exchanges seem deeply intimate. And in what has become the most dubious of achievements, I have finally beat my sister at something. Lisa is often busy handling my parents' finances, which leaves me time to socialize. Since I've endeared myself to the gals, Lisa is referred to as "the other sister." I am number one sister with the coffee klatch at Tel Aviv Gardens.

My mother has requested not to have visitors because she doesn't want to be seen when she's not at her best, but all the residents are following her recovery. Prior to her hospitalization, there were some incidents that I'm not able to confirm but might have occurred. The dining room, like the dress code, operates a lot like middle school. Everyone wants to be invited to sit with the cool kids, which in this case refers to the table where the majority have enough short-term memory left to gossip about those seated at other tables.

According to Mom, you have to be invited to sit at the table, and someone made it known that she was talking too much or talking too loudly or complaining too much. I've tried not to follow the drama too closely. When my son was four, at our local park, a kid with a crew cut and a runny nose, always a bad sign, informed my son that he couldn't play in the sandbox. I wanted to punch the little punk. Needless to say, we just went to another part of the park, but I've asked my mother not to tell me which of the women said she couldn't sit at their table, because there is no other sandbox, and someone's walker might suddenly have a loose screw, which could be very dangerous.

Luckily, the dining room incident is behind us. It might have been like prison hazing, where you have to prove how tough you are, because when the Shirleys and Lillians heard that Mom has stage-four cancer, everything made sense to them—why my parents, who are younger than the majority of the residents, had moved in, something they were all wondering about—and the gals were impressed by Mom's fortitude. If she can just recover, perhaps they will give her a hero's welcome, like that scene in the prison classic *Billy Jack*. I picture the residents of Tel Aviv Gardens lined up along the driveway, some of them propped up with their walkers, doing the slow clap as she hobbles inside.

After catching up with the gals, I see my dad up to his apartment, stopping in to slip a palm-sized dusty rose–colored lychee, my favorite of Mom's Chinese porcelain altar fruit collection, into my purse. Hopefully, she'll make enough of a recovery that she'll be able to notice that Sticky Fingers has pocketed something. Dad and I planned to go to the recovery center together, but first I jog around the campus, jump in the shower, and walk the few yards to the center, which takes the same amount of time for my father to use the restroom and drive his car over. We creep, which is the only word I can use to describe my father's form of locomotion, into the center together.

The lobby of the center has the same grand piano and bright artwork as the apartment building, but once you get into the wards upstairs, there are hospital-style rooms connected by nurses' stations and patients in wheelchairs lined up along the hallways. We pass the shape of a man in a chair with a sheet over his head, *Scooby-Doo* cartoon ghost style. He is doing something underneath the sheet that I am so thankful we can't see. Some of the patients are sleeping, but unlike the nappers in front of the apartment building, they are only partially dressed. If they had trousers on, they have a hospital-gown top; if the top half was street wear, then the bottoms are pajamas. A Yetta with a kerchief on her head, face like a potato, sits upright with perfect posture, but she is completely still, eyes wide open.

No one is parked in the hallway of the wing in which my mother is recovering, but there is a man moaning for help from an adjacent room. There is never a time during my visit when he isn't moaning, except for a brief interlude in which a nurse wheels him down the hall and parks his wheelchair behind the desk next to the staff.

Is this kind of thing unique to this facility or to Miami? I don't know. It's not the first time we've been treated to a front-row seat for the health care industry in Florida. A few years ago, my mother had a brain tumor removed at Jackson Memorial Hospital, a facility that specializes in bullet wounds to the head. Given Florida's heat and humidity and history of racial tension, combined with an open-carry law and castle doctrine (the so-called stand your ground law), is it any wonder that my mother was the only patient in the ward who wasn't handcuffed to her bed and accompanied by a police escort?

We enter my mother's room, and although she looks tiny, she is channeling the suffering of the entire Jewish people. "The nursing staff would do well at Buchenwald! The food is worse than Auschwitz!"

She is visibly shrunken. Her bony hand is clutching *Shirley's Little Book of Big Indignities*. She wants to show me the latest entries: scribbled in slanted script are times she'd called for nurses and they hadn't come, medications, random words, and assessments. There are circled notations, exclamation points, question marks, and underlines, and a list of births and deaths and dates of entry to this country.

11:02 11:04 11:05!!!!!! 11:06
Rang Bell
3:00 3:03 3:04 3:05
Mamushka

xeloda

Anna Akhmatova, Russian tenement poet

zometa

NO????!!!

Didn't show!!!!!

Faslodex, exemestane, aromasin, Procrit, levothyroxine

3:30 3:31 3:32 3:33 3:34 3:35

Dr. Rodrequez? Which one?

Attitude

Call

3:35 3:36 3:36 3:37 3:38 3:39 3:40

Zede 10/18/83 8/19/62 Geisen, Russia, entered U.S. 2/2/13

Bubbe 8/20/82 11/7/58 Aman, Russia, entered U.S. 8/5/14

Ironing

"Why ironing?"

"I can't find anyone to iron your father's shirts."

"You iron Dad's shirts?" I can't believe that after all these years, with so much history between them and her illness, she's been ironing his shirts. "Mom, please, that's the last thing you should worry about right now."

I too have kept lists. Because of the numerous hospital stays we weathered during Ezra's babyhood, friends facing medical crises often ask my advice. "Keep a notepad handy," I always recommend, "because when nursing shifts change, things can get dicey," although I've never felt the need to include the dates of births and deaths of family members.

"I don't understand why I have two colostomy bags. Why did they do this to me?"

I know that things have been explained to her but I carefully and slowly reiterate why the surgery was needed. Then she fires me for not having my shirt tucked in. It is annoying for her to look at me with the shirt untucked. This is when I am exiled to Ross Dress for Less.

There is something perverse in this assignment. Growing up, my mother deemed my taste in clothing too eccentric, and as recently as two months ago, she implored me to wear classic twinsets in demure colors like my sister. If I'd been tasked with this chore even two months earlier, I might have seen it as an opportunity to punish her for her failure to be anything more than the best mother she was able to be. Still, when I see a T-shirt on the rack that reads *Keep Calm and Smoke Weed*, or the one proclaiming *Yes We Cannabis*, for only $9.99, I can't resist imagining the horrified look on her face when I tell her, "This is the shirt you'll be wearing to Sunday brunch."

Yes, we cannabis.

"You can shoot a teenager in a hoodie who's strolling through your neighborhood but you can't purchase marijuana to relieve nausea from chemotherapy in Florida, which is why I'm proud to be my mother's drug mule." That's what I intend to say should I ever be questioned by the DEA as to why I am transporting drugs across state lines.

Of all the unexpected experiences I've had over the last year, becoming a patient of DOC420 is one I really didn't see coming. The doctor, who advertises with glamorous head shots on billboards in Los Angeles, has the only medical office I've ever visited that sells Flamin' Hot Cheetos. "Arthritis," I said, holding up my crooked right pinky finger, and promptly received my "doctor's note," which looks as official as any of the student-of-the-month certificates my son earned in kindergarten.*

It was almost as easy to get this weed as it was to score pot in high school. Back then I just walked down the hall to my parents' bedroom. The only time-consuming part was rifling through their belongings until I located the joints in a plastic baggie inside a shoe. Drugs hidden in your parents' closet? Please, every teenager knows that's an invitation to partake! I didn't bother to count them out, assuming that over time they'd smoke some and I'd smoke some and they'd never notice. The thing I hadn't counted on was that they didn't actually like it and I was the only one hitting their stash. Years later they told me that it was their way of keeping an eye on how much I was smoking.† "So you see, I owe them, Officer," I'll add to the DEA agent. I picked out lemon-drop THC-infused candy for my mother and I've successfully traveled with it twice. I told my parents when I arrived I'd brought more with me.

"Thank goodness, those are a godsend, you don't know how much they're helping," my dad said.

"Would you like one now, Mom? It might help you relax."

"Oh, no, your mother doesn't like them." Now his easier acclimation made more sense.

Back at the Gardens, I show her the long shirts that should cover

---

* For an industry trying to go legit, I'm not convinced my local dispensary is doing themselves any favors selling "medicine" labeled Blue Space Zombie Resin or Pineapple Trainwreck, although it would be more fun to call in a refill for Yoda's Brain than duloxetine, my antidepressant.

† Who was more naïve? Me, assuming they were smoking the joints as well, or them, assuming that the only pot I was smoking was their stash?

the colostomy bags, light jackets that won't wrinkle, and several pairs of black pants, as requested. She wants layers so people won't notice the bags, but ones that won't make her look heavy. Her obsession with weight has overtaken her cleanliness obsession.

"Do you know that your cat is fat?"

"Yes, Mom. We prefer 'husky,' but we've noticed that."

"Well, he's fat."

"We'll be sure to tell him you said so."

"I read that book you sent me by Jon Cryer. I just loved him in *Pretty in Pink*. Is he still slim?"

"Yes, he is, Mom."

"Good for him. Is he gay?"

"No, Mom, he's not gay."

"Are you sure? He seems gay."

"Mom, I know his wife, and I knew his first wife and other . . . he's just not gay."

"Well, I think he is."

"I'll be sure to tell him you said so."

"Have you taken anything from the apartment, Sticky Fingers?"

"You'll have to get better so you can find out for yourself, Shirley."

I get down to business. I've picked up some cucumber facial wipes and lavender room spray to help her feel refreshed, as well as hair clips to hold up her blouses so they don't get soiled as the bag is emptied. I explain to her that this is something that people refer to as "hacks," or self-styled tips to make things easier.

The nursing staff doesn't have much experience with colostomies, and as can happen, the surrounding skin is irritated and bleeding. Because my son had a colostomy bag for the first year of his life, I've got firsthand knowledge of all things ostomy. She and my dad have been badgering the staff to send an expert, but I know there is no one coming. The only help I received came from my tribe of mothers of children born without anuses, the most unexpected chosen family I've ever been a part of. Ezra's medical odyssey took place so many years ago that I have to work hard to pull up the information that I filed away in the "Information I Hope to Never Have to Use Again" area of my brain.

I explain how to air out the skin, how powder helps to keep it dry, and how to efficiently open and close the bag, but she's confused and keeps repeating that she doesn't understand why they did this to her and that the bags are filling too often.

"What are you eating?" I ask.

"Cherries and plums."

"That's the worst thing to eat, especially the cherries. Berries have more skin and fiber than other fruit. Try eating more processed food. Dad, please stop bringing her cherries."

"I want to bring my beautiful wife cherries!"

He is trying so hard to be kind. On their anniversary, he brought a small bottle of champagne to the hospital. He has also made her promise not to "predecease" him. As much as her mercurial housekeeping is driving him nuts, some deep well of love has been reawakened, and he is also terrified of being alone. There has been a rupture in the fabric of the universe. I am in bizarro world, the alternate universe that Dr. Handsome McBirkenstock lectured on at Sunday Assembly, trying to talk my father out of doing nice things for my mother.

"I've spent half my life with her and now I want to bring her cherries," he says, voice rising with indignation.

"Okay, Dad. Why don't you take a break," I suggest, and send him off with a bag of THC-infused lemon drops.

She is nervous about what will happen when she needs to use the bathroom. Because she is so worried that no one will come to help her, she rings for someone to come before she needs to go just in case it takes a long time. This means she is constantly ringing, which is why the *Little Book* reads like she is the timekeeper for a track and field team. It's a terrible cycle.

"That's why I'm here, Mom."

We use a walker to get her to the bathroom. I take her diaper off before I sit her down. The colostomy bag needs emptying and I open it up and start to gag. I am instantly transported back in time.

One Easter, my husband, son, and I attended a service at a Unitarian church that Jeff had been attending sporadically. Ezra's surgically reconstructed bowels hadn't stabilized yet. Halfway through the service, he got terrible diarrhea. I rushed him into the bathroom, but his clothes were completely ruined. I pulled a curtain down from the church's bathroom window, wrapped him in it, and carried him out to the car. I was determined to have a nice holiday, so we went home, got new clothes, and headed to a Chinese restaurant. Before the food arrived, he had to use the bathroom again. The smell was so strong that I started throwing up in the stall next to his. "Jesus, what is going on in here?" another patron said, coughing and gagging and quickly fleeing the bathroom. My son called out from his stall that he wished he could glue a toilet seat to his butt.

This odor is even more noxious than I remembered, perhaps because of the drugs in her system. I tell her that I am having allergies. My mother knows I don't have any allergies, but either because of the drugs or because she wants to believe me, she accepts this explanation. We close the bag up and settle her back into the bed. I execute a convincing "My phone is buzzing in my pocket" move and pretend to see an important number flash on the screen.

"Oh, I have to take this. I'll be right back," I say, then jauntily turn and exit her room.*

I wander through Wheelchair City on the hunt for a visitors' waiting room, but there is none. I find an unused corridor. A steel door slams shut, locking me in a vestibule with an antediluvian transport bed that has metal stirrups and leather hand restraints. I look out of the window to try to get my bearings and I see a bird that has been flattened by time and the decomposing process on the window ledge. I want to call my sister, but I can't get phone service in my isolation tank. What could she or anyone, for that matter, say that would help? Nothing. Except it would be nice if there were a call center for people taking care of their parents manned with volunteers who listen to you vent and then repeat, "I know, I know," over and over in a soothing voice. I lie down on the inside ledge and allow myself a good long cry. The window doesn't open, which is unsurprising; it would be too tempting.

One of my pitiful apartments in New York had an ancient hand-operated radiator. You had to open a valve to let the steam out and put a bowl underneath, otherwise water would drip onto the floor. I have turned into that radiator, requiring regular draining. A nurse's aide lets me out after only a few minutes of banging on the

---

* If that psychic's prediction were accurate, a camera would have been rolling, because this performance was Academy Award worthy.

door and I am strangely comforted by the sound of the man moaning for help down the hall.

When I get back to her room, my mother is asleep, not that you would know it, because the lights are on and she sleeps with her glasses on. She doesn't want the staff to forget that she's still alive. When she rouses, she reminds me to go to Friday night services with Rhoda, her temple buddy.

I'm not really crazy about going. I'm not convinced that the rabbi isn't a memory care patient. He rarely remembers me despite having met me a dozen times, but it can't be easy shepherding an elderly flock. You're basically a hospice worker. I couldn't do it. Still, I wondered whether "Shirley, you must be dying to get out of here" was his best choice of words when paying a visit to my mother after her surgery.

I massage her temples, her scalp, and the back of her neck. She makes happy sounds and only pauses from her enjoyment once to inquire if a certain cousin has gotten as heavy as she's heard. She resembles her mother more and more with each passing day, and I ask if she's thinking about Frances. She tells me a memory of holding hands with her sister, Gloria, both of them in pigtails, skipping down the street in Philly, while visiting their grandparents with her mother.

"You could walk by yourself on the street, because everyone in the neighborhood knew Bubbie and Zeyda. The street was always bustling. We'd peer into the open kitchens of restaurants; there was always something wonderful simmering on the stoves. Irish policemen were walking their beats and they'd tip their hats to us, and someone from the bakery would come out; they knew we lived in Delaware and they'd say, 'Hello, Miss DuPont,' and give us treats."

She falls asleep dreaming of warm cookies and her tribe.

Rhoda is waiting in the lobby for me. The Lils mentioned that she's "losing it" and I have noticed a marked decline. Details are getting a bit fuzzy. This morning she told us she was rushing to get to the bus for an out trip to a daytime concert. The bus was leaving at one thirty p.m. and it was only nine. No one stopped her, though, because you never know at the Gardens; it might take someone from nine until one thirty to make it from the dining room to the driveway, and no one wants to embarrass her.

I don't know a thing about Rhoda, where she comes from, who she loved or who loved her, or what has transpired in her life to bring her to the same place as my mother, but we hold hands and walk the few steps to the shul.

Outside the building, there's some new landscaping. A garden gnome in lederhosen is lounging in a hot-pink conch shell. A butterfly with a two-foot wingspan covered with multicolored LED lights and a dog wearing oversized reflective sunglasses frolic nearby. I believe I saw a similar scene when I took mushrooms in Washington Square Park in 1982. It seems like this display could test the mental health of residents whose hold on reality is already waning, but I am just a part-timer here, so what do I know?

Rhoda and I sit together. She doesn't seem familiar with any of the prayers. Is that memory loss, or has she, like my mother, only recently returned to the fold? Some people sleep, a few recite the prayers, and there's one guy who insists on singing loudly, calling out page numbers, and correcting the rabbi. Whether or not the rabbi lives in the memory care unit is unimportant; he has the patience of a saint.

Tonight the service is in English, courtesy of my dad. He led a

Gardens-wide campaign for the services to be held in English once a month and the rabbi indulged him, even though Dad makes it through only a half an hour before either falling asleep or departing for the casino. Even that is astonishing. It's possible that he is connecting to his roots, like he's gotten a contact Judaism from the home. He's been dreaming of Grandma Rose. In his dreams, she calls him by his Hebrew name, Hershel. "Hershela," she says, "you didn't get me the right coffin, the worms are getting in, please come and get me." As morbid as it sounds, he seems comforted to be hearing from her. It's probably a terrible sign—you hear about this kind of thing when people are nearing the end of their lives—but it could be that he's hitting those lemon drops hard or actually listening to the rabbi's sermons.

The rabbi tells us that night is a scary time in our tradition and we often don't know if we'll make it to the morning. No wonder my mother keeps the lights on; she must have heard this one a few times. My muscle memory kicks in and I'm swaying to the familiar melodies and I'm even grateful for Page-Number Guy, because it really is helpful. At the conclusion of our natural sciences lecture, I kiss Rhoda on the cheek, wishing her Shabbat shalom. She smiles and asks politely, "Who are you?" I'm ready for another cry break but a few seconds later she's remembered who I am and introduces me to the rabbi, who has again forgotten. As much as I want to ask him more about the fearsome properties of Judaic darkness, I can't, because he asks how my mother is doing and says he's going to visit her in the morning. I take out my phone, intending to take a picture of Rhoda and me to show my mother, but the rabbi stops me. "No pictures in the temple," he says. Tomorrow we will be sitting in the same seats, posing for pictures, because the temple room is also the

Sunday brunch room, but the sun has gone down and everyone knows now how scary a time it is for Jews, so I leave it at that. It's seven thirty p.m. and I'm so exhausted that I drink two mini bottles of cheap airline Merlot and fall asleep with the lights on in my mother's honor. I'm on Gardens Time.

In the morning, we attend the Father's Day brunch, and although there's no carving station, the spread includes smoked salmon and whitefish, which my dad and I agree is not at all shabby. We sit at a table with the residents of our building—even within the Gardens, you stick to your own. I've got a plane to catch, so I pack and hurry over to the recovery center to say good-bye.

My mother is dressed and seated in a wheelchair, waiting for me by the elevator. She wants to show me she is rallying. She's wearing one of the outfits I purchased, a zebra-patterned jacket with epaulets, lending her appearance a slightly militaristic air. Shirley Gurwitch, member of the Senior Brigade, reporting for duty.

"I don't want to leave you, I like taking care of you, Mom."

"You have to go and live your life and help your father."

"Bye, Mom, I love you."

I step into the elevator. I am memorizing my mother's face. We have said good-bye so many times over the last few years, I never know if this is going to be the last one. I press the button for the ground floor. The elevator doors close, and then they open.

"Bye, Mom," I say again.

She blows me a kiss. The doors close. And they open.

"Be sure to put your cat on a diet."

"We will, Mom."

"Don't tell Jon Cryer I said he might be gay."

"I won't."

"Are you going to write about this?"

"You know I am."

The doors close. And open again. Neither of us knows what to do.

"It's okay, Mom, why don't you go back to your room and get some rest?"

But she won't leave. She wants to wait until I'm gone. Maybe she is memorizing my face.

The door closes. Fourth time's a charm.

Back at the building, I call for a cab, roll my suitcase past the grand piano, and see that the Shirleys and Lillians are assembling for exercise class at the far end of the lobby. "Shake it but don't break it!" I yell to them. It's unclear if they've heard me, but they smile and wave.

I'm so emotionally drained that I slump onto one of the lawn chairs in front of the building. The water in the fountain splashes against the tile, cooling the air and making a satisfyingly crisp slapping sound. Just beyond the cypress, Mayim E. Flamingo's dazzling mosaics shimmer in the sunlight, like sequins.

My cousin will make you rich!

I'm Harry Gurwitch, Chairman of EMC Film Corporation. My cousin, M. A. Ripps, is President.

I manage the business and financial affairs. Mike is a motion picture producer-distributor — talented and highly motivated. Exhibitors make money with pictures he promotes. Our track record is THE ROAD TO THE BANK.

EMC Film Corporation is our company. Its services are unique, its people are creative, its style is innovative. And our connections are in all the right places. Let us put your picture on the right track, THE ROAD TO THE BANK.

WHEN EMC DISTRIBUTES, EVERYBODY CAN MAKE MONEY.

Have a cigar, Harry.

emc FILMS

EMC Film Corporation
444 Brickell Avenue
Miami, Florida 33131
(305) 358-7830

©Copyright 1976, EMC Film Corporation

have a cigar, harry

My mother made a remarkable recovery and happily returned to her exercise and poetry classes, but we should have known that my father wasn't long for this world when the raincoat money, the poker cash he kept stashed in a London Fog trench coat, ran out. I got to see him play once. Everyone at the casino, the players and dealers, even the parking valet, asked about my mother's health.

On that trip to Miami, I went by our old house and the current residents kindly let me in. The house had been updated, in keeping with the neighboring estates on Sunset Island II. My childhood bedroom is now an outdoor shower. The new owner gives me our hand-shaped brass doorknocker. My mom is still convinced that Sticky Fingers struck again.

I tracked down the artist who made Mayim E. Flamingo, who turns out to have been a student of my high school drama teacher.

She intended for the flamingo's name to be spoken aloud so that it sounds like the city of Miami—MayimE—but I never got a chance to tell my father that the mystery of the middle name had been solved.

My dad had a heart attack. In typical fashion, when he woke up in the hospital, he wanted Jack Daniel's and gumbo. When I asked my father if he was okay with my writing his stories, he said, "If you think there's money in it, go for it." He lived long enough to see his grandsons and to tell me that he'd always hoped to get back to the low country. He asked me to put on Linda Ronstadt's "Blue Bayou," which I did. Handsome Harry is missed at Tel Aviv Gardens.

I inherited his gun, which I sold, a couple of poker chips, and a container of his last batch of gumbo. My sister gave her sons his designer ties, and my son got a Gucci belt buckle from the 1970s.

Perkins, our husky cat, has gone missing. A friend suggested that he was waiting on the Rainbow Bridge to escort my father over. I highly doubt it. If there were an afterlife, my father would be ordering a steak, getting a lap dance, and playing poker with his cousin Billy.

Dear mom & Dad

I'm fine
    How are you?
I'm fine
miss ya
Don4 have
time
Love,

Anne

ACKNOWLEDGMENTS

I am forever indebted to Bill Maher for introducing me to David Rosenthal and the Blue Rider posse, including this amazing trifecta: Aileen Boyle, Milena Brown, and Linda Cowen. I can't express enough appreciation to my intrepid editor, Sarah Hochman, and my agent, Laura Dail, for their faith and patience during the writing of this book. So thankful for readers and friends: Maria Speidel, Jillian Lauren, Hadley Rierson, Ben Decter, Jeanne McConnell, Claudette Sutherland, Janelle Brown, Tonya Pinkins, Bart DeLorenzo, Keshni Kashyap, Diana Dinerman, Suzanne Rico, Dani Klein, Wendy Leibman, Aimee Lee Ball, Meghan Daum, Heather Havrilesky, and Scott Carter. I'd be lost without the Suite 8LA writers' collective, founded by Erica Rothschild and Carina Chocano.

Thank you to my family for sharing stories and DNA: Lisa Gurwitch, Ezra Kahn, Jeff Kahn, Sandy Gurwitch, Shirley and Neal Buchman, Barry Ripps, Marci Ballin, Robin Gurwitch, Ruth Gurwitch,

Shari Frankfurt, Robin Rosenbaum, cousin Monique, Michael Gurwitch, and Muriel Zimmerman.

Thank you, Hawara family, for inviting me into your home. Much gratitude to Rabbi Israel, Inez, Irene, David, Lil, Csilla, Pearl, Marty, Kaye, Anna, Ernie, Helen, and all of the Yettas, Shirleys, and Lillians at Tel Aviv Gardens. I appreciate all of those whose wisdom contributed to this book: Lisa Randall, Robert Reich, Barbara Ehrenreich, Dauphin Island Mayor Jeff Collier, Bill and Slavica Harper, Manette Silberman and the Ahavas Chesed Sisterhood, Ian Dodd and Sunday Assembly Los Angeles, Allen Boobar, Reason Rally 2016, Cheryl Bianchi, Coleman Hough, Christine Blackburn, Christine Romeo, Kimberly Rubin-Spivak, Michelle Joyner, Richard Schechner, the Brittany Foundation, Phyllis Michelle Greenhouse, Glenn Rosenblum, Mark Freeman, and Craig Bierko and his dog Boo, who raises money for cancer: Text KIDS at 27722 and donate $10 to Loma Linda University Children's Hospital from your phone bill. I value the continued support of the Kaplan-Stahler Agency, Melissa Campbell, Bradley Glenn, Metropolitan Talent Agency, and A.K.A. Talent. Big love to all the show people with whom I've shared dressing rooms, holiday meals, and Equity regulation cots; the Golden Bridge Community Choir for the songs and community that keep me going; and the ancestors on whose shoulders I slouch.

ABOUT THE AUTHOR

Annabelle Gurwitch is an actress, an activist, and the author of *I See You Made an Effort* (a *New York Times* bestseller and Thurber Prize finalist); *You Say Tomato, I Say Shut Up* (coauthored with Jeff Kahn); and *Fired!* (which was also a Showtime Comedy Special). Gurwitch gained a loyal following during her stint cohosting *Dinner and a Movie* on TBS and years as a regular commentator on NPR. She's written for *The New Yorker, The New York Times, The Wall Street Journal, Los Angeles Times, McSweeney's,* and *The Hollywood Reporter.* Gurwitch was the news anchor on HBO's *Not Necessarily the News* and hosted *WA$TED* on Planet Green network. Her acting credits include *Better Things, Seinfeld, Boston Legal, Dexter,* and *Melvin Goes to Dinner.* A veteran of many lauded and even more misguided theatrical productions, she regularly performs at arts centers around the country. Gurwitch is a Jewish mother, a reluctant atheist, and an ardent environmentalist. She is empty-nesting in Los Angeles.